A James Joyce *Miscellany*

SECOND SERIES

THIS VOLUME WAS PREPARED UNDER THE SPONSORSHIP OF THE JAMES JOYCE SOCIETY IN NEW YORK. THE MEMBERS OF THE PUBLICATIONS COMMITTEE OF THE SOCIETY ARE HERBERT CAHOON, PADRAIC COLUM, LEON EDEL (CHAIRMAN), MALCOM MERRITT, FRANCES STELOFF, AND WILLIAM YORK TINDALL. EX OFFICIO MEMBERS ARE MARIA JOLAS AND JAMES JOHNSON SWEENEY.

CONTENTS

LIST OF ILLUSTRATIONS

Introduction

MARVIN MAGALANER

T H E publication of a James Joyce *Miscellany* by a university press in the United States is of more than passing significance. In the half century during which the Irish author has received critical attention, the bulwark of support for his unusual artistry has been established almost exclusively in American colleges and among the intellectuals of this country. This is not to say that French critics, for instance, withheld their approval, or even that such distinguished English writers as E. M. Forster, though puzzled and a bit shocked, failed to take seriously their eccentric contemporary. It is to say, however, that mainly in the university climate of the United States there grew and flowered (and, some say, decayed) a responsible, technically demanding, time consuming, close examination of Joyce's works, undertaken by serious scholars to find out what Joyce was saying in his difficult books. Often the world has scoffed and smiled at the zeal with which professors and students swarm over Joyce's pages, but these academic labors have largely determined the now almost universal acceptance of Joyce as not only an important author but a readable one.

It is in the university too that Joyce is read — not only in specialized courses devoted entirely to his work such as are given from time to time at Columbia and Harvard universities, the University of Chicago, and New York University, but, even more important, in required courses offered to students whose major interest is not literature. *Dubliners* supplies stories for almost all contemporary anthologies. A *Portrait of the Artist* is a classroom text which many hundreds of young people — engineering students all — study at one New York college. And even *Ulysses* holds few terrors any more for enterprising undergraduates.

Now that Joyce is established as a major writer — dissenting opinions by V. S. Pritchett and Gilbert Highet notwithstanding — Joyce scholarship has taken a new turn. The guidebook approach, so valuable once, has been replaced by the specialized studies which are the province of the university presses. The past year has seen the publication of several: William Schutte's *Joyce and Shakespeare* and William T. Noon's *Joyce and Aquinas*. J. Mitchell Morse's *The Sympathetic Alien: James Joyce and Catholicism*. Finally, *Modern Fiction Studies*, published at Purdue University, devoted a number entirely to an explication of Joyce's works and to the most useful critical bibliography yet compiled (Spring, 1958). In this *Miscellany*, contributions by Ruth von Phul and John O. Lyons extend this trend.

If any catch-phrase can sum up scholarly activity with respect to Joyce during the fifties, it may be characterized as "the work of consolidation." The emphasis has been on making available to the interested public data hitherto inaccessible or difficult to examine. These years have seen the establishment or enrichment of Joyce collections, notably at Yale University and the University of Buffalo, and more recently at Cornell and Kansas universities, and in England at the British Museum. The importance of the university in this task is obvious from a mere glance at the list.

Furthermore, university presses have taken the lead in making available a large part of the contents of these collections to scholars who are unable to visit distant campuses. Buffalo undertook to publish Thomas Connolly's bibliography of *The Personal Library of James Joyce* and followed it with O. A. Silverman's edition of Joyce's *Epiphanies*.

A James Joyce *Miscellany*

SECOND SERIES

EDITED BY Marvin Magalaner

 Southern Illinois University Press

Carbondale, 1959

© 1959 BY SOUTHERN ILLINOIS UNIVERSITY PRESS
LIBRARY OF CONGRESS CATALOGUE CARD NUMBER 59-6903
MANUFACTURED IN THE UNITED STATES OF AMERICA
BY VAIL-BALLOU PRESS, INC., BINGHAMTON, NEW YORK
Designed by Andor Braun

To the memory of
PAUL LÉON
devoted friend and tireless adviser of
JAMES JOYCE

EDITOR'S NOTE

THE EDITOR owes a debt to many people for their splendid co-operation in helping to prepare this miscellany. Specifically he wishes to record his gratitude to Mr. Leon Edel, Chairman of the Publications Committee of the James Joyce Society, and to Mr. Herbert Cahoon, Curator of Autograph Manuscripts at the Pierpont Morgan Library, for good advice. Dr. H. K. Croessmann has been especially generous of time and of the resources of his Joyce Collection. To my wife Brenda I am indebted for encouragement and practical assistance.

For permission to quote from letters and unpublished manuscripts the editor wishes to acknowledge the kindness of Miss Harriet Weaver and the Administrators of the Joyce Estate; Mr. George Healey and the Cornell University Library; Mrs. Claire Gorman, Mr. Bennett Cerf, Mrs. Lucie Noel, Miss Gladys M. Palmer, Miss Phyllis A. Palmer, and Mr. Frank Budgen.

This book owes its appearance to the James Joyce Society and its policy of sponsoring historical and critical studies of the Irish writer.

M. M.

Northwestern University has issued Adaline Glasheen's *Census of Finnegans Wake*. The extensive bibliography of Joyce's own writings, edited by John J. Slocum and Herbert Cahoon, was Yale's contribution. Following this general trend toward consolidation, even commercial presses have accented the scholarly — Viking in bringing out Joyce's *Letters*, a second volume of which is now in preparation; and, from the same press, Stanislaus Joyce's *My Brother's Keeper* and the long sought collection of Joyce's critical writings, edited by Ellsworth Mason and Richard Ellmann. Columbia University Press has issued Kevin Sullivan's *Joyce among the Jesuits*. Abelard-Schuman Ltd. has recently published Louis Gillet's articles on Joyce in English translation, and the same firm will shortly bring out a detailed study of Joyce's early fiction by the present writer.

Significantly, this *Miscellany*, hardly by design, continues the tendency toward consolidation of scattered and hitherto unevaluated evidence. The inclusion of additional unpublished pages of *Stephen Hero* will afford scholars a preview of their contents until the pages can be incorporated in a new edition of the whole work. The exchange of letters regarding the schema of *Ulysses* makes available new material for biographers. In Joseph Prescott's analysis of Joyce's use of language, students are enabled to compare several versions of Joyce's final product in earlier stages — a project which would involve extensive travel, time, and expense if primary sources were to be consulted at first hand. Similarly, the contributions of Walton Litz, Richard M. Kain, and Michael J. O'Neill attempt to bring together and to categorize information never before sifted so effectively.

As the content of Joyce criticism has changed, there has been a concomitant alteration in its tone. Barring the shrill voices of his detractors, most writers on Joyce today go at their tasks with quiet confidence. There is no longer a need for the extravagances of literary manifestoes — for loud proclaiming of the rightness and seriousness of their labors.

In fact, the chapters in this *Miscellany* by Henry Morton Robinson, J. Mitchell Morse, and Herbert Howarth will show that a sense of humor and a sense of perspective are intruding happily on what used to be a scene of self-conscious high seriousness.

Biography remains the disturbing problem in Joyce criticism. Nor do the recent books on the subject help to uncomplicate it, for they are the product of people who are themselves highly individual and complex. The questions remain: what is the true relationship between Stephen Dedalus and James Joyce, biographically; between Bloom and his creator; between Joyce and his family. The National Council of Teachers of English recently devoted an entire convention session to these problems without reaching conclusive agreement. Nor will the chapters by Michael J. O'Neill, Maurice Beebe, Julian B. Kaye, and James Stern in this *Miscellany* provide definite answers. They are, however, tiny fragments of mosaic which, it is hoped, will contribute to the developing biographical pattern.

The *Miscellany* is testimony to the continuing acute interest in James Joyce. In the year and a half since the appearance of the first number, inquiries regarding contributions have come from such places as India, New Zealand, Austria, Ireland, England, and from all over the United States. It is probably fair to say that no other contemporary English or Irish writer is of sufficient stature to command the exclusive attention of a quarterly *Review* and, at the same time, a continuing series like the *Miscellany*. And though it would be foolish to equate popularity with merit, at this stage in the career of Joyce's literary reputation, the question is unlikely to arise.

April, 1959

A James Joyce *Miscellany*

SECOND SERIES

Five More Pages of James Joyce's *Stephen Hero*

JOHN J. SLOCUM

HERBERT CAHOON

L A T E in 1955, New Directions published a new edition of James Joyce's *Stephen Hero*, part of the first draft of his *A Portrait of the Artist as a Young Man*.[1] This new edition, edited by John J. Slocum and Herbert Cahoon, added twenty-five pages to the text that had been edited by Professor Theodore Spencer and first published in 1944. Mr. Slocum purchased these new pages in 1950 from Stanislaus Joyce, brother of James Joyce, and they are now in the Yale University Library. They precede numerically the three hundred eighty-three pages edited by Professor Spencer and are numbered 477–8, 481–89, 491–97, 499–505; the first page of the manuscript edited by Professor Spencer is numbered 519.

Messrs. Slocum and Cahoon attempted to locate missing pages with the numbers 479–80, 490, and 498, necessary to complete the continuity of the new text, but met with no success. In the belief that these pages had probably been destroyed they edited the major portion of the episode that had survived. The episode itself is of considerable interest to all readers of Joyce: Stephen's visit to his godfather, Mr. Fulham, in Mullingar, Westmeath, sometime after he had begun his studies at University College in 1898. Additional details of and background for this episode are given in the foreword to the 1955 edition.

In 1957, Cornell University Library announced the acquisition of a large collection of Joyce manuscripts and letters
from the estate of his brother Stanislaus. Among the manuscripts were the four pages missing from the episode published
in 1955 and one page numbered 506 which continues but does
not complete the episode. Although unhappy that the Cornell pages did not turn up in time for incorporation and
publication with the Yale pages the editors feel that they
should not wait for a new edition of *Stephen Hero* to make
these five new pages available to the public. With the kind
permission of the estate of James Joyce and the Cornell University Library they are printed here for the first time. When
Stephen Hero is next reprinted the editors hope that the
Cornell pages will be included in the book.

The pages as printed here, out of context, must be read
with the New Directions text in which the gaps have been
indicated. The story of the lame beggar and the argument
with Mr. Heffernan are now complete and we know what
was on the paper near the corpse of the woman from the
asylum. But the page added at the end of the episode leaves
us in greater suspense than ever, for Stephen seems about to
begin a romantic scene with Miss Howard. Perhaps in time
more pages of *Stephen Hero*, like fragments of Aquinas, will
appear to add to our knowledge and satisfy our curiosity.

Page 479

(*New Directions, p. 238; Cape, p. 241*):

of the ticket-collectors he paused for a few moments in in-
decision before he was sighted by the driver of a small dark-
green trap. The driver asked was he the young gentleman
for Mr Fulham and on Stephen's answering "yes" invited
him to climb up beside him on the seat. So they set off easily.
The trap which was not very clean [and it] jolted a good

deal and Stephen looked once or twice anxiously at his os-
cillating valise but the driver said he need have no fear. The
driver when he had said this a few times in the same words
fell silent a while and then asked didn't Stephen come from
Dublin. Re-assured on this point he fell silent again[st] and
began [to] with a deliberate whip to flick flies off the ill-
groomed hide between the shafts.

The trap went up the long crooked main street of the town
and crossing over the bridge of the canal made out for the
country. Stephen remarked that the houses were very small
but catching sight of a large square building that stood in
grounds closely walled [he asked]

Page 480

(*New Directions, p. 238; Cape, p. 241*):

he asked the driver what building it was. The driver told him
it was the lunatic asylum and added impressively that there
were a great many patients in it. The road wound through
heavy pasture lands and in [mea] field after field Stephen
saw herds of cattle fattening. Sometimes these cattle were in
the charge of a drowsy peasant but oftener they were left to
themselves and moved slowly from marsh to dry land and
from dry land to marsh as the will took them. The little cot-
tages along the road were covered with overblown roses and
in many of the doorways there would stand a woman gazing
silently over the flat country. Now and again a peasant plod-
ding along the road would give the driver the time of day
and if he judged Stephen worthy of the honour fumble at his
hat. Proceeding in this manner along the dusty road the trap
gradually drew near Mr Fulham's house.

It was an old irregular house, barely visible from the road,
and surrounded by a fair plantation. It was reached by an
untended drive and the ground behind it thick with clumps
of faded rhododendrons sloped down to the shore

Page 490

(New Directions, p. 243; Cape, p. 245):

they were almost Mongolian types, tall, angular and oblique-
eyed. Stephen whenever he walked behind a peasant always
looked first for the prominent cheek-bones that seemed to cut
the air and the peasants in their turn must have recognised
metropolitan features for they stared very hard at the youth
as if he were some rare animal[s]. One day Dan was sent into
the town to buy some medicine at the druggist's and Stephen
went in with him. The trap stopped in the main street before the druggist's and Dan handed down the order to a
ragged boy telling him to take it into the shop. The ragged
boy first showed the paper to an equally ragged friend and
then went into the shop. When they came out they stood
at the door of the shop gazing alternately from Stephen to
the horse's tail and back again. While they were thus gazing
they were confronted by a lame beggar who advanced towards them gripping his stick:

— It was yous called out names after me yestherday.

The two children huddling in the

Page 498

(New Directions, p. 247; Cape, p. 249):

have, of course after the love of God, is love of his native land.

— Jesus was not of your opinion, Mr Heffernan, said
Stephen.

— You speak very boldly, young man, said Mr Heffernan
reprovingly.

— I am not afraid to speak openly, answered Stephen, even
of the parish priest.

— You use the Holy Name glibly for one so young.

— Not in execration. I mean what I say. The ideal presented to mankind by Jesus is one of self-denial, of purity, and of solitude; the ideal you present to us is one of revenge, of passion and of immersion in worldly affairs.

— It seems to me that Stephen is right, said Miss Howard.

— I can see, said Mr Fulham, what these movements tend to.

— It is impossible for us all to live the lives of hermits! exclaimed Mr Heffernan desperately.

— We can combine the two lives by living as a Catholic should, doing

Page 506

(New Directions, p. 251; Cape, p. 253):

printed: The Lamp, a [mazn] magazine for . . . the rest was torn away and several other pieces of paper were floating about in the water.

The afternoon was well advanced before the young men separated. Stephen bade his friends goodbye, promising to renew acquaintance very soon, and took a path through the fields. The ground was very treacherous and he slipped often into bog-water. However he found a broad highway over the bog and here he was as secure as on the road. The sun was declining and against the deep gold of the western sky the figures of some bending turf-cutters were outlined. He reached Mr Fulham's house by a back road and climbing over the fence came up through a little wood. As he walked on the soft grass he made no noise. At the edge of the wood he stood still. Miss Howard was leaning on the high painted gate facing the sunset. The full glow of the sunset had covered her sombre vesture with streaks of rust and scattered spangles of rust upon her sombre hair. Stephen came towards her but when he was a few paces

NOTE

1. James Joyce, *Stephen Hero;* edited from the manuscript in the Harvard College Library by Theodore Spencer. A new edition incorporating the additional manuscript pages in the Yale University Library; edited by John J. Slocum and Herbert Cahoon (New York: New Directions, 1955). Also published by Jonathan Cape, London, in 1956.

2

Joyce, Gorman, and the Schema of *Ulysses:* An Exchange of Letters — Paul L. Léon, Herbert Gorman, Bennett Cerf

H . K . C R O E S S M A N N

S I X T E E N years before Herbert Gorman published his biography of Joyce in 1940, he had written another book, now less well remembered, entitled *James Joyce: His First Forty Years*, the first book-length study of the author. At that time, 1924, the two men had not met; but when Gorman proposed, the following year, to publish a revised edition, Joyce agreed to correct the inaccuracies in the first if Gorman would keep secret the fact of his collaboration. He did in fact draw up notes, now in my collection.

Gorman's plans were delayed, however, and before the first book was ready for republication, Joyce urged him to undertake instead a full biography, and promised to co-operate with him fully. Gorman was willing enough, but crises in his personal life hindered him. Joyce, meeting with crises of his own, was impatient; in letters we find him writing: "Gorman is confined to bed"; "Gorman seems to have vanished"; "Gorman *says* . . . he will . . . start on the book again"; "Gorman seems to be in bad health"; etc. For his part, Gorman felt that Joyce had not given him as much help as promised, and that the many trips around Europe to verify facts, which Joyce kept proposing he make, were beyond his means. Occasionally the tension between them rose to bitterness, as in

9

the affair of the schema of *Ulysses*, with which these letters from my collection are concerned. The schema also is in my collection.

References to the schema ("chart") appear here and there in Stuart Gilbert's *Letters of James Joyce*, notably in the letter to John Quinn, 3 September 1920 (145), and again, on the following page, in the letter to Carlo Linati, 21 September 1920. Doubtless it was on his mind from the beginning, proliferating and becoming more elaborate as he proceeded. In the letter to Linati, he comes closer to actual physical description of the document as finally prepared, with his reference to the sheets of paper. The schema measures approximately 40 inches horizontally by 7⅞ to 7¼ inches vertically, and consists of five typed sheets, from left to right, 8½, 8½, 8½, 8, and 8½ inches wide respectively, pasted together forming a scroll wound loosely around a mailing-tube, and covered by an unattached sheet of paper for protection.

An example of the inordinate jealousy with which Joyce surrounded this document, through the years previous to Stuart Gilbert's *James Joyce's Ulysses: A Study*, in 1930, is shown in the letter to Edmund Wilson, written for Joyce by Sylvia Beach, 20 August 1928 (264), in which Wilson is refused a copy. Valery Larbaud was furnished a copy and of course Stuart Gilbert had one. How many copies besides these and Gorman's were distributed is unknown, but it is certain that the number was very small. In spite of Joyce's secrecy, a few copies were bootlegged and reproduced more or less accurately from authorized copies.

In the initial letter of this series, Paul L. Léon writes to Herbert Gorman, on 22 November 1933, as follows:

Dear Mr Gorman,
    Mr Joyce wishes me to write to you on the following matter:
    He is being pestered by his American publishers about the inclusion in the American edition of *Ulysses* of a chart which he had drawn up some eleven years ago establishing the parallel episodes between *Ulysses* and the *Odyssey*. This

chart which had been written for Mr Valery Larbaud at the
time, had an absolutely private character and was not meant
for publication, least of all as an addition or interpretation
of the text. It had been communicated to you confidentially
and nobody in America knew of its existence at least as far
as the publishing circles are concerned.

The present publishers of *Ulysses* have obtained it, as they
tell us, from you and despite the repeated and absolute refusal
of Mr Joyce to allow them to print it in their edition they
keep on insisting on its inclusion.

This chart was communicated to you for the purposes of
the biography of Mr Joyce which you intended to write at
the time. I do not know if you intend to use it still or to
write the biography at all but as you have thus been
instrumental to this new plan would you please be good
enough to write to Random House, to your editor and to
Mr Joyce himself stating that the chart was communicated
to you and that you showed it and as it seems parted with
it without any authority and much to Mr Joyce's annoyance
as it seems the only way to put an end to their perpetual
insistence.

Stung by this display of temper, Gorman replies as follows:

43 MANCHESTER STREET,
MANCHESTER SQUARE,
LONDON, W.1.
NOV 25 1933

Dear Mr Joyce,

I have received this morning a letter from Mr. Paul Léon
evidently instigated by you in which it is assumed that I
have given a copy of the chart outlining the parallels between
Ulysses and the *Odyssey* to Random House, which, I believe,
is to publish the American edition of *Ulysses*. There is no
truth whatsoever in this assumption. I have neither seen nor
been in communication with Random House for years. If
they have the chart they must have received it from another
quarter than myself and if they say that I gave it to them
or authorized them to get or agreed to their publishing it
they are barefaced liars. I have written to Mr. Cerf of
Random House and I enclose herewith a copy of the letter.

Mr. Léon, much to my surprise, informs me in his letter
that the chart was communicated to me for the purposes
of the biography but as I have possessed the chart for six

or more years and the biography was broached only two
years ago I must point out that he is at fault. This chart
was sent me a long time ago to aid me in what was intended
to be a corrected edition of "James Joyce: His First Forty
Years." It was not "communicated" to me confidentially.
There was never anything said about showing or not showing
it. Naturally I possessed sense enough (which evidently you
and Mr. Léon doubt) not to publish it or suggest its
publication. It is true that I have shown it to certain friends
in the privacy of my study (Edmund Wilson, among them)
and it is possible that one of these friends copied it. I should
like very much to know myself and I have asked Mr. Cerf
to tell me where he got the chart. Under these conditions,
therefore, I can hardly acquiesce to Mr. Léon's rather absurd
demand that I write to Random House, my editor and
yourself "stating that that chart was communicated to me
and that I showed it and as it seems parted with it without
any authority." I have the chart with me in London.

Mr. Léon also says that he does not know whether I intend
to write the biography at all. Neither do I. I have asked you
the courtesy of a direct withdrawal of your permission in
this matter but as yet I have heard nothing from your or
your representative.

Gorman, having written Random House, receives this letter, of 12 December 1933, from Bennett Cerf:

Dear Herbert:
First let me dispose of this Ulysses chart business. I am
terribly sorry that you should have been drawn into this
controversy in any way, shape, or form, and I am writing
to Paul Léon at once telling him that it was no fault of yours
that this chart fell into our hands. At the time the chart
was shown to me I thought it such an excellent piece of
work that I immediately wrote to Paul Léon and asked him
to get Joyce's permission for us to include this chart in the
American edition of Ulysses. I expected his permission to
come as a matter of course, and was amazed at the vehemence
with which he refused. I still think that the publication of
such a chart could only result in increased sales of the book,
and what is more important, in increased understanding on
the part of the people who actually read the book. There
was no arguing with either Joyce or Léon in this matter,

however, so we dropped the idea. In light of the fact that
they became so angry about the whole business, I don't
think it would be fair for me to tell where I saw this chart.
I can only say that the man who showed it to me was acting
in perfect good faith and never had the slightest intention
of betraying anybody's confidence. I am enclosing a copy
of my letter to Léon about this matter, and I hope that you
will suffer no further inconvenience because of it. You must
believe that I never dreamed you would be drawn into this
matter in any way. As a matter of fact, the first time I had
the faintest knowledge that you were involved was when
Léon seemed to take for granted the fact that it was you
who had given the chart to me.

I cabled you this morning asking whether or not you had
made definite plans for the publication of the biography
you are doing of James Joyce. I suppose I am much too late
in this business and that you have already signed a contract
with somebody, but if you have not, I want to emphasize
how interested we would be in arranging with you for the
publication of this book. Now that the Ulysses case was
decided in our favor, we could sell the Biography and
Ulysses hand in hand. Probably one book would help the
other.

It occurs to me that you might be interested in seeing the
historic decision that Judge Woolsey handed down on the
Ulysses case, and I am enclosing a copy of it for you. It was
a great victory and has been hailed as such by every newspaper
in New York. We will publish the book complete and
unabridged on January 25, 1934, and at last Joyce will receive
some royalties on the American edition of his master work.

Looking forward to hearing from you, I remain . . .

The letter Cerf wrote to Léon, also on the 12 December
1933, is here reproduced in its entirety:

Mr. Paul Léon
24 Rue Casimir-Perier,
Paris, France
Dear Mr. Léon:

I was very much surprised to receive a letter from Herbert
Gorman this morning in which he told me that you had
accused him of turning over to us the Ulysses chart about
which we have had so much correspondence in the last few

weeks. I am writing to you at once to assure you that I have
neither seen nor heard a word from Mr. Gorman in the
last two years. The chart was shown to me some weeks ago
by someone who did not tell me where he had gotten hold
of it. Furthermore, he asked for no money for this chart and
was convinced that he was doing Mr. Joyce and ourselves
a great favor in letting us see it because he felt that its
inclusion in our edition of the book would result in greater
sales and what was even more important, would help clarify
the book for every reader. It is unnecessary for me to repeat
again that I thoroughly agree with this opinion, and regard
it as extremely unfortunate that Mr. Joyce would not give
us permission to use this chart.

The purpose of this letter, however, is not to reopen this
question. It is simply to assure you and Mr. Joyce once and
for all that Mr. Gorman had no knowledge whatever that
this chart was given to us, or for that matter, that a copy of
it even existed here in New York.

Cordially yours,
Bennett Cerf

RANDOM HOUSE

3

Stylistic Realism in Joyce's *Ulysses* *

JOSEPH PRESCOTT

I

A S the paper which follows represents a chapter of a longer study, I should like to make a few introductory and, later, a few concluding observations on the place of this chapter within the study as a whole.

Herbert Gorman's biography of James Joyce, containing valuable information and documents, Stuart Gilbert's analysis of the published text of *Ulysses*, Frank Budgen's record of Joyce's conversation and correspondence during the composition of *Ulysses*, and the writings of others have greatly increased our understanding and enjoyment of the novel. No one, however, has yet analyzed the materials of *Ulysses* as they were going through the creative process in Joyce's now widely scattered manuscripts, typescripts, proof sheets, and other preliminary drafts.

The purpose of this study is to analyze the technique of *Ulysses* as it is revealed by the growth of the text through

* An abbreviated version of this paper was read at the triennial congress of the International Federation for Modern Languages and Literatures, at the University of Heidelberg, on August 27, 1957. The writing of the paper was made possible, in part, by a sabbatical leave of absence from Wayne State University and a grant from the Committee on Research Activities of the Modern Language Association of America. Joyce's revisions are quoted by permission of the James Joyce Estate.

the innumerable, extensive, and significant changes which the author made in various stages in the writing of the book. The revisions constitute an enormous body of material which yields much new light on Joyce's intentions and methods.

The present study takes account of such things as the manuscript notebooks and sheets in the University of Buffalo Library, the manuscript of *Ulysses* owned by the late A. S. W. Rosenbach, a certain number of the scattered typescript sheets, the partial and untrustworthy serial version in the *Little Review*, a large collection of proof sheets now in the Harvard Library, and other documents in private hands. The fact that the proofs in the Harvard Library alone offer from one to eight galleys for any given segment of *Ulysses* should indicate how the materials afford a fascinating insight into Joyce's methods as well as a basis for observations on the entire history of the evolution of the novel.

This paper is one of two chapters on style. The other chapter, on "Varieties of Style," will, I trust, offset any impression that Joyce's writing can be ticketed with a single label.

II

In any discussion of style which concerns Joyce, one would do well to bear in mind Stendhal's definition: "le style est ceci: ‹Ajouter à une pensée donnée toutes les circonstances propres à produire tout l'effet que doit produire cette pensée.›" [1]

Of primary importance in the achievement of style, it need hardly be said, is precision in the use of words. Joyce's reputation on this score has eclipsed even that of his master Flaubert. The process of revision demonstrates beyond peradventure the fundamental role which the *mot juste* plays in Joyce's extraordinarily faithful realism.

For example, in a manuscript notebook we are told that under the leaf of his hat Stephen Dedalus "watched through quivering peacock lashes the southing sun." Joyce moves from "quivering peacock" to "peacockquivering", then to "peacocktwinkling", and finally, achieving the published version, to "peacocktwittering".[2]

Miles Crawford, the newspaper editor, wishes to see his dayfather:

Where's what's his name?
He looked about him round his loud unanswering machines.
— Monks, sir?
— Ay. Where's Monks?

After "sir?" Joyce adds in galley proof, "a voice asked from behind the castingbox." [3] The impression of unbodied source made by the speech of an unseen speaker is exactly reproduced.[4]

Later in the day, from "the window of the D. B. C. Buck Mulligan gaily, and Haines gravely, gazed down on the viceregal carriages". Joyce alters "carriages" to "equipage",[5] giving us, instead of undistinguished vehicles, a carriage of state with all that accompanies it, in this case horses, outriders, and the following carriage — the whole scene.

When the citizen takes "out his handkerchief to swab himself dry", we read:

The muchtreasured and intricately embroidered ancient Irish facecloth attributed to Solomon of Droma and Manus Tomaltach, authors of the Book of Ballymote, was then carefully produced and called forth prolonged admiration. The scenes depicted on it are as wonderfully beautiful and the pigments as delicate as when the Sligo illuminators gave free rein to their artistic fantasy long long ago in the time of the Barmecides.

Among other changes, Joyce replaces the colorless "it" with "the emunctory field".[6] With this impressively exact phrase he punctures the passage even as he inflates it.

To enter his home, at the end of the day, Bloom "raised the

latch of the area door by the exertion of force at its free arm".
For "free arm" Joyce substitutes "freely moving flange".[7]

As we all know, however, precision does not denote only
exactness with the independent word. There is also precision
within a context — appropriateness. In this kind, too, Joyce
excels.

At twilight,

A lost long candle wandered up the sky from Mirus bazaar
in aid of funds for Mercer's hospital and broke, drooping,
and shed a cluster of violet but one white stars.

Joyce alters "aid" to "search",[8] adapting a phrase from the
placard advertising the bazaar [9] to one which, fitting into its
context more appositely, gives the whole sentence a unity of
effect it formerly did not possess, and at the same time ac-
cords with the anthropomorphic impressions which Bloom
has, in his drowsy state, of other inanimate things mentioned
in the same paragraph.

In another passage we may watch Joyce at work selecting
the precisely appropriate word. To men's praises of Bloom,
Joyce adds the following:

Women whisper eagerly.)

A MILLIONAIRESS

(*richly*) Isn't he simply wonderful?

A NOBLEWOMAN

(*nobly*) All that man has seen!

A FEMINIST

(*masculinely*) And done! [10]

The adverb qualifying the first speech did not come to Joyce
at one stroke. He first wrote "entl" ("ent[husiastically]"?
[the *t* is uncrossed, the presumed *h*, only half-completed]),
then he deleted that and wrote "(adoringly)", and finally he
deleted that for the highly appropriate "*richly*" which consists with the millionairess as "*nobly*" does with the noblewoman and "*masculinely*" with the feminist.

Among Bloom's memories of Milly as an infant, is "a doll, a boy, a sailor she threw away:". Joyce alters "threw" to "cast".[11] And how much more appropriate it is that the sailor should have been *cast away*.

When he can do so without violence to dramatic propriety, Joyce even manipulates the style of his characters in the interest of precision. The reader who deals with the final text cannot be aware of the improvement.

Even Bloom, who might well be forgiven a lack of precision, is not immune to such revision. In the morning he considers: "Dislike dressing together. Cut myself shaving." Joyce alters "Cut" to "Nicked".[12]

At the funeral Bloom recalls Dignam's appearance: "Blazing face: redhot. Cure for a red nose. Drink like the devil till it turns puce." For "puce" Joyce substitutes "adelite" [13] — and, since adelite is gray, while puce would still give us red (though a weak red), the cure is now complete.

Later in the same episode, we again see Joyce at work adding precision through the mind of Bloom. An interpolation begins as "Only a mother and child ever buried in the one coffin." Then, before "child" Joyce adds "newborn". Finally, he changes "newborn" to "deadborn",[14] achieving complete accuracy.

Bloom recalls a snatch from *The Young May Moon*: "Glowworm's lamp is gleaming, love." Changing "lamp" to "la-amp",[15] Joyce accounts exactly for the two notes to which the word is sung.[16]

But genius can err, and in a number of revisions Joyce confutes Stephen's proud claim to the contrary,[17] for these changes create difficulties, particularly with respect to precision.

Mr. Deasy, in paying Stephen Dedalus, lays two notes on the table. "— Two, he said, stowing his pocketbook away." In manuscript, Joyce inserts "strapping and" before "stowing" [18] without eliminating the awkwardness of "strapping . . . his pocketbook away."

Bloom has hurried downstairs to save the burning kidney:

"By prodding a prong of the fork under the kidney he detached it and turned it over on its back." For "over" Joyce substitutes "turtle" [19] — in itself certainly an improvement, except that it introduces a tautology which Joyce does not eliminate.

In the passage describing Bloom's exit from All Hallows Church, the following sentence is added: "He stood a moment unseeing by the cold stone stoup while before him and behind two worshippers dipped furtive hands in the low tide of holy water." [20] Later "cold stone stoup" becomes "cold black marble bowl",[21] which, while it adds precision in further qualifying the basin, eliminates the specific ecclesiastical "stoup" for the general "bowl".

Lenehan has just told M'Coy how Tom Rochford once saved a man's life:

— The act of a hero, he [Lenehan] said.
At the Dolphin he halted.
— This way, he said, walking to the right. I want to pop into Lynam's to see Sceptre's starting price. What's the time by your gold watch and chain?

Joyce changes the second sentence to read: "At the Dolphin they halted to allow the ambulance car to gallop past them." [22] He fails, however, to make the now necessary revision, in the third sentence, of "he said" to "Lenehan said". As it stands, the statement leaves the reader uncertain who the speaker is, and the doubt is resolved only later, when M'Coy replies.

In the penultimate episode, a confusion is introduced as another difficulty is eliminated.

What marks of special hospitality did the host [Bloom] show his guest [Stephen]?
Relinquishing his right to the moustache cup of imitation crown Derby presented to him by his only daughter, Millicent, he drank from a cup identical with that of his guest and served to his guest and, in reduced measure, to himself, the

cream usually reserved for the breakfast of his wife Marion (Molly).

Were there marks of hospitality which he contemplated but suppressed, reserving them for another and for himself on future occasions?

The reparation of a fissure of the length of 1½ inches in the right side of his guest's jacket. A gift to his guest of one of the four lady's handkerchiefs, if and when ascertained to be in a presentable condition.

Was the guest conscious of and did he acknowledge these marks of hospitality?

His attention was directed to them by his host jocosely and he accepted them seriously as they drank in silence.

The third answer, in this version, implies that the guest could *accept* marks of hospitality which the host contemplated but suppressed. Joyce therefore transposes the last two units of question and answer,[23] so that the acceptance now relates to marks of hospitality actually shown.

The revision, however, introduces a confusion of reference. In the old version, it was perfectly clear that Bloom was "he" who "contemplated but suppressed", for the subject of the preceding answer — "he" — , as well as the seven other pronominal forms in the statement, referred to "the host" of the first question. But in the new version, both subjects of the preceding sentence — "His attention" and "he" — refer to "the guest". To clear up this detail required only the substitution of "the host" for "he" before "contemplated" — an improvement which Joyce failed to make here and did not fail to make in neighboring passages.[24]

Through a mirror Bloom sees the "optical reflection of several inverted volumes with scintillating titles on the two bookshelves opposite." After "volumes" Joyce adds "improperly arranged and not in the order of their common letters".[25] As a result, "with scintillating titles" is awkwardly distant from "volumes" and uncomfortably close to "letters".

But these few lapses should not blind us to the fact that the great mass of Joyce's innumerable revisions represent improvement of one kind or another. And now I pass to another kind, namely, specification. A writer who strives for precision will probably also aim at being concrete and specific. In a whole group of changes Joyce moves steadily from the general to the particular.

Near the opening of the first episode, Stephen, leaning on the parapet of the Martello tower, "looked down on the water." From a preceding sentence we know that "the water" is "Dublin bay",[26] but it is unqualified; we know nothing more about it than that it is the water of Dublin Bay. Joyce deletes the period to add "and on the mailboat clearing the harbour mouth of Kingstown." [27] — and at once the bay has assumed the detailed features of a particular scene. The further specification by kind of boat and by place-name needs no comment. But the location of the boat introduces perspective. Stephen's general view, starting with the whole undifferentiated expanse of the harbor, converges upon a particular point, the mouth; and his awareness of the mouth implies awareness of the shores running round to it, and of the sea beyond. More important still, with the boat in the act of leaving the harbor, the hitherto inert scene has taken on motion. Again and again, as we shall see,[28] Joyce introduces movement.

And the mailboat goes on moving. Toward the close of the episode, Haines "gazed over the bay, empty save for a sail tacking by the Muglins." After "for" Joyce adds "the smokeplume of the mailboat vague on the bright skyline and".[29] The ship has sailed, in the course of the episode, from the harbor mouth to a point near the horizon on the open sea.

When the Citizen threw the tinbox at Bloom, the "observatory at Dunsink registered in all eleven shocks and there is no record extant of a similar seismic disturbance in our island since the earthquake of 1534, the year of the rebellion of Silken Thomas." After "shocks" Joyce adds technical specifications: ", all of the fifth grade of Mercalli's scale,".[30]

At midnight, in answer to a stern summons from the watch,

Bloom, "(*Scared, makes Masonic signs.*)".[31] Between this galley and publication, for the indefinite last three words Joyce substitutes specific signs: "*hats himself, steps back then, plucking at his heart and lifting his right forearm on the square, he gives the sign and dueguard of fellowcraft*".

Bloom is about to have his babies:

A NURSETENDER

Embrace me tight, dear. You'll be soon over it. Tight, dear.

Joyce changes the anonymous "A NURSETENDER" to "*Mrs Thornton*", whom we have already met.[32]

Almost immediately afterward, Bloom hints that he may be a messiah:

A LAYBROTHER

Then perform a miracle.

Joyce changes "A LAYBROTHER" to "BROTHER BUZZ",[33] whom, also, we have met before.[34]

Soon afterward, again, a general occupational term is replaced by the name of a specific practitioner already known to us:

A BUSHRANGER

What did you do in the cattlecreep behind Kilbarrack?

For "A BUSHRANGER" Joyce substitutes "*Crab*".[35]

Later in the same episode, "(*The widow woman, her snubnose and cheeks flushed with deathtalk, fears and Tunny's tawny sherry, hurries by in her weeds, her bonnet awry.*" For "*The*" Joyce substitutes "Mrs Dignam," [36] whose husband's funeral Bloom had attended in the morning.

When Bloom and Stephen had their cocoa, we learn, Bloom drank his more quickly, "having the advantage of ten seconds at the initiation and taking three sips to his opponent's one." Joyce deletes the period and adds ", six to two, nine to three." [37] By this addition the figures first given are transformed from an abstract mathematical ratio into part

of a specific relative progression by the drinkers, one of whom,
it now appears, emptied his cup in nine sips, the other in
three.[38]

Bloom and Stephen construct scenes suggested by the
former's unrealized project of an advertising showcart.[39]
Then Stephen narrates his *Pisgah Sight of Palestine* or *Parable of the Plums*, which,

with the preceding scene [Stephen's construction] and with
others unnarrated but existent by implication, to which add
essays on various subjects composed during schoolyears,
seemed to him [Bloom] to contain in itself and in conjunction with the personal equation certain possibilities of financial, social, personal and sexual success,[40]

After "subjects" Joyce adds "or moral apothegms (e.g. *My
Favourite Hero* or *Procrastination is the Thief of Time*)".[41]

As for precision, so for specification, Joyce unobtrusively
manages the thought of his characters. Thus, Bloom, thinking
about the railway lost property office, generalizes:

Astonishing the things people leave behind them in trains
and cloak rooms. What do they be thinking about? Women
too. Incredible. There's a little watch up there on the roof
of the bank to test those glasses by.

After "Incredible." Joyce adds a pair of specific examples:
"Last year travelling to Ennis had to pick up that farmer's
daughter's bag and hand it to her at Limerick junction. Unclaimed money too." [42]

Bloom is thinking about menstruation: "All kinds of crazy
longings. Girl in Tranquilla convent that nun told me liked
to smell rock oil." Between the generalization and the specimen Joyce inserts another specimen: ". Licking pennies." [43]

Bloom's thoughts are again on women:

Poor idiot! His wife has her work cut out for her. Sharp as
needles they are. When I said to Molly the man at the corner
of Cuffe street was goodlooking, thought she might like,
twigged at once he had a false arm. Had too. Where they get
that? Handed down from father to mother to daughter, I
mean.

The rest of the paragraph contains further specimens of feminine sharpness. But let us confine ourselves to the changes in the passage cited. Here Joyce works Bloom's thought up to the generalization on sharpness by introducing specific examples before it: ". Never see them sit on a bench marked *Wet Paint*. Eyes all over them. Look under the bed for what's not there." [44] In a later galley, after "that?", Joyce adds still another specimen: ". Typist going up Roger Greene's stairs two at a time to show her understandings." [45]

Molly looks back upon her courtship:

then [Leopold] writing a letter every morning sometimes twice a day I liked the way he made love then he knew the way to take a woman then I wrote the night he kissed my heart at Dolphin's barn I couldn't describe it simply it makes you feel like nothing on earth

After "woman" Joyce introduces another specimen of Bloom's knowledge: "when he sent me the 8 big poppies because mine was the 8th".[46]

Molly recalls her last day with Mulvey: "I was a bit wild after coming back". Following "after" Joyce introduces a specimen of Molly's wildness: "when I blew out the old bag the biscuits were in from Albertis and exploded it Lord what a bang all the woodcocks and pigeons screaming".[47] Another specimen, already embedded in the text, follows shortly after.[48]

Molly plans to buy fish for the day which has just begun: "anyway Im sick of that everlasting butchers meat or [it occurs to her] a picnic". After "butchers meat" Joyce begins to specify by inserting "from Buckleys".[49] Later, after "Buckleys" he adds specimens of the meat: "loin chops and leg beef and rib steak and scrag of mutton".[50] Later still,[51] after "mutton" he adds further "and calfs pluck".

Perhaps the most interesting introduction of the specific through the mind of a character occurs in the penultimate episode. The type of advertisement represented by Plumtree's Potted Meat, which Bloom has twice condemned,[52] is cited as one which he would not use. The statement, in manu-

script, concludes as follows: "The name on the label is Plumtree." After this sentence, Joyce adds: "A plumtree in a meat-
pot, registered trade mark." [53] Following this addition, the
first galley proof contains the phrase "Beware of imitations.",
after which Joyce adds further: "Plumtree." [54] We have here,
at this stage, either a quotation from the advertisement [55]
or a verbalized image of the label (either as reproduced in the
advertisement or perhaps as attached to the pot). In a later
galley Joyce replaces the newly introduced "Plumtree" with
"Peatmot. Trumplee." [56] And between this second galley and
publication, after "Trumplee." he must have added further:
"Montpat. Plamtroo." In other words, the passage shifts
ground. For the quotation from the advertisement or the
visualization of the label, as the case may be, now ends with
the warning "Beware of imitations.", and the words following represent specimen names of possible imitations which
echo the name of the genuine product. These specimens,
considered in themselves and especially in their context,[57]
must be regarded as indirect quotation of Bloom's thought
on the warning.

Not only does Joyce move from the general to the specific.
In many revisions, he adds vivid picture-making details.

A number of these additions consist of single individualiz-
ing touches which vivify the hitherto undefined or vaguely
realized. Bloom sees a boy smoking: "A smaller girl eyed him
[the boy], listlessly holding her battered caskhoop." After
"girl" Joyce adds "with scars of eczema on her forehead".[58]

Bloom passes "over a hopscotch court." Joyce deletes the
period to add "with its forgotten pickeystone." [59]

"Horses with white frontlet plumes" come round a corner
as Bloom is riding to Glasnevin. Joyce changes the "Horses"
to "White horses".[60]

In another group of changes, Joyce introduces movement
or heightens action already present. Bloom, in the butcher's
shop, considers the nextdoor girl: "Strong pair of arms.
Whacking a carpet on the clothesline. She does whack it, by

George." Following this, Joyce adds: "The way her crooked, skirt swings at each whack." [61] — giving us repeated motion. Shortly afterward, we read: "The crooked skirt swinging whack by whack by whack." [62] And later in the day, the thought of punishment reminds Bloom of "The crooked skirt swinging, whack by." [63]

Bloom visualizes: "Drinkers, drinking, laughed." Joyce deletes the period and adds "spluttering, their drink against their breath." [64]

In the library: " — Are you going, John Eglinton's eyebrows asked." Before "eyebrows" Joyce adds "active".[65]

The tale of Bloom's encounter with the Citizen is drawing to a close: "Begob he [the Citizen] made a swipe and let fly." After "he" Joyce adds "drew his hand and".[66]

Among Bloom's accusers we hear:

A FEMALE INFANT

And under Ballybough bridge?

Before "And" Joyce adds "(shakes a rattle)".[67]

Bloom's grandfather is described: "(*Profuse yellow spawn foaming over his bony epileptic lips.*)" Joyce alters the opening to read: "(*Agueshaken, profuse*".[68]

Bloom and Stephen observe a "star precipitated with great apparent velocity from Vega in the lyre above the zenith beyond the stargroup of the Tress of Berenice towards the zodiacal sign of Leo." After "velocity" Joyce adds "across the firmament" [69] — so that we now see the star against its background, without which the picture of its motion would be incomplete.

Molly remembers: "she [Mrs. Galbraith] was a lovely woman magnificent head of hair on her down to her waist like Kitty O'Shea". After "waist" Joyce adds "tossing it back like that".[70]

As may already have been observed, Joyce makes things present to various senses. Thus, Bloom looking toward his bath, "foresaw his pale body reclined in it at full, naked, oiled by scented melting soap, softly laved." After "naked," Joyce adds ", in a womb of warmth," [71] — without which what bath of Bloom's could be complete? [72]

Another case in point follows an addition in which Joyce introduces into Molly's thought: "and when the priest was going by with the vatican to the dying blessing herself for his Majestad". After "with" he adds further "the bell bringing" [73] — and we hear as well as see.

In his desire to present reality as precisely, as specifically, and as vividly as possible, Joyce often abandons narrative for drama. This is true not only in part of the library episode [74] and in that welter of reality, the brothel scene, but also in many isolated passages which suddenly take flight, as it were, from the narrator's, or the character's, mouth,[75] and present themselves independently.

Thus, Stephen recalls an early experience with water: "When I put my face into it in the basin at Clongowes. Out quickly, quickly." In this version, the second sentence may be read as Stephen's present narrative thought compressed: 'I wished to take my face out of it very quickly.' But between the two sentences Joyce inserts: "Can't see! Who's behind me?" [76] Not only do these speeches introduce straightforward, immediate dramatization, or historical drama in the form of quotation; they also draw into their orbit "Out quickly, quickly!", which can now mean only one of two things: 'I wish to take my face out of it quickly, quickly!' or, more urgently, 'Take it out quickly, quickly!'

Bloom checks a didactic impulse: "Tell him if he smokes he won't grow. O let him! His life isn't such a bed of roses!" Following this, Joyce adds: "Waiting outside pubs to bring da home. Come home to ma, da." [77] The speech converts the scene into drama.

In church Bloom thinks: "Confession. Great weapon in their hands." Between these sentences Joyce inserts: "Everyone wants to. Then I will tell you all. Punish me, please." [78]

Bloom goes on in the same vein: "Pray at an altar. Flowers, incense, candles melting." Again, between these sentences, Joyce inserts a dramatizing agent: "Hail Mary and Holy Mary." [79] And there is more drama in the context.[80]

Bloom is now thinking, characteristically, of the income of the Church: "Bequests also: to say so many masses." For the narrative "to say so many masses" Joyce substitutes a quotation from a specific bequest: "to the P. P. for the time being in his absolute discretion. Masses for the repose of my soul to be said publicly with open doors." [81]

Soon afterward Bloom discovers that two buttons of his waistcoat are open: "Women enjoy it. Never tell you." Between these sentences Joyce inserts: "Annoyed if you don't. Why didn't you tell me before." [82] Here, also, there is more drama in the context.[83]

Bloom has just explained to Mrs. Breen why he is in black: "Going to crop up all day, I foresee. Turn up like a bad penny." Between these sentences Joyce adds: "Who's dead, when and what did he die of?" [84]

Bloom recalls a nurse: "Old Mrs Thornton was a jolly old soul." Following this, Joyce adds: "Got her hand crushed by old Tom Wall's son. His first bow to the public. Head like a prize pumpkin." Then, before "Got" Joyce adds two dramatic specimens of the nurse's jolliness: "All my babies, she said. The spoon of pap in her mouth before she fed them. O, that's nyumnyum." [85] Interestingly enough, Bloom had once before presented Mrs. Thornton in her own words.[86] And we have already seen her enter the drama of the brothel.[87]

The sight of Sir Frederick Falkiner, recorder of Dublin, moves Bloom to think: "Old legal cronies cracking a magnum. I suppose he'd turn up his nose at that wine I drank." Between these sentences Joyce inserts: "Tales of the bench and assizer and annals of the bluecoat school. I sentenced him to ten years." [88]

Toward the close of the library scene Buck Mulligan chaffs Stephen for having attacked the work of Lady Gregory:

Couldn't you do the Yeats touch?
He went on and down, chanting with waving graceful arms:
— I have conceived a play for the mummers, he said solemnly.

After "arms:" Joyce adds a dramatized specimen of the Yeats touch:

— The most beautiful book that has come out of our country in my time. One thinks of Homer.[89]

The narrator of the *Cyclops* episode is discussing Blazes Boylan: "Dirty Dan the dodger's son that sold the same horses twice over to the government to fight the Boers. That's the bucko that'll organize her, take my tip." Between these sentences Joyce inserts: ". Old Whatwhat. I called about the poor and water rate, Mr Boylan. You what? The water rate, Mr Boylan. You whatwhat?" [90]

At twilight Bloom reflects: "Sad however because it lasts only a few years till they [girls] settle down to potwalloping and fuller's earth for the baby when ah ah." After "potwalloping" Joyce adds "and papa's pants will soon fit Willy and".[91]

Shortly afterward, Bloom considers the plight of a Mrs. Duggan: "Husband rolling in drunk, stink of pub off him like a polecat. Have that in your nose all night, whiff of stale boose. Bad policy however to fault the husband." After the second sentence Joyce adds: ". Then ask in the morning: was I drunk last night?" [92]

In one change, a shift from the author's to a character's point of view represents a shift from narrative to dramatic presentation of the character's thought. Bloom thinks of the young student whose acquaintance Milly has made: "O well: she knows how to mind herself. But if not? No, nothing had happened. Of course it might. Wait in any case till it did." Joyce alters "had" to "has" and "did" to "does".[93] Apparently,

Joyce had nodded into the conventional indirect mode of presenting thoughts, and here caught himself, as on another occasion he did not.[94]

Allied to all the aids to realism which I have thus far discussed — precision, specification, vividness, and dramatization — is Joyce's primal and unremitting interest in onomatopoeia.[95]

Stephen, in a passage which was part of an addition in a manuscript notebook containing an early version of the third episode, recalls a Parisian experience: "the barrier of the post office shut in your face by the usher." [96] In proof, Joyce fills this soundless memory with the clamor of the actual event as he alters the passage to read: "the banging door of the post office slammed in your face by the usher." [97]

In the same manuscript notebook, Joyce adds:

Listen: a fourworded wavespeech: seesoo, hrss, rsseeiss, oos. Vehement breath of water amid seasnakes, rearing horses, rocks. In cups of rocks it slops: flop, slop, slap; bounded in barrels. And, spent, its speech ceases: it flows purling, wide-flowing, floating foampool, flower unfurling.[98]

Bloom, in proof, considers the way women prepare a corpse for burial: "Huggermugger in corners. Then getting it ready." Between these sentences Joyce inserts: "Slop about in slipper-slappers for fear he'd wake." [99]

On the way to Dignam's funeral, the carriage bearing Bloom stops to allow a drove of cattle to pass: " — Huuu! the drover's voice cried, his switch sounding on their flanks. Huuu out of that!" Joyce alters both "Huuu!" and "Huuu" to "Huuuh!" [100] — adding, with the aspirate, the final expulsion of breath which the prolonged cry necessitates.

At the cemetery, it occurs to Bloom that a gramophone might help one remember the dead: "Have a gramophone in every grave or keep it in the house. Remind you of the voice like the photograph reminds you of the face." Between these sentences Joyce introduces a dramatic performance:

After dinner on a Sunday. Put on poor old greatgrandfather. Kraahraark! Hellohellohello amawfullyglad kraark awfully-gladaseeagain hellohello amawf krpthsth.[101]

Almost immediately afterward, Bloom becomes aware of a rat by the noise it makes: "Ssld! A rattle of pebbles. Wait. Stop." Joyce changes "Ssld!", which is rather like a hiss, to "Rtststr!",[102] which bursts with "rattle" (itself felicitous for its inclusion of the animal's name) and ratness.

At the tale of Pyrrhus' failure to "retrieve the fortunes of Greece": " — Boohoo! Lenehan wept with a little noise." Following this, Joyce adds in proof: "Poor, poor, poor Pyrrhus!" [103] The whimpering explosive and the lugubrious vowel, effectively repeated, galvanize Lenehan's dream of passion. An entirely different effect is achieved in manuscript with the same explosive when, later in the day, Molly Bloom, "plump as a pouter pigeon", becomes "plump as a pampered pouter pigeon".[104]

In the Burton Restaurant Bloom sees a man at lunch: "Scoffing up stewgravy with bread." Before the last word Joyce inserts "sopping sippets of".[105] The added sibilants, reinforcing those already present, render the effect almost physically.

Another man in the Burton blows the froth from his tankard: "Well up: it splashed yellow near his boot." Following this, Joyce adds:

A diner, knife and fork upright, elbows on table, ready for a second helping stared towards the foodlift. Other chap telling him something with his mouth full. Sympathetic listener. Table talk. I munched hum un thu Unchster Bunk un Munchday. Ha? Did you? [106]

Joyce's comment on an earlier mouthful is pertinent to this one as well. The author is reading to Budgen from the third episode:

"Sir Lout's toys. Mind you don't get one bang on the ear. I'm the bloody well giant rolls all them bloody well boulders,

bones for my steppingstones. Feefawfum. I zmells de bloodz
oldz an Iridzman."

Joyce read this with stammering, cluttered utterance, then
stopped with a laugh at the odd sounds he made. . . .

". . . My Sir Lout [said Joyce] has rocks in his mouth
instead of teeth. He articulates badly." [107]

Towards the close of the *Cyclops* episode, we hear of the
enraged Citizen cursing "bell book and candle in Irish and Joe
and little Alf trying to peacify him." After "Irish" Joyce adds
"spitting and spatting out of him".[108]

In the brothel scene, between 'REUBEN J's' "Nip the
first rattler." and a speech by Brother Buzz, Joyce must have
introduced, between the galley in which Brother Buzz's words
are added [109] and the Hanley proof, the speech of

THE FIRE BRIGADE

Pflaap! [110]

Later in the same episode, Virag *"chases his tail.)* Piffpaff!
Popo! (*He stops, sneezes.)* Pchp!" Following this, Joyce adds:
"(*he worries his butt*) Prrrrht!" [111]

The Croppy Boy, about to be hanged, has just said:

I bear no hate to a living thing,
But I love my country beyond the king.

The executioner, after a professional speech,

*jerks the rope, the croppy boy's tongue protrudes violently.
A violent erection of the hanged sends gouts of sperm spout-
ing through his death clothes on to the cobble stones.*

Between these sentences Joyce adds closing and opening
parentheses respectively, and between the parentheses he inserts:

THE CROPPY BOY

Horhot ho hray hor hother's hest [112]

The speech that is strangled with the young martyr is an
abbreviated version of a line in the ballad from which he is

quoting himself, as he echoes Benjamin Dollard's performance of an earlier hour: [113] "And forgot to pray for my
mother's rest." [114]

As has been observed,[115] one form of innovation which Joyce
uses is distortion. In connection with personal names, this
takes the form of variation for purposes suitable to given contexts. Two such variations introduced in proof, create a de-
sired atmosphere by sound effects. At Stephen's explanation
of Shakespeare's cuckoldry: " — Cuckoo! Cuckoo! Buck Mulligan clucked lewdly. O word of fear!" Joyce alters "Buck" to
"Bird",[116] and, later, "Bird" to "Cuck".[117]

Soon afterward, "Puck" Mulligan exclaims about John
Eglinton: " — O, the chinless Chinaman!" After this, Joyce
adds: "Chin Chon Eg Lin Ton." [118]

But Joyce's most interesting imitative contributions are yet
to come. In the brothel scene, Molly appears in Turkish
costume, beside her a camel: *"Fiercely she slaps his haunch,
scolding him in Moorish.)"* After *"haunch,"* Joyce adds
", her goldcurb wristbangles angriling,".[119] The vividly ono-
matopoeic verb (note the ting-a-ling of "angriling"; and the
clash of "-bangles angril-", to get which Joyce produces "wristbangles" on the analogy of *wristbands*) is coined by conversion, *angrily* giving rise to "angriling" as *almost* earlier
gave rise to "almosting".[120]

A hunt is on. Simon Dedalus *"makes the beagle's call giving
tongue.)* Bulbul! Burblblbrurblbl! Hai, boy!" Almost directly
afterward: *"The fox, brush pointed, runs swift, brighteyed,
under the leaves. The crowd bawls of dicers, crown and
anchor players, thimbleriggers, broadsmen."* Between these
sentences Joyce inserts: *"The pack follows sniffing their
quarry, beaglebaying, burblbrbling to be blooded."* [121] Here
Joyce carries onomatopoeia through two stages. In Mr.
Dedalus' speech he catches the beagle's cry; in the added
stage direction, he converts the cry into a verb. By the same
process he gives us the sound "Clipclap",[122] and verbifies it
in *"Clipclaps"*.[123]

But Joyce does not limit himself to sound effects. In order to imitate experiences as accurately as possible, he resorts to the use of rhythms. Thus, he once told Budgen that he had "been working hard all day" on two sentences:

"You have been seeking the *mot juste?*" I [Budgen] said.
"No," said Joyce. "I have the words already. What I am seeking is the perfect order of words in the sentence. There is an order in every way appropriate. I think I have it."
"What are the words?" I asked.
". . . I am now writing the *Lestrygonians* episode, which corresponds to the adventure of Ulysses with the cannibals. My hero is going to lunch. But there is a seduction motive in the Odyssey, the cannibal king's daughter. Seduction appears in my book as women's silk petticoats hanging in a shop window. The words through which I express the effect of it on my hungry hero are: 'Perfume of embraces all him assailed. With hungered flesh obscurely, he mutely craved to adore.' You can see for yourself in how many different ways they might be arranged." [124]

On the same page in *Lestrygonians*, Bloom, in the Burton Restaurant, sees a "man spitting back on his plate: gristle: no teeth to chew it." Before "gristle" Joyce adds "halfmasticated", which prepares for his replacement of "chew" by "chewchewchew".[125] A hitherto inert statement now puts us vicariously, and vividly, through a dynamically realized process. And in this one change we have the shaping spirit of such other reduplicates as "ripple", [126] "creecries", [127] "Clapclop. Clipclap. Clappyclap." [128] and "Clapclap. . . . Clappyclapclap. . . . Clapclipclap. . . . Clapclopclap." [129] and *"Clipclaps"*,[130] "gigglegiggled",[131] "spillspilling",[132] "Jigjag. Jigajiga. Jigjag.",[133] "pullpull",[134] and "curchycurchy".[135]

To revert to an earlier episode, the technique of a whole group of passages is illustrated by Joyce's treatment of Bloom in the jakes. The session with the old number of *Titbits* is on:

Something new and easy. Our prize titbit. . . . He allowed his bowels to ease themselves quietly as he read, reading patiently that slight constipation of yesterday quite gone. . . . He glanced back through what he had read and envied kindly

Mr Beaufoy who had written it and received payment of three pounds thirteen and six.

When Joyce has done revising, this passage reads:

Something new and easy. No great hurry. Keep it a bit. Our prize titbit. . . . Quietly he read, restraining himself, the first column and, yielding but resisting, began the second. Midway, his last resistance yielding, he allowed his bowels to ease themselves quietly as he read, reading still patiently that slight constipation of yesterday quite gone. . . . He glanced back through what he had read and, while feeling his water flow quietly, he envied kindly Mr Beaufoy who had written it and received payment of three pounds thirteen and six.

Alternately interrupting identically timed themes, Joyce has caught with superb precision the effect of simultaneity.[136]

The evolution of a speech by Mulligan, in the library scene, further illustrates Joyce's sensitiveness to rhythm. Mulligan addresses Stephen in a parody of Synge:

— It's what I'm telling you, mister honey, it's queer and sick we were, Haines and myself, the time himself brought it in. And we one hour and two hours and three hours in Connery's sitting civil waiting for pints apiece.

Between these sentences Joyce inserts:

'Twas murmur we did for a gallus potion would rouse a friar, I'm thinking, (laissez ici un espace suffisant pour six, sept paroles de la fin de la phrase) [137]

In a later galley for this passage, the space is left, and into it Joyce writes: "and he limp with leching." [138] What happened? I suspect that in the first galley, after bringing his sentence to the point at which he left it, Joyce felt that the rhythm of Synge's prose called for some such ending as he later formulated. The rhythm of the ending was perhaps running through his head. Perhaps even the construction (which occurs frequently in Molly Bloom's speech) had already been decided upon. But it may have refused at the time to take a verbal habitation. Therefore — to follow my suspicion through — Joyce left space for the words which should, and finally did, come.

In the afternoon, in manuscript, a "cavalcade in easy trot along Pembroke quay passed, outriders leaping gracefully in their saddles." [139] In proof, the phrase ends with "outriders leaping, leaping in their, in their saddles, in their saddles." Joyce deletes the first "their saddles".[140] Shortly afterward we hear: "In saddles of the leaders, leaping leaders, rode outriders." [141]

The rhythms of equitation engage Joyce again in the brothel scene. Bello "*thrusts out a figged fist and foul cigar.*) Here, kiss that. Both. Kiss." Following this, Joyce adds:

(*he throws a leg astride and, squeezing with horseman's knees, calls in a hard voice*) Gee up! I'll ride him for the Eclipse stakes. (*he horserides ridehorse, leaping in the, in the saddle*). The lady goes a pace a pace and the coachman goes a trot a trot and the gentleman goes a gallop a gallop a gallop a gallop.[142]

Later in the same episode, in manuscript, "*Dwarfs ride them* [horses in a race], *rusty armoured, leaping in their, in their saddles.*" [143] In proof, the sentence ends: "leaping, leaping in their, in their saddles."; [144] in the published version: "leaping, leaping in their saddles."

Another type of prancing rhythm is employed in Molly's monologue. Molly remembers Leopold, during their courtship,

begging me to give him a tiny bit cut off my drawers . . . of course hes mad on the subject of drawers thats plain to be seen [etc.] . . . anything for an excuse to put his hand anear me drawers all the time till I promised to give him the pair off my doll to carry about in his waistcoat pocket

After the last "drawers" Joyce adds "drawers".[145]

In the Ormond Bar, Miss Douce addresses Lenehan: " — You're the essence of vulgarity he [sic] said in gliding." Joyce alters the ending to read: "she in gliding said." [146] — giving us a keener sense of simultaneity of speech and movement.

Blazes Boylan is about to leave the Ormond:

— Wait a shake, begged Lenehan, drinking quickly, I
wanted to tell you. Tom Rochford . . .
— Come on to blazes, said Blazes Boylan, going.
Lenehan gulped to go.
— Got the horn or what? he said. Half a mo. I'm coming.

Joyce changes "Half a mo." to "Wait." [147] A man who is
drinking quickly and has just gulped to go is not likely to
waste words. What we now have, in Lenehan's dialogue, is
an audible quickening of pace. "Wait a shake" comes down
to "Wait."

Dollard is singing:

— *When love absorbs my ardent soul* . . .
— War! War! cried Father Cowley. You're the warrior.

Between these sentences Joyce inserts the following paragraph:
"Roll of Bensoulbenjamin rolled to the quivery loveshivery
roofpanes." [148] By balanced repetition Joyce has caught the
rhythm of full rolling waves of sound (Dollard is a bass
baritone [149]) and of delicate answering vibrations from the
roofpanes.

While Dollard is singing, Bloom recalls:

Night he ran round to us to borrow a dress suit for that concert. Trousers tight as a drum on him. Musical porkers.
Molly did laugh when he went out. Threw herself back across
the bed, screaming, kicking. With all his belongings on show.
O, saints above, I'm drenched! O, the women in the front
row! O, I never laughed so much!

Joyce changes "much" to "many" [150] — and we can visualize
Molly across the bed, screaming and kicking, gasping out,
exhausted, or perhaps before suddenly going off into another
transport, not a complete sentence, but an hysterical fragment. The rhythm of wild laughing speech is achieved by
the characteristically abrupt interruption.

In the brothel scene, a moth flies *"Round and round"*.[151]

At, and for, *"the everflying moth"* [152] (though here it "doth
rest anon"), Virag recites:

> I'm a tiny thing
> Ever flying in the spring
> Round and round a ringaring.
> Long ago I was a king,
> Now I do this kind of thing
> On the wing, on the wing!
> Bing!

Joyce restores a "tiny" after "tiny" [153] — and the circularity
of the moth's flight begins to make itself felt in the first line
of the superbly appropriate utterance.

Between Bloom and Stephen's leavetaking, with "the lines
of their valedictory arms, meeting at any point and forming
any angle less than the sum of two right angles.", and the
question "Alone, what did Bloom hear?", Joyce inserts:

What sound accompanied the union of their tangent, the
disunion of their (respectively) centrifugal and centripetal
hands?
The sound of the peal of the hour of the night by the chime
of the bells in the church of Saint George.[154]

It is almost superfluous to remark on the chiming rhythm of
"The sóund of the péal of the hóur of the níght by the chíme
of the bélls in the chúrch of Saint Geórge." [155]

In the same episode, between Bloom's memory of the face
of his father-in-law and a question concerning Molly's
clothes, Joyce inserts:

What recurrent impressions of the same were possible by
hypothesis?
Retreating, at the terminus of the Great Northern Railway,
Amiens street, with constant uniform acceleration, along
parallel lines meeting at infinity, if produced: along parallel
lines, reproduced from infinity, with constant uniform retarda-
tion, at the terminus of the Great Northern Railway, Amiens
street, returning.[156]

Comment on this passage is certainly superfluous.

At one point in Molly's reverie we hear: "wait by God he [Stephen] was on the cards this morning". Into the initial uncertainty of this memory Joyce introduces fluctuation: after "God" he adds "yes wait yes".[157] In a later proof he further curbs the tugging assertion by introducing, after "yes wait yes", "hold on".[158] And part of an addition in the context carries the uncertainty forward, with appropriately diminished force: "yes wait it all came out".[159]

In the numerous changes which we have thus far observed, Joyce, with some exceptions,[160] already has the words. But there are so many words that he does not have,[161] and consequently creates, that they merit separate treatment. These neologisms, as will become clear, increasingly adumbrate the style of *Finnegans Wake*, but I shall here treat them only as they bear upon the composition of *Ulysses*.

In coining his words, Joyce employs techniques of long standing. He extends the meaning of already existing words. Mulligan, after shaving, "with stroking fingers felt the smooth skin." After "stroking" Joyce adds "palps of".[162] The only current meaning for the noun *palp* is the zoological 'palpus' or 'feeler.'[163] Yet it is understandable that the word should be applied to the tip of the finger, with which one *palpates*.

Composition, ubiquitous in *Ulysses*, inspires a number of changes. Two or more already existing words, in combination, often achieve, besides the compactness to be expected, a wider radius of suggestiveness, a stronger sense of identification or of simultaneity, than their components had. Two specimens which I have presented in another connection are introduced when Dollard's voice "rolled to the quivery love-shivery roofpanes."[164] On the analogy of such words as *love-smitten* and *love-fond*, Joyce gives us not only "loveshivery" but also "lovesoft";[165] while "roofpanes" follows the model of *roof-windows*.

At twilight, Bloom thinks: "O sweety all your little white

up I saw dirty girl". So reads the passage in galley, but between this galley [166] and a later proof, "white" becomes "girlwhite".[167] And Joyce also coins "Girlgold".[168]

In the brothel, a dog *"growls, his scruff standing, a gobbet of pig's knuckle between his molars."* Joyce fills in his picture by deleting the period and adding "through which rabid scumspittle dribbles." [169] Here, again, there are analogues, in *scum-board and scum-soap.*

Before Bloom and Stephen part at the end of the day, they stand silent, "each contemplating the other in both mirrors of the flesh of fellowfaces." Before the final word Joyce inserts "his nothis".[170] Later the newly added words give way to "theirhisnothis".[171]

The bells of St. George's Church chime, Stephen walks off, and Bloom, "Alone," feels the "cold of interstellar space . . . the incipient intimations of proximate dawn." Following this, Joyce adds: "Of what did bellchime and handtouch and footstep and lonechill remind him?" [172] In this instance, the coinage, "lonechill", bringing up the rear of a line of already current compounds, comes upon us in a receptive, even expectant state.

But Joyce does not only combine already existing words; he also extends their use — again, as in previous instances,[173] by conversion. Simon Dedalus "took off his silk hat and, blowing out impatiently his bushy moustache, began to rake through his hair with his fingers." For "began to rake through" Joyce substitutes "welshcombed".[174] Before this change *Welsh comb* had only one meaning: 'the thumb and four fingers.' [175] With the dual function of *comb* to encourage him, and on the analogy of such a word as *Christian-name,* Joyce converts the compound noun into a compound verb. By the same process he verbifies *"Easter kiss"* [176] in *"Easter-kissing".*[177]

Besides compounds, Joyce also creates by analogy single words. In the penultimate episode we learn that Bloom was once prevented from completing a song, in part, by "oscillation between events of imperial and of local interest, the diamond jubilee of Queen Victoria (born 1820, acceded 1837) and the opening of the new municipal fish market:". Thus the second of three available proofs [178] for this passage. In the third, Joyce introduced "anticipated" before "diamond" and, in its wake, "posticipated" before "opening".

And now for the type of neologism which, based upon "an occasional mode of word formation," [179] ultimately carried Joyce farthest from the current language. Specimens of blending in *Ulysses* are plentiful; and a number of them were added late. In an addition already cited, the simple statement 'I met him in the Ulster Bank on Monday' is chewed into "I munched hum un thu Unchster Bunk un Munchday." [180]

"John Eglinton", before mentioning the views of two Shakespeareans, becomes "John Eclecticon".[181] And we have already seen this Irishman Orientalized as "Chin Chon Eg Lin Ton." [182]

In the brothel scene, Virag says: "Insects of the day spend their brief existence in reiterated coition, lured by the smell of the inferiorly pulchritudinous fumale Pretty Poll!" After the appropriate "fumale" Joyce adds "possessing extendified pudendal nerve in dorsal region." [183] Between proof and publication, "pudendal nerve" becomes, pertinently, "pudendal verve".[184]

Near the close of the same episode, Corny Kelleher, after rescuing Stephen from the watch, is leaving the scene:

With thumb and palm Corny Kelleher reassures that the two bobbies will allow the sleep to continue for what else is to be done. With a slow nod Bloom conveys his gratitude as that is exactly what Stephen needs. The car jingles round the corner of the lane. Corny Kelleher again reassures with his hand. Bloom with his hand assures Corny Kelleher that he is reassured. The tinkling hoofs and jingling harness grow fainter.

After *"jingles"* and before *"lane"* Joyce adds *"tooraloom"*; he changes the second *"reassures"* to *"reassuralooms"*, *"as-*

sures" to *"assuralooms"*, and *"reassured"* to *"reassuraloom-tay"*; after *"fainter"* he deletes the period to add *"with their tooralooloo looloo ay."* [185] And between this galley and publication, the last addition becomes *"with their tooralooloo looloo lay."* [186] Joyce first introduces simultaneity by alternating two themes (a device we have already met [187]), the movement of the car and Kelleher's lilting. Then, apparently, observing the vowel sound common to *"reassures"*, *"assures"*, *"reassured"*, and *"tooraloom"*, he builds up a series of blends that synchronize even more closely the gestures of assurance and the lilting, which he carries forward. His perception of the common vowel would not surprise us under ordinary circumstances, and it surprises us not at all here, since, before the car jingles off, Kelleher has sung his *tooraloom* no less than ten times,[188] and Bloom has thought it at him twice,[189] as well as sung it four times on his own.[190] The coincidence of four occurrences of the root *-sure-* with the character responsible for all these *tooraloom's*, and those just added,[191] undoubtedly set off Joyce's amalgamating impulse. And the impulse goes on to telescope Kelleher's last recital, the third of this particular snatch, in the last added blend. To put it mathematically:

"tooralooloo looloo" = "tooraloo-" + "-loo-" + "-loo-" + "-loo-" of "With my tooraloom tooraloom tooraloom tooraloom." [192]

The final *"lay"* brings up the rear with a blend of "tay" [193] and *lay* (in the sense of 'song'), as the liquid follows up its line of predecessors.

In one passage we may watch a pair of blends in process of formation. The catechism reads:

Did they [Bloom and Stephen] find their educational careers similar?
Bloom had passed successively through a dame's school and the high school; Stephen through the preparatory, junior, middle and senior grades of the intermediate and through the matriculation, first arts and degree courses of University.

For "Bloom had" Joyce substitutes "If Stephen had been
Bloom he would have"; for "Stephen", "if Bloom had been
Stephen he would have passed successively".[194] With the
hypothetical interchange of identities, the stage is set, for
later Joyce points up the interchange by blending the names
of the characters through the transposition of initial consonants (a device which he has used before [195]). The answer
becomes:

Substituting Stephen for Bloom Stoom would have passed
successively through a dame's school and the high school.
Substituting Bloom for Stephen Blephen would have passed
successively [etc.] [196]

Joyce has thus come a long way from the simple interest
in orthodox precision which I discussed at the opening of
this paper. In effect, he has travelled the whole road from
Dubliners to *Finnegans Wake*. Even in *Ulysses*, he crosses
established borders. And though his excursions are still relatively infrequent, he is clearly moving toward the full adop-
tion of what one critic, quoting *Ulysses*, has described as the
language of the outlaw.[197]

III

Joyce's revisions represent almost exclusively a process of
elaboration. Great numbers of additions gravitate into pat-
terned constellations of purpose and method, and innumerable details, in the final text as well as in the additions, become luminous with meaning.

In the matter of style, Joyce is extraordinarily alert to the
possibilities of greater success in the achievement of a multitude of effects.

His primary concern is for realistic representation. To this
end he adds continually, rare lapses notwithstanding, precision in the use of words, specification, vividness, dramatization, onomatopoeia, and rhythms. In these efforts, as I

have suggested, we may trace his development from *Dub-liners* to *Finnegans Wake.*

But to Joyce style means far more than realistic representation. In his quest for the perfect union of matter and manner, he evolves a variety of techniques for a variety of episodes. In the process of revision, he intensifies the incubism of the graveyard, the journalistic atmosphere of the newspaper office, the gastronomic effects of lunch, the Elizabethan wrapping around the discussion of Shakespeare, the musical properties of the Ormond Bar, the language of the pub. He heightens the sentimental aura around Gerty MacDowell, as also the accompanying rhythm of tumescence and detumescence, the 'embryonic development' of English style for the lying-in, the jerky rhythm appropriate to the brothel, the climate of exhaustion which envelops the cabman's shelter, the cold impersonality of the penultimate episode, the turning movement of the throbbing final episode.

Briefly, the revisions afford a direct view into the mind of Joyce in the process of creation. This insight, fascinating in itself as an adventure in psychological analysis, yields two contributions of critical importance. By making us aware of fresh and dominant relationships, it enables us to effect a fuller synthesis in our apprehension of the finished work of art. By making clearer the kinship of that work with Joyce's earlier and later works, it enables us to appraise more justly Joyce's total achievement.

ABBREVIATIONS

Editions of *Ulysses*

S   *Ulysses*, Paris, Shakespeare and Co., February, 1922. The first edition, set up from the proof sheets treated in the present study.

EP   *Ulysses*, published for The Egoist Press, London, by John Rodker, Paris, October, 1922. All citations from

this the first English edition (struck off from the original
plates) take account of the seven pages of errata laid in.

S4   *Ulysses,* Paris, Shakespeare and Co., fourth printing,
January, 1924. All citations from this edition take account of the list of "Additional corrections" on pp.
733–36.

S6   *Ulysses,* Paris, Shakespeare and Co., sixth printing,
August, 1925. All citations from this edition take account of the list of "Additional corrections" on pp.
733–36. Both the text and the list, in all passages for
which I cite this edition, are identical with those of S4.

S9   *Ulysses,* Paris, Shakespeare and Co., ninth printing, May,
1927. This edition follows that of May, 1926, for which
the type was entirely re-set. The "Additional corrections"
mentioned under S4 and S6 were, with some exceptions,
incorporated.

U   *Ulysses,* New York, Random House, sixth printing,
February, 1934. This edition is based upon a corrupt
pirated text. The publishers included it in the Modern
Library — after the exposure of their mistake. Since,
however, it is the only edition generally available to
American readers, I am compelled to use it for citation
from the final text. Whenever, in collating editions, I
mention *U,* I do so for the convenience of the reader,
not for authority.
       In citing from *Ulysses,* whatever the edition, for the sake
of complete accuracy I give all opening and closing
punctuation marks as in the text quoted and place outside the quotations all opening and closing punctuation
marks that are mine. In citing the Random House edition, I refer to it as *U,* following it directly with the page
number, e.g., *U*5.

OP   *Ulysses,* 2 vols., Hamburg-Paris-Bologna, Odyssey Press,
third impression, August, 1935. The first impression of

this edition called itself the "definitive standard edition . . . specially revised, at the author's request, by *Stuart Gilbert.*" In the second impression, the text was made more accurate. For the superiority of the third impression to the first two, see J. F. Spoerri, "The Odyssey Press Edition of James Joyce's 'Ulysses,' " *Papers of the Bibliographical Society of America,* L (Second Quarter, 1956), 195–98.
I owe some of the information used above to R. F. Roberts, "Bibliographical Notes on James Joyce's 'Ulysses,' " *Colophon,* New Series, 1 (Spring, 1936), 565–79.

Manuscript and Other Materials

B   Manuscripts of parts of *Ulysses* exhibited at the Librairie La Hune, Paris, in 1949 and acquired by the Lockwood Memorial Library of the University of Buffalo. Numbers following the symbol B will refer to entries in the La Hune catalogue *James Joyce: sa vie, son œuvre, son rayonnement* (Paris, 1949), items 252–53, 255–59. (Item 254 was lost in transit between Paris and Buffalo.) These manuscripts are also described in John J. Slocum and Herbert Cahoon, A *Bibliography of James Joyce* [1882–1941] (New Haven, 1953), E5b.

H   Proof sheets of *Ulysses* described by Slocum and Cahoon, E5f, quoting the private catalogue of Edward W. Titus as follows: "Complete and final proofs of the first edition of this stupendous work with the author's profuse autograph corrections, emendations and additions exceeding sometimes 160 words on a single page. These important additions are not found in the manuscript of the work, that had been the sensation of the memorable Quinn Sale in 1924." Made available to me by Mr. T. E. Hanley.

I   Miles L. Hanley and others, *Word Index to James Joyce's Ulysses* (Madison, Wisconsin, 1937). A list of "Errata in Random House Edition" occurs on pp. xiii–xix.

R   Manuscript of *Ulysses* made available to me by the late A. S. W. Rosenbach and now in the Rosenbach Foundation. Described in Slocum and Cahoon, E5a, quoting the catalogue of the Quinn sale, no. 4936: "Original autograph manuscript of 'Ulysses,' written on over 1200 pages." — etc.

W   Proof sheets of *Ulysses* made available to me by Miss Marian G. Willard and now in the Houghton Library of Harvard University. Miss Sylvia Beach, publisher of the first edition of *Ulysses*, has described this material as follows: "A complete set, and several incomplete sets of the proofs abundantly corrected and added to by the author. About 600 pages contain 5 to 10 lines of autograph corrections, others are almost completely covered with manuscript.

      "These proofs show the important changes that James Joyces [sic] made in his ‹Ulysses› while it was printing, and his manner of continually adding text to successive sets of proofs up to the very moment before going to press." — *Catalogue of a Collection Containing Manuscripts & Rare Editions of James Joyce . . .* (Paris, 1935), p. 3.

      Miss Willard numbered the galleys from 1 to 212. The pagination of the galleys underwent so many changes that it seems best to refer to the pages of each galley by a fresh count. A specimen reference follows: W187:4 indicates galley numbered 187, fourth page.

NOTES

1. In "Du Style," *Œuvres complètes de Stendhal* (*Henry Beyle*), p. 311 of vol. (Paris, 1854) which includes "Racine et Shakespeare." For a pertinent commentary, see J. M. Murry, *The Problem of Style* (London, etc., 1925), pp. 78 ff. Especially to our purpose is the following excerpt: "The first thing to remember in examining this definition is that 'thought' (as I have said before) does not really mean 'thought'; it is a general term to cover intuitions, convictions, perceptions, and their accompanying emotions before they have undergone the process of artistic expression or ejection. A man like Stendhal, brought up in the French sensationalist philosophy of the late eighteenth century, lumps them all together under the name of thoughts. . . . The second point is in the phrase, 'the whole effect which the thought ought to produce.' A more truly accurate translation, I think, would be: 'the whole effect which the thought is intended to produce.' At all events, the French hovers between the two meanings." (p. 79). Murry mistakenly cites Stendhal's definition as from "Racine et Shakespeare."

2. U50; B253, p. 16.   3. U120; W42:4.

4. Cf. U56: "His [Bloom's] hand took his hat from the peg over his initialled heavy overcoat, and his lost property office secondhand waterproof."; p. 60: "His [Bloom's] hand accepted the moist tender gland and slid it into a sidepocket. Then it fetched up three coins from his trousers' pocket and laid them on the rubber prickles."; p. 149: "His [Bloom's] slow feet walked him riverward, reading." In each of these passages, a part of Bloom's body takes on independent activity while his mind is busy elsewhere. In each, the information is conveyed with admirable precision and economy.

5. U249; W69:8.

6. U325–26; W92:6. The rest of the paragraph is built up here in W92, in W91:7, W95:7, and H.

7. U653; W178:3.   8. U372; W106:5.

9. Cf. U180: "In aid of funds for Mercer's hospital." The phrase recurs on p. 251.

10. U472; W137:2.

11. U677; W173:8. Note how "a doll, a boy, a sailor" repro-

duces the groping process of Bloom's memory as, with increasing individuation, it recalls the discarded toy.

12. U69; W20:2.

13. U94; W34:8. Here, also, after the first sentence, Joyce adds: "Too much John Barleycorn."

14. U108; W25:4.

15. U165; W49:7. Since R reads "laamp", Joyce appears to be restoring text.

16. Cf. *Moore's Irish Melodies, with Symphonies and Accompaniments by Sir John Stevenson* (Boston, 1852), p. 126.

17. U188: "A man of genius makes no mistakes."

18. U30; R.   19. U65; W24:8.

20. U82; W19:1.   21. H.

22. U229; W66:6. In W65:6, after "them" he adds further "for Jervis street."

23. U660–61; W163:2. Here, also, Joyce changes "drank from" to "substituted"; before "cream" he adds "viscous"; after "occasions" he deletes the question mark and adds "to complete the act begun?" In W175:2, after "Millicent," he adds "(Milly)". The rest of the text was introduced in H.

24. Consider the following:

U651; W177:2:

"Once in 1892 and once in 1893 with Julius Mastiansky, on both occasions in the parlour of his house in Lombard street, west."

After "his" Joyce adds "(Bloom's)".

N.B. The same addition, in the same passage, is made in W178:2. W177 and W178 are identically dated (see below).

U658; W178:8:

"Because of the surety of the sense of touch in his firm full masculine feminine passive active hand.

"What quality did it possess but with what counteracting influence?"

After "it" Joyce adds "(his hand)".

U664; W163:5:

"How many previous encounters proved their preexisting acquaintance?

"Two. The first in the lilacgarden of Matthew Dillon's house. [sic] Medina Villa, Kimmage road, Roundtown, in 1887, in the

I Telemachia

	TITLE	SCENE	HOUR	ORGAN	ART	COLOUR	SYMBOL	TECHNIC	CORRESPONDENCES
1	Telemachus	: The Tower	: 8 a.m.	:	theology	white gold	: hair	narrative (young)	(Stephen - Telemachus - Hamlet : Buck Mulligan - Antinous : Milkwoman - Mentor)
2	Nestor	: The School	: 10 a.m.	:	history	brown	: horse	catechism (personal)	(Deasy : Nestor : Pisistratus . Sargent : Helen : Mrs O'Shea)
3	Proteus	: The Strand	: 11 a.m.	:	philology	green	: tide	monologue (male)	(Proteus - Primal Matter : Kevin Egan - Menelaus : Megapenthus : the Cocklepicker)

II Odyssey

	TITLE	SCENE	HOUR	ORGAN	ART	COLOUR	SYMBOL	TECHNIC	CORRESPONDENCES
1	Calypso	: The House	: 8 a.m.	: kidney	:: economics	orange	: nymph	narrative (mature)	(Calypso - The Nymph. Dlugacz : The Recall : Zion : Ithaca)
2	Lotuseaters	: The Bath	: 10 a.m.	: genitals	botany,chemistry		: eucharist	narcissism	(Lotuseaters : Cabhorses, Communicants, Soldiers, Eunuchs, Bather, Watchers of Cricket)
3	Hades	: The Graveyard	: 11 a.m.	: heart	religion	white black	: caretaker	incubism	(Dodder, Grand and Royal Canals, Liffey - The 4 Rivers : Cunningham - Sisyphus : Father Coffey - Cerberus : Caretaker - Hades - Daniel O'Connell - Hercules Dignam - Elpenor : Parnell : Agamemnon : Mentor : Ajax)
4	Eolus	: The Newspaper	: 12 noon	: lungs	rhetoric	red	: editor	enthymenic	(Crawford - Eolus : Incest - journalism : Floating Island - press)
5	Lestrygonians	: The Lunch	: 1 p.m.	: esophagus	architecture		: constables,	peristaltic	(Antiphates - Hunger : The Decoy : Food : Lestrygonians - Teeth)
6	Scylla and Carybdis	: The Library	: 2 p.m.	: brain	literature		: Stratford,London	dialectic	(The Rock - Aristotle, Dogma, Stratford : The whirlpool : Plato, Mysticism,London Ulysses : Socrates, Jesus, Shakespeare)
7	Wandering Rocks	: The Streets	: 3 p.m.	: blood	mechanics		: citizens	labyrinth	(Bosphorus - Liffey : European bank - Viceroy : Asiatic bank - Conmee : Symplegades Groups of citizens)
8	Sirens	: The Concert Room	: 4 p.m.	: ear	music		: barmaids	fuga per canonem	(Sirens - barmaids : Isle - bar)
9	Cyclops	: The Tavern	: 5 p.m.	: muscle	politics		: fenian	gigantism	(Noman - I : Stake - cigar : challenge - apotheosis)
10	Nausikaa	: The Rocks	: 8 p.m.	: eye,nose	painting	grey,blue	: virgin	tumescence detumescence	(Phaecia - Star of the Sea : Gerty - Nausikaa)
11	Oxen of Sun	: The Hospital	: 10 p.m.	: womb	medecine	white	: mothers	embryonic development	(Hospital - Trinacria : Lampetie, Phaethusa - Nurses : Helios - Horne : Oxen Fertility : Crime - Fraud)
12	Circe	: The Brothel	: 12 midnight	: locomotor apparatus	magic		: whore	hallucination	(Circe - Bella)

III Nostos

	TITLE	SCENE	HOUR	ORGAN	ART	COLOUR	SYMBOL	TECHNIC	CORRESPONDENCES
1	Eumeus	: The Shelter	: 1 a.m.	: nerves	: navigation	:	: sailors	narrative (old)	(Eumeus - Skin the Goat : Sailor - Ulysses Pseudangelos : Melanthius - Corly)
2	Ithaca	: The House	: 2 a.m.	: skeleton	: science	:	: comets	catechism (impersonal)	(Eurymachus - Boylan : Suitors - scruples : Bow - reason)
3	Penelope	: The Bed	: ——	: flesh			: earth	monologue (female)	(Penelope - Earth : Web - Movement)

This schema of *Ulysses* is the copy that Joyce gave Herbert Gorman and is the subject of the exchange of letters between Paul L. Léon, Gorman, and Bennett Cerf which is reproduced in this book. This and the other illustrations appearing in this book are all from the collection of H. K. Croessmann.

company of his mother, Stephen being then of the age of 5 and reluctant to give his hand in salutation. The second in the coffeeroom of Breslin's hotel on a rainy Sundy [sic] in the January 1892, in the company of his father and his granduncle, Stephen being then 5 years older."

Before "mother", "father", and "granduncle", Joyce changes "his" to "Stephen's". (Also, after "January" he adds "of".) U686; W172:6:

"His logical conclusion?" (The preceding question and answer, except for irrelevant differences, read as in U.)

After "His" Joyce adds "(Bloom's)". (The rest of the text is added in W171:6.)

The dates of the galleys containing the above changes (W177 and W178: "15 décembre 1921"; W163: "16 décemb. 1921"; W172: "21 décembre 1921") and the fact that the very galley (W163) in one part of which Joyce fails to clarify his reference, contains just such a clarification in another part, make it perfectly plain that, at the time, his mind dwelt on such improvement. Moreover, Joyce takes pains in this episode as a whole to express his meaning with exaggerated lucidity.

25. U692–93; W170:4. Other lapses follow:
U49–50:

"He lay back at full stretch over the sharp rocks, cramming the scribbled note and pencil into a pocket, his hat tilted down on his eyes. That is Kevin Egan's movement I made nodding for his nap, sabbath sleep. *Et vidit Deus. Et erant valde bona.* Alo! *Bonjour,* welcome as the flowers in May. Under its leaf he watched through peacocktwittering lashes the southing sun."

The excessive distance of "its" from its antecedent is the result of a sequence of associative interpolations. In a manuscript notebook (B253, p. 16), the passage reads: "He stretched backward at full over the sharp boulders, his hat tilted down on his eyes, cramming the scribbled note and pencil into a pocket. Under its leaf he watched through quivering peacock lashes the southing sun." Joyce transfers "his hat tilted down on his eyes" to a position following "pocket.", and between the sentences inserts: "That is Kevin Egan's movement, nodding for his nap. Hlo! *Bonjour*" (The fact that "movement," replaces "gesture." as an afterthought and that "nodding for his nap" is written, with a guide-line, in the margin of p. 17 of the notebook, may explain the need for the repeated addition of the participial phrase in R.)

R reads: "He lay back at full stretch over the sharp rocks, cramming the scribbled note and pencil into a pocket, his hat tilted down on his eyes. That is Kevin Egan's movement I made. Hlo! *Bonjour.* Under its leaf he watched through peacocktwittering lashes the southing sun." After "I made" Joyce adds ", nodding for his nap." — and this text, with the addition incorporated and "Hlo" italicized, appears in *The Little Review*, VI (May, 1918), 43. (For the process by which "quivering peacock" became "peacocktwittering" in the manuscript notebook, see above, pp. 16–17.)

H, after a typographical correction, is identical with U.

U218:

"Moored under the trees of Charleville Mall, Father Conmee saw a turfbarge,".

U485:

"[Bloom] *turns each foot simultaneously in different directions,*".

26. U6.   27. U7; W1:3.

28. See esp. pp. 26 ff., above.

29. U20; W6:2. The passage will bear further comment (irrelevant to the point I am making in my text). The galley under discussion reads: "He gazed southward over the bay. Eyes, pale as the sea the wind had freshened, paler, firm and prudent. The seas' ruler, he gazed over the bay, empty save for a sail tacking by the Muglins." After "for" Joyce first adds "the smokeplume for [with deleting lines through it] vague on the bright skyline and". Then, after "smokeplume" he adds "of the mailboat".

First, about the change from "far" to "vague" in the very writing of the addition. A bald statement of distance is transformed into a statement not only of distance but also of its effect (as well as that of the brightness of the skyline) upon the appearance of the smokeplume *as Haines sees it.*

And now about the tardily inserted "of the mailboat". Apparently, Joyce, himself clearly visualizing his scene with the recently introduced mailboat in it, first proceeded directly to the smokeplume, and only later, realizing that his reader would expect to be supplied with the source of the smokeplume, added "of the mailboat" for clarification.

A further improvement occurs in H, where Joyce (besides correcting a compositor's error in the placing of the phrase "of the mailboat") eliminates the repetition of 'gazed over the bay', retaining only the one distinctive word in the two expressions about the gazing, namely, "southward": "Eyes, pale as the sea the wind had freshened, paler, firm and prudent. The seas' ruler, he gazed southward over the bay, empty save for the smoke-plume of the mailboat, vague on the bright skyline, and a sail tacking by the Muglins."

30. U337; W98:7.   31. U448; W118:1.

32. U484; W140:1. And before "Embrace" he adds "(in nursetender's gown)".

Bloom has thought about Mrs. Thornton twice before (U66, 159).

33. U485; W140:2.

In W133:8 (U487–88), another characteristic speech by Brother Buzz, with appropriate action, is introduced. The proof reads:

"Nip the first rattler.
   (*Lieutenant Myers of the Dublin Fire Brigade by general request sets fire to Bloom. Lamentations.*)"
After "rattler" Joyce adds:
                    "BROTHER BUZZ
(invests Bloom in a yellow habit with painted flames and high pointed hat. He places a bag of gunpowder round his neck and hands him over to the civil power, saying) Forgive him his trespasses."
Then, after "with" Joyce adds further "embroidery of". (The rest of the text must have been introduced between W133 and H. For comment, see above, p. 33, and below, n. 110.)

34. U82.

35. U486; W140:2. And before "What" he adds "(in bushranger's kit)".

Crab was a character in Mulligan's *national immorality in three orgasms* (U214).

36. U553–54; W129:6. The rest of the text must have been introduced between W129 and H, in which the final version is achieved. [R for this passage begins: "(The widow Dignam, her snubnose and cheeks flushed with deathtalk, tears and

Tunny's tawny sherry,",". H, like W129:6: *"fears"*. R's "tears" and OP's and U's *"tears"* follow B259, n.p., in which Joyce introduced the phrase "her face flushed with talk, tears & old tawny sherry,".]

The reintroduction of Mrs. Thornton, Brother Buzz, Crab, and Mrs. Dignam helps knit *Ulysses* together.

37. U661; W163:2. The rest of the text was introduced in H.

38. This interpretation is supported by Joyce's constant emphasis in the penultimate episode upon complete explicitness.

39. U152.

40. The kinds of success listed reflect the various aspects of Bloom's all-round failure.

41. U669; W174:1. Bloom's interest in moral apothegms does not manifest itself for the first time in the present addition. Early in the morning Bloom considered: "Might manage a sketch. By Mr and Mrs L. M. Bloom. Invent a story for some proverb which?" (U69). In the hospital scene he was taken to task for dispensing "apothegms of dubious taste to restore to health a generation of unfledged profligates" (p. 403; "apothegms of dubious taste" is part of an addition in H). And dominating these details, there is Bloom's triteness, which leans heavily on moral apothegms.

On the first of the newly introduced titles, Joyce composed during his own schoolyears, choosing Ulysses for his subject. (Valery Larbaud, "James Joyce," *La Nouvelle revue française*, April 1, 1922, pp. 404–5; Herbert Gorman, *James Joyce* [New York, 1948], p. 45.) This experience is utilized once more in *Finnegans Wake*, p. 306: "Your Favorite Hero or Heroine".

42. U164; W49:6.   43. U361; W105:4.

44. U365; W104:7. Here, also, after "Where" Joyce adds "do".

45. W105:7. Joyce first wrote "to show her calves", then replaced "calves" with "understandings", a slang term which is peculiarly suited to Bloom, considering his love of 'adaptations.'

In W105:7, also, after "there." Joyce gives Bloom an insight: "Longing to get the fright of their lives."

46. U732; W183:8. OP, U: "Dolphins", "couldnt".

47. U746; W198:2. In W194:2, Joyce changes "Albertis" to "Benady Bros".

48. "I wanted to fire his pistol" (U746).

49. U749; W197:4.

50. W198:4. In W195:4, after "mutton" Joyce adds "the very name is enough".

51. H.   52. U152, 169.

53. U668; R.   54. W163:8.

55. In the context of the passage under discussion, Bloom recalls verbatim the advertisement (or that part of it?) which he saw in the morning (cf. U73–74): "What is home without Plumtree's Potted Meat?" etc.

56. W175:8.

57. The question-and-answer unit in which the passage under discussion occurs, the preceding two units, and part of the third answer back, all render indirectly Bloom's "cogitations" on the "art of advertisement" (U667).

For an earlier performance of Bloom's at anagrams, see U662.

58. U70; W20:4.   59. U76; W21:2.

60. U94; W33:8.

61. U59; W24:2. The whole addition follows: into a blank space of four lines between "by George." (end of paragraph) and "The model farm" (beginning of next paragraph), Joyce writes: "The way her crooked skirt swings at each whack.

"The ferreteyed porkbutcher folded the sausages he had snipped off with blotchy fingers, sausagepink. [Note the splendid picture here added.] Sound meat there like a stallfed heifer."

Then, at the bottom of the page, Joyce inserts a new opening for the next paragraph: "He took up a page from the pile of cut sheets [sic]". "He", which seems to refer to the "porkbutcher", actually, and awkwardly, refers to Bloom. The sentence is apparently added to make clear the source of the following speculations, by Bloom, on the model farm.

From here on, I am lumping together all changes, whether made by the author as such or through the minds of his characters. I have already shown that Joyce himself does not make the distinction.

62. U59.   63. U275.

64. U165; W50:7.   65. U189; W55:5.

66. U337; W97:7.

67. U486; W140:2. It is in the context of this passage that

Joyce also introduces the pictorial "bushranger's kit" presented above, n. 35. A similar addition in the interest of picture-making is that of the "nursetender's gown", presented above, n. 32.

68. U510; W124:3.

69. U688; W172:8, continued in W169:1.

70. U736; W188:3. 71. U85; W19:3.

72. Bloom has just thought: "Enjoy a bath now . . . the gentle tepid stream." (U85). His interest in warmth also figures in one of the imagined recreations of "Flowerville": "discussion in tepid security of unsolved historical and criminal problems:" (p. 700).

73. U744; W195:1. Additions of vivid detail discussed in other connections follow: the change of "far" to "vague" (see above, n. 29), and the insertion of "across his stained square of newspaper" (see below, n. 106).

74. U206–7.

75. Evidently Joyce's characters share some of his predilections. Harry Levin has remarked on their "preoccupation with language." [*James Joyce: A Critical Introduction* (Norfolk, Connecticut [1941]), p. 126.]

76. U46; W10:6. Here Joyce also changes the second period to an exclamation mark.

77. U70; W20:4. U's comma after the second "da" is an erratum; cf. S, OP.

78. U81; W21:6. In W36 (single page) before "Punish" Joyce adds further "Penance.", which clarifies the shift in Bloom's thought from "Then I will tell you all." to "Punish me, please.", and balances off against "Confession." as an introductory thought.

It should be noted that only "Punish me, please." is an unquestionable dramatization. "Then I will tell you all.", which echoes the letter from Martha Clifford (U77), may be regarded as drama only if we assume that Bloom is not merely recalling Martha's sentence as an instance of the desire to confess but that he is dramatizing confession and putting the sentence into the mouth of the confessor. We may presume that he is dramatizing confession since, in the next sentence, in the same addition, he dramatizes penance; and the adaptation would be typical of Bloom.

Bloom recalls Martha's sentence once more at twilight (U366).

79. U81–82; W36.

80. "And I schschschschschsch. And did you chachachacha-cha? And why did you?" (*U*81)

81. *U*82; W21:6. The whole addition includes, as ending: "Monasteries and convents."

82. *U*82; W21:7. The period at the end of the addition is Joyce's — a mistake which he apparently failed to catch. Cf. S, OP, U.

83. "Excuse, miss, there's a (whh!) just a (whh!) fluff." (*U*82)

84. U154; W47:7.

85. U159; W49:3. The addition is so placed that it may be mistaken as coming between "Not stillborn of course." and "They are not even registered and Y.M.C.A." (*U*159 — in W50:3, Joyce deletes "and Y.M.C.A."). The printer made this mistake in setting up W50. In H, Joyce rearranged the text as he had originally intended it.

H, S, OP, U: "nyumyum". In W50:3 Joyce clearly corrected a misprint to "nyumnyum".

86. "Well, God is good, sir." (*U*66)

87. See above, p. 23.

88. U180; W53:4. Here, also, Joyce alters "wine" to "stuff", a demotion appropriate to the context of Bloom's thought, as witness the addition, also made here, after "drank.", of "Vintage wine for them, the year marked on a dusty bottle." In W54:4 Joyce alters "assizer" to "assizes".

89. U213–14; W61:4. The whole addition includes, as ending, the independent paragraph: "He stopped at the stairfoot." Between W62, a later galley containing this passage, and H, Joyce must have inserted "mopping," before "chanting".

90. U314; W86:4. Here, also, after "son" Joyce adds "off Island bridge".

U's "Government" is an erratum. Cf. R, S, OP.

91. *U*366; W104:8. Here, also, after "when" Joyce fills in the postern scene with "they hold him out to do".

92. U366–67; W104:8. In H Joyce eliminates the repetition of "night" by altering "all night" to "in the dark".

93. U66; W22:8.

94. "He [Bloom] stood by the nextdoor girl at the counter.

Would she buy it too, calling the items from a slip [in (see I, S, OP)] her hand. Chapped: washing soda." (*U*59; italics mine.)

95. Cf. Joseph Prescott, "James Joyce: A Study in Words," *PMLA*, LIV (March, 1939), 304–7, 310–12.

96. *U*42; B253, p. 8.   97. W10:2.

98. *U*50; B253, p. 17. R, W7:4, H: "waters" and "widely flowing". W7:4 and H, like *U*, have no comma before "oos", and have a colon before "bounded".

Besides onomatopoeia, note also Joyce's marvellous use of rhythms, to be treated above, pp. 35 ff.

99. *U*86; W34:1. Cf. p. 571: "*woman's slipperslappers*"; also, p. 466: "Mother Slipperslapper" [a variant — developed in W119:8 from "Mother Slipperslopper", presumably to form an echoing pattern with the other passages — on "old Mother Slipper-Slopper"; cf. Eric Partridge, *A Dictionary of Slang and Unconventional English* (New York, 1937), p. 783].

100. *U*96; W32:2. He does not touch "out". OP, *U*: "Out".

101. *U*112; W26:6. OP, *U*: "greatgrandfather Kraahraark!", "awfullygladaseeragain", "amarawf", "kopthsth".

102. *U*112; W25:6.

103. *U*132; W43:6. The rest of the speech, which is typical of Lenehan, must have been introduced between this galley and H.

104. *U*434; R.   105. *U*167; W51:1.

106. *U*167; W51:1. I have supplied the first "un" from W52:1, which incorporates the addition here made. In W51:1, there is a gap between "hum" and "thu", part of the page, in a folded corner of the proof sheet, being torn out. S, OP, *U*: "hum un thu".

In W52, after "you" Joyce adds ", faith". He completed the picture (with "across his stained square of newspaper") in H.

107. Frank Budgen, *James Joyce and the Making of ULYSSES* (New York, 1934), p. 52. The passage which Joyce read occurs in *U*45. (S, OP, *U*: "gigant".)

108. *U*335; W97:5. Here, also, after "Alf" Joyce adds "round him like a leprechaun". The rest of the text must have been added between this galley and H.

109. See above, n. 33.

110. *U*487. We are now prepared for the appearance of Lieu-

tenant Myers of the Dublin Fire Brigade who, shortly afterward, sets fire to Bloom (p. 488).

The brigade spoke at the close of the preceding episode: "Pflaap! Pflaap! . . . Pflaap! . . . Pflaaaap! . . . Pflaap! . . . Pflaaaap!" (pp. 420–21). And it appears twice again (pp. 427, 471 [added in W135:1]) before its speech is reintroduced.

111. U508; W124:2. OP, U: "*He*", "*butt.*"

112. U578; W132:4. Before the speech Joyce has the following instruction: "vers / ".

H, OP, U: "ho rhother's hest.", "*cobblestones*". H, OP, I (correcting U's "*clothes to*"): "*clothes on to*".

The division into "ho rhother's" seems to introduce a desperate gasping attempt to get out the last words in what otherwise might appear to be, under the circumstances, too regular an utterance.

In H, before "A *violent erection*" Joyce inserts "*He gives up the ghost.*" The rest of the text must have been introduced between this proof and publication. The leaping assistants echo p. 299: "there's two fellows waiting below to pull his heels down when he gets the drop and choke him properly" (part of an addition in W84:1).

113. Cf. U279: "Once by the churchyard he had passed and for his mother's rest he had not prayed."

114. "The Croppy Boy," by Carroll Malone, in M. J. Brown, *Historical Ballad Poetry of Ireland* (Dublin and Belfast, 1912), pp. 212–13.

115. E. R. Curtius, *James Joyce und sein Ulysses* (Zürich, 1929), pp. 57–58.

116. U210; W61:1. U omits the opening dash. Cf. S, OP.

117. H. U's "Buck" is corrected by I. Cf. also S, OP.

The final form of Buck's name in this passage may owe something to the similar-sounding variation to "Puck" which occurs twice shortly afterward (pp. 212, 213).

Other variations on Malachi ("Buck") Mulligan's name are "Monk Mulligan" (p. 203), "Sonmulligan" (p. 205), and "*Ballocky Mulligan*" (p. 214).

118. U213; W61:2. Eglinton's chin is also satirized in one of 'Puck's' verses: "*Magee that had the chinless mouth.*" (p. 213).

"John Eglinton" is the pseudonym of the essayist William

Kirkpatrick Magee. Other variations on his names follow: "little-john Eglinton" (p. 192), "John sturdy Eglinton" (p. 200), "Second Eglinton" (p. 201; "Second" replaces "John" in H), "ugling Eglinton" (p. 202), "*Eglintonus Chronologos*" (p. 204; "*Eglintonus*" replaces "Eglington" [sic] in W59:3), "MAGEE-GLINJOHN" (p. 206 – cf. below, n. 181), "Judge Eglinton" (p. 209), "Eglinton Johannes" (p. 211), "John Eclecticon" (*ibid.* – cf. above, p. 42) and "Tanderagee" (p. 499).

119. U432; W116:3.

120. (U47) — and *biscuit* to "biscuitfully" (p. 122), as also the adjective *alive* to the noun "alive" (p. 112).

121. U557–58; W130:2. The whole addition includes, after the sentence I have cited, the following: "*Ward Union hunts-men and huntswomen live with them, hot for a kill. From Six Mile Point, Flathouse, Nine Mile Stone follow the footpeople with knotty sticks, hayforks, salmongaffs, lassos, bearbaiters with tomtoms, toreadors with bullswords, grey negroes waving torches.*" Then, after "*pack*" Joyce adds further "*of staghounds*"; after "*follows*", "*, nose to the ground,*"; after "*lassos,*", "*, flock-masters with stockwhips,*".

Here, also, he changes the opening "*The*" to "A *stout*"; after "*fox*" he adds "*, drawn from covert,*"; after "*pointed,*", "*, having buried his grandmother,*"; after "*swift*", "*for the open*"; after "*brighteyed*", "*, seeking badger earth,*".

The Ward Union huntsmen and huntswomen hot for a kill, and the staghounds, echo Bloom's earlier thought: "Lady Mount-cashel has quite recovered after her confinement and rode out with the Ward Union staghounds at the enlargement yesterday at Rathoath. Uneatable fox. . . . Weightcarrying huntress. . . . First to the meet and in at the death." (p. 158). (In proof, Lady Mountcashel "rode out with the Meath hounds." The final version is introduced in W49:2.)

The fox's disposition of his grandmother echoes the riddle which Stephen put to his class in the morning and solved thus: " — The fox burying his grandmother under a hollybush." (pp. 27–28) The riddle recurs, with a significant variation, in the brothel scene (p. 544), not very long before the reintroduction of the solution.

Note the completeness of the picture which Joyce has built up from so meagre a beginning.

The final version (except for typographical details) must have been worked out between W130 and H.

122. U252. For analogues, cf. *clip-a-clap* and *clip-clop.*

123. U561. The coinage took place between B259, n.p. ("claps") and R ("clipclaps").

124. Budgen, pp. 19–20. The sentences discussed occur in U166. In R, they read: "Perfumes of embraces assailed him. His hungered flesh obscurely, mutely craved to adore."

125. U166–67; W51:1.   126. U85.

127. U189. Joyce had already made use of the first half of this word when a door "whispered: ee: cree." (p. 116). The form of the whole word might have come to him from the NED entry "Cree, crie" (= 'create'). Should evidence of Joyce's acquaintance with the NED be necessary, see below, n. 161.

128. U252.   129. U271.

130. U561.   131. U256.

132. U439.

133. U461. For analogues, cf. *jig-a-jig, jig-a-jog, jig-jig, jig-jog,* and *jog-jog.*

134. U524.

135. U562. Concerning Joyce's later partiality for reduplicates, see T. P. Beyer, "A Note on the Diction of *Finnegans Wake*," *College English,* II (December, 1940), 275–77.

136. U68–69; W20:2. Other specimens of this technique follow: "Excuse, miss, there's a (whh!) just a (whh!) fluff." (p. 82); "Sllt. The nethermost deck of the first machine jogged forward its flyboard with sllt the first batch of quirefolded papers." (etc. – p. 120); "All flushed (O!), panting, sweating (O!), all breathless. . . . And flushed yet more (you horrid!), more goldenly." (p. 256); "Shebronze, dealing from her jar thick syrupy liquor for his lips, looked as it flowed (flower in his coat: who gave him?), and syrupped with her voice: . . . Miss Kennedy passed their way (flower, wonder who gave), bearing away teatray." (p. 261); "So I just went round to the back of the yard to pumpship and begob (hundred shillings to five) while I was letting off my (*Throwaway* twenty to) letting off my load"

(etc. — p. 329); "Kiss and delighted to, kiss, to see you." (p. 362); "Mr Bloom inserted his nose. Hm. Into the. Hm. Opening of his waistcoat." (p. 369)

137. U197; W57:5.   138. W58:5.

139. U237; R.

140. W67:5. W68, incorporating this change, omits the first "in their saddles", as do S, OP, and U.

U's "Pembrook" is corrected by I. Cf. also S, OP.

141. U244.

142. U522; W125:5–6. Then, after "up!" Joyce adds: "A cockhorse to Banbury cross."; and he alters *"ridehorse"* to *"cockhorse"*.

OP and U omit "in the,"; S, EP, S4, S6 do not.

143. U558; R.

144. H. This is also the reading in B259, n.p.

145. U730–31; W182:7. Joyce appears to be restoring the prancing rhythm, for in typescript (made available to me by Mr. R. F. Roberts) he altered "anything for an excuse to put his hand near my drawers drawers all the time" to "anything for an excuse to put his hand anear me drawers all the time". (He eliminates the apostrophes and period in W184:7, and changes "all the time" to "the whole blessed time" in W185:8.)

The rhythm of insistence was employed at one stage in the composition of the Gerty MacDowell episode: "But Tommy said he wanted the ball and Edy told him no that baby was playing with the ball and if he took it there'd be wigs on the green but Tommy said it was his ball and he wanted his ball his ball and he pranced on the ground, if you please." (U346). In H, Joyce, for reasons best known to himself, eliminated the prancing repetition by deleting the second half of "his ball his ball", thereby restoring, for this phrase, the reading in B257 (p. 8) and R.

146. U262; W73:7. The conclusion of the sentence, in R, reads: "she said."

147. U263; W73:7.   148. U265; W76:2.

149. A "base barreltone" according to Molly (U759). Through Bloom's thought (p. 152) we learn that Molly has used the expression before. It occurs to Bloom thrice again during the day (pp. 266, 278, 510).

150. U266; W76:2.   151. U491.

152. U504.

153. U506; W123:7. When the moth's speech was added in B259 (opposite p. 12), the first line read: "I'm a tiny tiny thing,". In R, this version is incorporated in the text.

154. U688–89; W170:1. The whole addition includes, after the question and answer I have cited, the two units of question and answer which occur next in the final version. There is one variation between Joyce's addition and the final text: Joyce wrote "Ned Lambert (in bed), Tom Kernan (in bed),".

155. Since "Saint" is here used as a prefix, its vowel is unstressed.

156. U714–15; W167:6. OP, U: "by the hypothesis".

157. U760; W201:4.   158. H.

159. W200:5. Note also the groping questions in the context: "what was the seventh card after that" (likewise added in W200), "didn't I dream something too". Uncertainty moves with a different step through Molly's "wait O Jesus wait yes that thing has come on me yes" (p. 754).

160. Most of the exceptions occur, understandably, in Joyce's attempts to verbalize various sounds. See above, pp. 31 ff.

161. Cf. Frank Budgen, "James Joyce," *Horizon*, III (February, 1941), 107–8: "In my hearing he [Joyce] answered (perhaps for the hundredth time) the question: 'Aren't there enough words for you in the five hundred thousand of the English language?' 'Yes, there are enough of them, but they are not the right ones.'"

Cf. also Budgen, "Joyce's Chapters of Going Forth by Day," *ibid.*, IV (September, 1941), 177: "I have already quoted a saying of Joyce's (evidently a practised hand-off for a straight tackler), 'Yes, there are enough words in the Oxford Dictionary, but they are not the right ones.'"

162. U8; W2:4.   163. NED.

164. See above, p. 38.

165. U269. In *Finnegans Wake*, Joyce elaborates *lovesoft* into "lovesoftfun" (p. 607), to pun upon *lots of fun*.

166. U375; W107:8.

167. H. And "dirty girl" becomes "dirty bracegirdle". In other words, Joyce probably borrowed "girl" for "girlwhite" from "dirty girl", while with "dirty girl" he conflated the memory of

"Mrs Bracegirdle" (p. 363), who was herself introduced between W105:6 and H.

For "girlwhite" there are, of course, analogous *-white* compounds, of which Joyce uses the following: "lilywhite" (p. 675), "milkwhite" (p. 55, 335, 471), and "saltwhite" (pp. 50, 113).

168. U258. In *Finnegans Wake* he produces "girlglee" (p. 182) and "girlsfuss" (p. 430).

169. U446; W117:7. Cf. *Finnegans Wake*, p. 299, n. 2: "scumhead."

170. U687; W171:8. Cf. "nothandle" (U64; introduced as two words in W24:7, the addition appears as one word in W22:6 and H) and the history of the already current "notwithstanding" (used on pp. 634, 655). Cf. also *Finnegans Wake*, p. 161: "nothave" and "nothalf"; p. 175: "Notpossible"; p. 455: "Notshall"; and, on p. 124: "butnot".

171. H. (Here Joyce also added "reciprocal" before "flesh".) Cf. *Finnegans Wake*, p. 442: "ournhisn"; p. 446: "ouryour".

172. U689; W170:1. The whole addition includes the answer to this question. This answer is obviously modelled on that to the third question back, likewise added here (as pointed out above, n. 154).

For the chiming of the bells, also introduced here, see above, p. 39.

173. See above, p. 34.

174. U125; W42:8. Here, also, before the last "his" Joyce adds "raking".

175. *NED*.   176. U513.

177. *Ibid.* A similar piece of agglutination and conversion is "Sherlockholmesing" (p. 620), which antedates and differs from the only specimen given by the *NED* (*Supplement*) for the use of the full name as a verb.

Cf. *Finnegans Wake*, p. 121: "blackartful"; p. 122: "toomuchness" (cf. *NED* s.v. "Too," 6.a.) and "fartoomanyness"; p. 184: "noondayterrorised"; p. 199: "hungerstriking"; p. 513: "inandouting".

178. U662–63; W163:4, W175:4, and H. W163 bears the following inscription:

$$1 \begin{cases} \text{16 décemb. 1921} \\ \text{M}^{\text{lle}}\text{ Beach} \end{cases}$$

W175 bears the following inscription:

$$2 \begin{cases} \text{30 décembre 1921} \\ \text{M}^{\text{lle}}\text{ Beach} \end{cases}$$

179. Louise Pound, *Blends, Their Relation to English Word Formation* (Heidelberg, 1914), p. 2.

180. See above, p. 32. And cf. *Finnegans Wake*, p. 164: "so munch to the cud" (in a context involving "stomach" and "digesting" — p. 163); p. 317: "munchantman".

181. U211; W61:2. In H, before his statement "Names! What's in a name?" (U206) "JOHN EGLINTON" becomes "MAGEEGLINJOHN", a blend of *Magee* (his real name), *Eglinton*, and *John*.

182. See above, p. 34. Eglinton is joined, in *Finnegans Wake* (p. 81), by Napoleon and Wellington as "Nippoluono" and "Wei-Ling-Taou."

183. U504; W123:6.

184. S, OP, U. R, OP, U: "female"; but Joyce changed "female" to "fumale" in typescript (owned by Miss Sylvia Beach), hence S, EP, S4, S6, S9: "fumale". For other puns on *female*, cf. *Finnegans Wake*, p. 437: "femurl"; p. 539: "fimmel"; p. 564: "femecovert"; p. 617: "Femelles". For other puns on *fume*, cf. *ibid.*, p. 219: "perfumance"; p. 320: "blastfumed"; p. 333: "mewseyfume"; p. 413: "fumiform"; p. 624: "parafume".

185. U591–92; W143:6–7.

186. S, S4, OP, U: "*with their tooralooloolooloo lay.*"

187. See above, pp. 35–36.

188. U70 (in Bloom's memory), 588.

189. U104: "With your tooraloom tooraloom."

190. U481.

191. The coincidence occurred once before in a passage dealing with Corny Kelleher:

"Corny Kelleher fell into step at their side.

" — Everything went off A I, he said. What?

"He looked on them from his drawling eye. Policeman's shoulders. With your *tooraloom tooraloom*.

" — As it should be, Mr Kernan said.

" — What? Eh? Corny Kelleher said.

"Mr Kernan *assured* him." (U104. Italics mine.)

Joyce, who knit together *Ulysses* with preternatural care, surely bore in mind, if he did not return to, this preceding passage relating to Kelleher, when Kelleher reappeared in nighttown. Thus there would be operating in Joyce's brain two coincidences of *-sure-* and *tooraloom.*

192. U70, 481, 588. On p. 70 (as indicated above, n. 188) Bloom remembers Kelleher's singing of the snatch; on p. 481 (as indicated above, n. 190) Bloom sings it on his own; on p. 588 Kelleher himself sings it.

The punctuation I have given is that of pp. 481, 588; that of p. 70 includes commas in the series of repeating words. The divergence occurs in S and OP, also.

193. U70. This same "tay" no doubt accounts for the last syllable in "reassuraloomtay".

194. U666; W163:7. Here, also, after "first arts" Joyce adds "second arts"; after "courses of" he adds "the royal", at the same time uncapitalizing "University".

195. U516: "Nes. Yo." For other transpositions of initial letters, cf. above, p. 26, and *Finnegans Wake*, p. 16: "oach eather"; p. 106: "*Inglo-Andean*"; p. 144: "Jolio and Romeune"; p. 189: "wious pish"; p. 349: "pughs and keaoghs"; p. 460: "stuesser . . . Vanilla"; p. 569: "Nowno and . . . Brolano".

196. H.   197. Levin, p. 168, quoting U141.

4

Joyce and Stephen Dedalus: The Problem of Autobiography *

MAURICE BEEBE

CRITICISM, I suppose most of us would agree, ought to be based at least in part on scholarship. In the history of Joyce's reputation, criticism came first, and it is only recently that scholarship has begun to catch up with the many impressions and interpretations evoked by Joyce's conveniently few works. Perhaps, though, it is just as well that we have had to wait for the letters, the bibliographies, the memoirs, the fugitive writings, and the other primary materials which the past few years have brought us, because earlier we might have been frightened off them by the twin bogies named Intentional Fallacy and Biographical Heresy. If now the emphasis in criticism begins to swing the other way, it is partly because the very abundance of Joyce readings has taught us that the Selective Fallacy is as dangerous as the Intentional one: interpretations convincing enough in themselves tend to refute one another and to demonstrate that any skilled critic can find in the works of any complex writer whatever he is looking for.

As illustration, we have only to consider the critics' changing attitude towards *A Portrait of the Artist as a Young Man*.

* Both this essay and that by Julian B. Kaye, which follows, were originally delivered as talks before the Joyce Section of the 1958 convention of the National Council of Teachers of English in Pittsburgh.

A decade or so after its publication it was still standard practice to take Stephen Dedalus seriously, to identify him with Joyce, and to accept his theory of art as the programme for Joyce's later writings. Then Wyndham Lewis pointed out that Stephen "is 'the poet' to an uncomfortable, a dismal, a ridiculous, even a pulverizing degree," and other critics, tough-minded Joycean apologists embarrassed by the identification of Joyce with the allegedly unmanly and disagreeable Stephen, assured us that Stephen is not an artist at all, but a posturing esthete whose ideas on art are quite different from those of his creator. Stephen, we were told again and again, would have been incapable of writing *Ulysses*. His Shelleyan idealism on the one hand, his eating sausages and white pudding on the other provided sure proof of Joyce's irony in the depiction of Stephen. A book that played a key role in making rebellion from God, Home, and Country seem the necessary first step towards artistic integrity turned out to be a satire on the alienated artist.

The problem which this example illustrates remains one of the most crucial, if one of the most tired, issues in Joyce criticism: was Joyce committed to the viewpoint of Stephen, or was he, even in this early lyrical work, dramatically detached from his hero? Critics who equate Stephen with Joyce tend to feel that Joyce champions his hero. Critics who dissociate Stephen from Joyce tend to feel that Joyce repudiates his hero. But neither position is being argued with much fervor these days, and practically every Joycean seems willing to compromise. Because we find in the *Portrait* both exaltation of the artist-hero and a certain amount of irony in the depiction of Stephen as a human being, it is tempting to think in terms of *both . . . and* rather than *either . . . or*. However, there are at least three different ways of compromising. In this paper I should like briefly to review these three alternatives to *either . . . or*, none of which is original with me, and to judge them in terms of the new evidence. With the publication of such material as the *Letters*, bibliographies of Joyce's writings and his personal library, the early book reviews, Ellmann and Mason's forthcoming edition of the critical essays (which I am grateful to say that I have had a chance to see in advance of publication), memoirs by Stanislaus Joyce, the Colums, Byrne, Sheehy, and others, the biographical researches of Richard Ellmann, Patricia Hutchins, and Kevin Sullivan, and the many new scholarly studies of Joyce's sources, it has finally become possible to compare the fiction with the reality and to decide, with partial assurance at least, the extent to which Stephen is modelled upon the young Joyce. If in many respects Stephen now seems to be even more autobiographical than had been assumed, in other ways he is strikingly different from Joyce. Because the general autobiographical basis of the novel may now, I think, be conceded, it is the divergences from reality rather than the parallels which must concern us particularly.

Probably the most popular alternative to arguing that Stephen is Joyce or is not Joyce is to avoid the issue entirely by saying that the *Portrait* is an autobiographical novel — with equal emphasis on both words — that is, neither straight autobiography nor pure fiction. As Stanislaus Joyce, who was in a better position to know than anyone else, put it, Joyce drew "very largely upon his own life and his own experience. . . . But A *Portrait of the Artist* is not an autobiography; it is an artistic creation." Although no one can disagree with this statement, I am not sure that it helps us much, for it is based on a false comparison. If we put "autobiography" on one side, "artistic creation" on the other, where do we place the *Confessions* of Rousseau or *The Education of Henry Adams?*

Modified, the work-of-art compromise is relevant to our problem in at least one way. Many of the divergences between the reality and the fiction derive simply from Joyce's need to economize, to transform the multitude of wasteful and chaotic impressions which made up Joyce's experience

into a compact, unified novel. This process has been apparent
since the publication of *Stephen Hero*, which allows us to
isolate a midway stage between Joyce's experience and the
finished work of art. The most important example is perhaps
the almost entire omission from the *Portrait* of Stephen's
brother Maurice, who has an important part in the earlier
version. Playing down the role of Maurice helps to emphasize
the aloneness and the proud independence of Stephen and to
place greater emphasis on his search for vocation. But now
that the memoirs of the real Maurice, Joyce's brother Stanislaus, have been published, we can see an additional reason.
It turns out that Stanislaus was even more estranged from his
family, more bitter against his father, country, and church
than was his brother. It was Stanislaus, not James, who refused to make his Easter duty. If Joyce had wanted only to
strengthen the impression of Stephen's uniqueness and his
staunch withstanding of opposition, he could have given him
a brother who opposed his views, as Shaun opposes Shem in
Finnegans Wake. Joyce, in the *Portrait* still generally faithful
to his experience, though less so than in *Stephen Hero*, could
not go that far. Rather than oppose Stephen with a strong
spokesman for the other side or weaken his victory by provid-
ing moral support within his family, Joyce combined certain
aspects of his brother's character with his own and thus gave
Stephen the strength of the two young Joyces. In this way
the need for artistic economy results in a distortion of reality
that is in Stephen's favor.

The second alternative to deciding whether Joyce champions Stephen or repudiates him is to fall back on the convenient critical doctrine of the irony of noncommittal. In
his later works, certainly, Joyce is free of opinions and value
judgments, and it may well be that in the *Portrait*, too, Joyce
attempted deliberately to avoid either favoring Stephen or
making him the object of ridicule. Whether deliberate or
not, much of the author's seeming aloofness from his subject

is the inevitable detachment of time. The Joyce writing is a different person from the Joyce depicted. If Stephen's life parallels Joyce's, the story ends in 1902. Joyce did not finish writing the novel until 1914. The mixture of irony and sympathy may be explained as the half-apologetic, half-proud attitude of an older man looking back after a decade on the foibles of his youth. This, I take it, is the sense of Joyce's frequently quoted remarks to Frank Budgen — his assertion that people too often forget the words "as a young man" in his title, and his statement, "I haven't let this young man off very lightly, have I?" In neither statement does Joyce disown the autobiographical relation nor imply an attack upon the character of Stephen. The words "as a young man" do not eradicate the word "artist." And Joyce immediately followed his other remark with two sentences that are never quoted by the Stephen-detractors: "Many writers have written about themselves. I wonder if any of them has been as candid as I have?" All that Joyce probably meant by saying that he had not let Stephen off lightly was that he had tried to draw an uncompromisingly truthful portrait of his earlier self. The objectivity of the picture, which veers neither too far in the direction of self-glorification nor too far in the direction of self-attack, demonstrated Joyce's artistic ideal of the author's detachment from his subject.

Even this means of compromise — though it is preferable to the *either . . . or* answers — does not stand up entirely against the new evidence. The surprising thing about the changes from reality is that more often than not they are in the direction of self-exaltation rather than self-criticism. Joyce, far from maintaining consistently the ironical attitude of a mature man looking back on the errors of youth, actually gave to Stephen many beliefs and convictions which Joyce did not come by until after 1902. Although he remains juvenile in some ways, the Stephen of 1902 has the learning, the wisdom, the cunning of the Joyce of 1914. For example, when Joyce gave his paper on "Drama and Life" in

1900 he replied to his critics at length and with considerable spirit. In *Stephen Hero*, Stephen after the reading of his paper and the attack upon it maintained a calm, dignified silence in keeping with Joyce's later theory that the artist ought to be aloof, self-assured, indifferent to his critics.

The "Drama and Life" essay, like the others Joyce wrote while he was at University College between 1898 and 1902, shows him moving gradually and steadily towards the mature philosophy of art attributed to Stephen, but still a long way from it. When Ellmann and Mason's collection of these essays is published, it will be seen, I think, that though there is a clear progression in his attempt to define "drama" — and, with it, his concept of the artist's relation to life — there is no evidence that Joyce possessed fully and with realization the esthetic attributed to Stephen. In 1898, drama is simply interplay of emotions. Two years later, in "Drama and Life," it has become the "underlying laws" rather than those "accidental manners and humours" which characterize mere literature. Drama, he now feels, is outside the dramatist: "it exists, before it takes form, independently," a kind of pre-existent Platonic "spirit" which Joyce seems to feel is the sum-total of all human experience. It is something which the artist may hope to capture — the theory of epiphanies which Joyce came later to reject seems to be a development of this view — but not create. Great artists such as Ibsen, Joyce argues, have a mystic insight into the spirit of drama, and what distinguishes their art is the kind of life they capture rather than the technical control over life which Joyce, the artist as artificer, later recognized as his own mission as artist. Thus "Drama and Life" has an exhortatory, life-exalting, let-in-fresh-air message that makes it seem dated and juvenile beside the cool exposition of drama which Stephen expounds in his talk on the three stages of art, from lyrical to epical to dramatic.

Although Joyce gave Stephen a more invulnerable esthetic than he himself possessed at the equivalent time of his life, he may be said to have balanced this by making Stephen a more disagreeable person than Joyce seems to have been. According to Stanislaus, Joyce was fairly athletic, a good swimmer, and so good-natured as a child that he earned the nickname "Sunny Jim." Stephen, of course, shuns the playing field, is frightened of the water (for symbolic reasons), and no one would call him sunny of temperament. Unlike Stephen, Joyce, far from being shunned or ridiculed by his classmates, was voted by them to the most important elective office at Belvedere College. Stephen is intelligent and presumably a good student, but he is not presented as being so distinguished a student as was Joyce, who, in competition with all the boys of his grade in Ireland, for two consecutive years took first prize in the English examination. Changes like these can be explained satisfactorily through neither the work of art nor the irony of noncommittal compromise. This brings us to the third alternative — the one which I happen to favor.

Joyce, it is clear, was a better rounded — alas, better adjusted — person than his fictional surrogate. It is the lack of roundedness which makes many readers dislike Stephen. If Joyce had given him more of his own features — had, that is, been even more truthful — Stephen would not have seemed the poet to so dismal and pulverizing degree as he struck Wyndham Lewis and the other Stephen-haters. The whole point, though, is that Stephen is *the poet* or, as Joyce's carefully worded title tells us, *the artist*. One of Joyce's first critics, Valery Larbaud, said that the *Portrait* should be read as "l'histoire de la jeunesse de l'artiste en général, c'est à dire de tout homme doué du temperament artiste." One way in which Joyce sought to detach himself from his hero was to depict not James Joyce, but the universal, representative, archetypal artist, the ideal which Joyce could only partially achieve in reality. Thus he had to omit certain features of his personality that seemed out of keeping with the conventional stereotype of the artist. As far as the stereotype available to Joyce is concerned, a well-rounded, athletic poet would have seemed an anomaly, and everyone knows that poets are supposed to be gloomy rather than sunny. The stereotype had it that artists were too absorbed in their own dream worlds to be good students, too indifferent to conventional religion of any kind to serve willingly as prefects of their sodalities, and therefore Joyce had to remove these aspects of his own youthful career from his depiction of Stephen. The Stephen-haters may recognize this, but they make the error of assuming that because Stephen is the stereotyped poet he cannot be a true artist. The cumulative weight of the stereotype, the frequency with which it appears in other portraits of the artist, may, on the contrary, convince us that whether we like the type or not, it may well characterize the essential, universal qualities of the artistic temperament. Byron, Baudelaire, Rimbaud, Baron Corvo, and a good many other artists of distinction had unbalanced and disagreeable personalities; and to dislike Stephen because of his lack of human roundedness does not justify saying that he cannot therefore be an artist. Proust's Marcel is a sickly, effeminate, posturing creature whom few of us would care to know personally, but that he was also an artist is proved by the novel in which he appears.

There is hardly a feature of Stephen's personality or attitude which is entirely original with Joyce, and A *Portrait of the Artist* may be considered the apotheosis of a movement rather than the beginning of one. It is, of course, impossible in a paper of this length to deal adequately with the many sources that Joyce used, but a mere list of those writers who most interested him helps to suggest the extent to which the stereotype was already well established when Joyce wrote the *Portrait*. The *Kunstlerdrama* form proved especially influential during the college years, and works like Ibsen's *When We Dead Awaken*, Hauptmann's *Michael Kramer*, and Sudermann's *Magda* (of which Joyce said to his family, "The subject of the play is genius breaking out in the home and against the home. You needn't have gone to see it. It's going to happen in your own house"), all with the common theme of the artist versus society, helped to establish in Joyce's mind the conviction that the artist is inevitably in conflict with his domestic environment. There was Giordano Bruno, proud and eccentric rebel, who helped Joyce form his scorn of the "rabblement" and may even have suggested the name "Daedalus." There were Byron, Blake, and the other early Romantics; Pater and Wilde; the French writers Flaubert, Baudelaire, Rimbaud, Verlaine, and Mallarmé; the Irish poet James Clarence Mangan, on whom Joyce wrote two essays, in 1902 and 1907, which may be considered his first imaginary portrait of the artist-type; Goethe's *Wilhelm Meister*, which not only founded the tradition of the portrait-of-the-artist novel but established within it the convention of *Hamlet* criticism which Joyce, in *Ulysses*, was not the first writer to continue; the artist stories of Yeats; Butler's *The Way of All Flesh* with its obvious appeal for revolt against the fathers; the cool detachment of a Henry James, whose *Portrait of a Lady*, Stanislaus tells us, suggested the title of Joyce's novel. Many of these influences have been studied at length, and the list could be extended, but this is enough to show that Stephen, far from being a new kind of hero, had a good many ancestors.

But aside from known sources of Joyce, the Stephen-as-archetype thesis is supported by a comparison of Stephen with the artist-heroes of other novels which Joyce may or may not have read. The standard elements of the artist type as it appears in the long tradition of the portrait-of-the-artist novel would include sensitivity, passivity, egoism, introversion, the faculty of concentration and absorption in a single activity, a sense of divine vocation, aloofness from society, and the ability as artist to stand detached even from the self. Stephen shares all these traits. Critics have objected to the fact that he is a passive hero, but he is no more passive than David Copperfield, Jacob Stahl, or Ricky Elliot. Some readers object to his egoism, but he is less self-centered than Jean Christophe or Shaw's Owen Jack. Even minor points of

character are paralleled in other portraits of the artist. The
hero of *Changing Winds*, St. John Ervine's neglected and
powerful portrait of another Irish artist as a young man, is,
for instance, afraid of dogs. Edwin Clayhanger (and scarcely
anyone would consider that Joyce and Arnold Bennett had
much else in common) is as sensitive and passive as Stephen;
Edwin reacts against his family and religion, he reads *The
Count of Monte Cristo*, and he first learns to distrust his
elders in a tea party scene similar to the Christmas dinner
scene of the *Portrait*. I could go on, but let me instead describe at greater length but one example of a work that
demonstrates that the atmosphere of Joyce's novel was simply
in the air during the time when the novel was gestating in
Joyce's consciousness.

I do not know that Joyce read George Moore's excellent
novel, *The Lake*, though it was published in 1905 and in 1907
Joyce called Moore "an intellectual oasis in the Sahara of
the false, spiritualistic, Messianic, and detective writings
whose name is legion in England." But even if Joyce did not
read the book, he would have been amused to discover later
the curious parallels, some in reverse, to his *Portrait*. *The
Lake*, which is dedicated to Edouard Dujardin, is focussed
largely in the mind of a provincial Irish priest named, interestingly enough, Oliver Gogarty. He falls in love with a young
woman whom he has driven out of his parish for alleged immorality and with whom he begins a long, painful correspondence. Partly for esthetic reasons, for she weans him
away from the Church through culture, art, and progressive
ideas, Father Gogarty loses his faith. In a moving conclusion,
he feigns drowning in the lake which serves as central symbol
in the novel, but actually swims across it, puts on layman's
clothes, and departs for America. His immediate goal, however, is a place on the other side of the lake, a village named
Joycetown. Coincidence? Undoubtedly. Nonetheless, the
center-of-consciousness method of the two novels, the way in
which the heroes move from priesthood and commitment to

art and detachment, much of the moon, water, and bird symbolism, and the obvious baptismal scenes in the climaxes of both novels tempt one to feel that if Joyce did not know Moore's novel, then he was right in saying that drama "exists, before it takes form, independently."

In conclusion, then, I would say that in depicting the character of Stephen Joyce drew not only on his own character and experience modified by the artistic need for selection and economy, but also on the artist-heroes of life and fiction. From these many sources he developed the image of an archetypal artist, gave it the appropriately symbolic name of "Dedalus," and carefully removed from the composite figure any traits of his own character that conflicted with the stereotype. But reading is experience, and readers, like critics, tend to find what they are looking for. In developing his composite artist, Joyce, who had long been seeking a pose, provided for himself a personal model, a Mallarméan mask, which he seems to have put on once he knew what it looked like. In this sense, the Joyce writing in 1914 was depicting not so much the Joyce of the past as the Joyce of the future. Many reviewers of the *Letters* have commented on their strange, cool aloofness, the almost neutral personality revealed in letters that show an absorption of self in the role of artist. The Joyce of the *Letters* is quite different from the touchingly fallible young man depicted by his brother and others. Thus the "autobiographical problem" in Joyce is not only a question of how life influences art; it is also a question of how art influences life.

5

A Portrait of the Artist as Blephen-Stoom

JULIAN B. KAYE

I N the last few years we have learned a great deal about the theme and techniques of *Ulysses*, with the result that older studies often seem the work of cultivated amateurs. Most recent work has been professional indeed; but I have been disappointed by the fact that a whole group of critics — whom, for the sake of convenience, I shall call the Kenner school — have drawn conclusions about *Ulysses* against the evidence which they have gathered. To them *Ulysses* is a book, not about the quick, but about the dead, the burden of which is "no I said no I won't No." For those who think my version of the concluding words of *Ulysses* unfair, let me quote Mr. Kenner's *Dublin's Joyce:*

The "Yes" of consent that kills the soul has darkened the intellect and blunted the moral sense of all Dublin. At the very rim of Dante's funnel-shaped Hell is the imperceptible "Yes" of Paola [*sic*] and Francesca; they are blown about by the winds, but Molly lies still at the warm dead womb-like centre of the labyrinth of paving-stones. Her "Yes" is confident and exultant; it is the "Yes" of authority: authority over this animal kingdom of the dead.[1]

Quite logically, Mr. Kenner views both Stephen Dedalus and Leopold Bloom as dead: Stephen is disposed of by the statement that Joyce changed his name from the Daedalus of *Stephen Hero* to the Dedalus of *A Portrait* and *Ulysses* because Dedalus chimes with dead (39); and Bloom is dead because he is immersed in matter, which is the "curse God has laid on the Jewish people, according to Jacques Maritain" (185). No wonder Bloom is compared with the monstrous apparition in James's "The Jolly Corner" (164) and with the criminal Magwitch — Pip's father from the antipodes in *Great Expectations.*

Both Mr. William Schutte, the author of *Joyce and Shakespeare*, and Father William Noon, the author of *Joyce and Aquinas*, are scholarly and judicious, and they express themselves more temperately than Mr. Kenner, but neither disagrees with his conclusion that both Stephen Dedalus and Leopold Bloom are failures.

Can these critics be proved wrong? I think so. How? By showing — for this is the heart of the matter — that Stephen Dedalus and Leopold Bloom are fictional representations of James Joyce.

Perhaps it would be best first to limit the area of disagreement. I think that all Joyce scholars would agree that Stephen and Leopold are fictional representations — i.e., that Joyce presents himself in fictional terms and that he is concerned with his surrogates primarily as characters in a work of fiction. On the other hand, I doubt whether anyone would say that Stephen Dedalus, at any rate, is no more autobiographical than Robinson Crusoe. Thus, the question becomes: Granted that Stephen's portrait is *A Portrait of the Artist as a Young Man*, which emphasizes Stephen's immaturity, is Stephen a portrait of the artist at all? Mr. Kenner says that "Joyce was never the Stephen Dedalus of his 1914 *Portrait*, mirror of nineteenth-century romantic idealism: Byron, Shelley, Axel, Frédéric Moreau" (44). Therefore, Bloom is not Joyce's other self, but a horrible example of the other side of nineteenth-century romantic estheticism. He gives the example of Sherlock Holmes and Dr. Watson, with Bloom, of course, as Dr. Watson, the admiring bourgeois (170).

What I should like to do is to study Bloom rather than Stephen, whose affinities with Joyce have been ably treated by other critics.[2] First, Bloom, because he is a Jew, is considered a foreigner by most of his associates even though he is a native-born Irishman. The parallel with Joyce's exile from Ireland is obvious. But perhaps even more important is Mr. Bloom's opposition to everything in Ireland that the young Joyce detested.

That this is not mere conjecture is borne out by a study of Temple in *Stephen Hero* and in *A Portrait*. Temple has been correctly identified by Chester G. Anderson [3] as a surrogate for Stephen; for Temple does possess many of Stephen's qualities. For example, his parable of the monkeys in *Stephen Hero* is similar in tone to Stephen's parable of the plums in *Ulysses*,[4] and both parables are concerned with Irish sterility. But Temple also possesses many of Bloom's attributes. He is a humanitarian, a Utopian, a rationalist who is skeptical about church and clergy. In *Stephen Hero*, Joyce — who is economical with symbols, images, situations — observes Temple looking with interest at some crubeens in a butcher's window (109), and Bloom purchases some crubeens which figure in the Circe episode of *Ulysses* (427, 430, and 445). Temple's olive complexion and gipsylike appearance recall the dark Bloom, an exotic in Ireland.

Most important of all are Temple's name and his relationship to Cranly. *Temple* is a synonym for synagogue, and Temple is — in name, at least — a Jew although he is not racially Jewish. This is confirmed by the actions of Cranly, who represents those forces which Stephen fears and distrusts — Ireland, asceticism, Virgin, mother, and Church. Cranly detests Temple because he feels that Temple encourages Stephen in his rebellion against the Church and also because he is offended by Temple's crude anticlericalism. In *A Portrait* Cranly twice chases Temple away from Stephen with a stick. When one considers that almost every gesture of Cranly's has been shown to have symbolic overtones, one may conclude that Cranly is recapitulating the triumph of the Church over the Synagogue, the subject of many stained glass windows and much statuary in the cathedrals of medi-

eval Europe.[5] In *A Portrait*, Stephen appears between Cranly
and Temple; in medieval religious art, Jesus is seen between
the Church and the Synagogue.[6] But in *A Portrait* Cranly
triumphs by threats of violence, and our sympathies — and
presumably Stephen's and Joyce's — are with Temple, despite
his crudity and muddleheadedness.[7]

The relationship in *A Portrait* of Cranly-Stephen-Temple
is analogous to that of Mulligan-Stephen-Bloom in *Ulysses*.
Stephen believes that both Mulligan and Cranly are treacherous usurpers. Mulligan as physician and Cranly as eccle-
siastic, they usurp the rightful primacy of the artist as priest
of the imagination. He also believes that they personally
disparage, denigrate, even betray him. Against these figures
are set the clumsily articulate, unpopular Temple and Bloom
who both express personal affection for Stephen and admiration for his gifts. And Mulligan attempts to disparage Bloom
as "sheeny" and pederast, just as Cranly constantly criticizes
Temple. Another conclusion one may draw from Joyce's
treatment of Temple is that if Temple possesses traits of
both Stephen and Bloom and if he is Stephen's *alter ego*,
then Stephen and Bloom are one person.

Of course, it is generally agreed that Bloom is Stephen's
other self. Mr. Schutte's *Joyce and Shakespeare* is conclusive
there. Bloom and Stephen both are Shakespeare, and they are
at the same time father and son as, respectively, the Ghost
of King Hamlet and Prince Hamlet.[8] Father Noon identifies
them as analogous to God the Father and God the Son in
the Trinity. But both critics refuse to make the identification
with Joyce. To Mr. Schutte, Stephen and Bloom together
make a paralyzed Shakespeare, not the author of *Ulysses*
(144–45). Father Noon finds Stephen guilty of the Sabellian heresy — i.e., that Stephen and Bloom are not one and
at the same time two, according to the orthodox interpretation of the Trinity, but rather that they represent different
aspects of the same person, which is the heresy of Sabellius,
sometimes called modalism.[9] Mr. Kenner's view of Bloom as

Stephen's nightmare self — i.e., a judgment upon Stephen
for being Stephen — I have already described.

What I should like to do now is briefly to observe the
development of the principal Joyce *alter ego* as he grows up
and reaches maturity, and his relationship with the author
James Joyce. In doing this I shall emphasize what I believe
was important to Joyce — ages, dates, coincidence, correspondence, and so forth.[10]

First, the Joycean *alter ego* is almost always Joyce's age.
Even the exceptions, such as Gabriel Conroy, prove the rule,
for Gabriel is Joyce's portrait of the man he might have become if he had stayed in Ireland. The boy narrator of "The
Sisters" seems to be about thirteen years old, Joyce's age in
1895 when the story takes place;[11] Stephen Dedalus is of
course Joyce's age throughout A *Portrait* and *Ulysses*; Richard
Rowan is about thirty, like Joyce in 1912; Leopold Bloom is
in his late thirties, Joyce's age when he was writing *Ulysses*;[12]
and HCE seems vaguely fiftyish, like the man writing *Finnegans Wake*.

That the boy narrator of the first three stories of *Dubliners*
is the adolescent Stephen Dedalus would be generally accepted.[13] It is the transformation of Stephen into the man
who possesses many of Bloom's qualities which is difficult to
understand. Here the transitional figure of Richard Rowan
is important, for in *Exiles* we can see Stephen Dedalus becoming Leopold Bloom. Maurice Beebe, in his excellent
"James Joyce: Barnacle Goose and Lapwing," has linked for
us, by using Joyce's notes for *Exiles*, Gretta Conroy of "The
Dead," Bertha of *Exiles*, and Molly Bloom of *Ulysses* with
Mrs. Joyce.[14] And if Leopold Bloom is Mrs. Joyce's husband,
who can he be but Joyce? That Joyce, whose obsession with
dates is notorious, married Molly to Leopold on October 8
(720), the date of his elopement with Nora Barnacle, strongly
confirms this speculation.

If we were to accept Mr. Kenner's argument that *Exiles* is
the end of Stephen Dedalus and of Joyce's exile, we would of

course have to abandon Bloom as an *alter ego* for Joyce, for
Bloom is in exile in Dublin. The theme of *Exiles,* "The soul
being unable to become virgin again" [15] may well be an excellent argument for conventional marriage, which, according
to Mr. Kenner, is "as much of a fulfilment as is allowed"
rather than a retreat from the romantic idealism of Joyce's
youth, but even Mr. Kenner's phraseology indicates rather
the resignation of Leopold Bloom than the support of traditional institutions that he asks us to infer from the play.[16]
That Joyce did not marry Nora legally until 1931, and then
only for testamentary reasons, seems to indicate that Joyce's
views were different from Mr. Kenner's; moreover, J. F.
Byrne's statement that Nora was unwilling even to suggest
a marriage ceremony after more than twenty years of married
life must be noted as proof that Joyce's conception of the
family and of marriage as institutions remained unorthodox.
The revelation of Mary Colum, who was the godmother of
Stephen Joyce, Joyce's grandson, that Joyce's family would
not tell him of his grandson's baptism (in 1932) certainly
does not indicate the end of Joyce's exile from his church.
And his physical exile from Ireland remained unbroken after
1912 despite the fact that he was relatively well-off, during
the twenties, and liked to travel. Not even his strong attach-
ment to his old, bedridden father could tempt him to revisit
Dublin.

How then does Richard Rowan differ from Stephen
Dedalus? First, he is growing older and he is "tired for a
while." He seems to be growing more tolerant of human
weaknesses and failures. Mr. Beebe's opinion that at this
point Joyce begins to separate his life as a man from his life
as an artist and to attempt to reconcile the man to the human
condition [17] seems correct to me. Certainly it leads in the
direction of Bloom.

One trait which Stephen, Richard, and Leopold share
with Joyce is masochism. In his notes to *Exiles,* Joyce speaks
of the play as a "rough and tumble between the Marquis de

Sade and Freiherr von Sacher Masoch," with Robert as sadist and Richard as masochist. "Richard's Masochism needs no example." [18] Stephen's masochism, the reader of *Ulysses* may say, also needs no example. As for Bloom, we know that he has read — or at least purchased — Sacher Masoch and that he is almost destroyed by his masochist fantasy in the Circe episode.[19]

"Richard," says Joyce, "wishes, it seems, to feel the thrill of adultery vicariously and to possess a bound woman Bertha through the organ of his friend." [20] In the Circe episode Leopold Bloom experiences an hallucinatory fantasy of "offering his nuptial partner to all strongmembered males" (525), and he imagines himself as suffering and enjoying erotic pleasures from the embraces of Molly and Boylan (550–53). It is after this experience that Bloom and Stephen are identified with Shakespeare in "the mirror held up to nature" (553). Although I am not able to go beyond the generality that love and suffering are often equated by Shakespeare as they are by many other writers — notably Marcel Proust — I can say that even the reading of Joyce's letters convinces me of his masochism. Certainly Joyce's miserable winter of 1902–3 — when his teeth were so bad that although he was usually half-starved the pain of eating was so great that he had to stop for several minutes after his first bite of food — must be attributed to his masochism as well as his determination to make a success of his "first flight." That he is able to laugh at himself as Leopold Bloom has escaped the notice of those critics who have in effect depicted him as sneering at his youth while being unable even to laugh with tolerant amusement at the weaknesses of his maturity, for that is the result of making Stephen a parody of the young Joyce and Bloom a nightmare self of Stephen.

We now know that Joyce experienced at least twice the torments of jealous love for his wife. First, he learned that as a young girl she had been in love with a boy who had died. This incident must have obsessed Joyce for some time, for

he used it as the climax of "The Dead," it is the subject of
"She Weeps over Rahoon," and he was still brooding over
it in 1913 when he wrote the notes for *Exiles*. The second
incident concerns the story which Vincent Cosgrave (Lynch
of *A Portrait* and *Ulysses*) told him in a Dublin bar in 1909
— namely, that he (Cosgrave) had been intimate with Nora
before her elopement to the continent with Joyce. Richard
Ellmann tells the story [21] and J. F. Byrne describes Joyce's
reaction to Cosgrave's fabrication. "He wept and groaned
and gesticulated in futile impotence as he sobbed out the
thing that had occurred. Never in my life have I seen a human
being more shattered." [22] Byrne succeeded in convincing
Joyce that Cosgrave had lied, but Joyce had gone to Byrne's
house at 7 Eccles Street, believing that he had been betrayed.
This experience is represented fictionally by Bloom's reaction
to his wife's unfaithfulness. And it is at 7 Eccles Street that
Mr. Bloom feels relief in resignation just as Joyce had felt
it in Byrne's assurances of Nora's innocence. That Joyce
used what was perhaps the most harrowing experience of
his life as the basis for Leopold Bloom's adventure may be
considered as another proof of their identity.

   The importance of the numerous correspondences between Joyce and Bloom must be pointed out again. Joyce,
in addition to giving Bloom his wedding anniversary, gave
Bloom's mother his grandmother's name Ellen [23] (which he
had already used fictionally for the mother of Gabriel Conroy [24]). Bloom's Catholic baptism takes place in the same
church as Stephen's and, presumably, Joyce's.[25] Moreover,
Joyce and Bloom are both managers of singers.[26]

   Perhaps more important is Bloom's role as a representation
of the bourgeois side of Joyce's nature. Herbert Gorman's
contrast of Joyce and Pound as opposing types — as aesthete
and bourgeois — is apparently correct.[27] Joyce's fondness for
de luxe hotels, *haute cuisine*, fashionable restaurants like
Fouquet's, temperate drinking of wines (no beer or whisky),
courteous manners, family portraits, and family parties makes

us think of Leopold Bloom. The "materialism" and "sentimentality" for which poor Mr. Bloom has been attacked are characteristics of Joyce as well as Bloom.[28] Although some critics of Joyce find these qualities faintly contemptible, I believe that Joyce found them hugely amusing, and I strongly suspect that Mr. Bloom's fantasy of a suburban paradise in the Ithaca episode is Joyce's good-humored parody of his own longings for the solid comfort of the well-to-do middle class — those longings which Thomas Mann depicts so solemnly in "Tonio Kröger."

Perhaps the most convincing argument for the identification of Bloom with Joyce is that it solves several of the problems of *Ulysses*. First, William Noon's interpretation of Stephen and Bloom as related to each other according to the terms of the Sabellian heresy — namely, as different modes of the same Being rather than as different Persons of the Trinity [29] — is, from this point of view, incorrect. Mysteriously, Stephen and Bloom are one since they are both James Joyce, and yet they are different persons. In other words, it would seem to me that this relationship is a good illustration of orthodox Trinitarianism.

William Schutte comments that Bloom and Stephen combined do not make another Shakespeare, but rather a paralyzed Shakespeare; [30] and it is true that their combination in a mirror-image makes a paralyzed Shakespeare. Add the two and you have paralysis. But if Stephen eventually does fulfill the promises he makes to himself at the end of *A Portrait* ("Welcome, O life! I go to encounter for the millionth time the reality of experience and to forge in the smithy of my soul the uncreated conscience of the race." [299]), then he is more than his old self (Stephen Dedalus) plus his new values and habits (Leopold Bloom). The two personae interpenetrate each other. Mr. Schutte conceives of the process as a mechanical combination, and therefore quite naturally he finds it implausible. What does happen daily is the re-creation of our psyches by the combination of new and old, present and past. By this process Stephen Dedalus and Leopold Bloom — become "Blephen-Stoom" (666) — are "redeemed" as the author of *Ulysses* and *Finnegans Wake*.

Mr. Schutte himself discusses a scene in which "is sounded the note of redemption." [31] Georgina Johnson, the prostitute whom Stephen intends to visit at Bella Cohen's house, has married.

> ZOE It was a commercial traveller married her and took her away with him.
> FLORRY (*Nods.*) Mr Lambe from London.
> STEPHEN Lamb of London, who takest away the sins of our world.

But Mr. Schutte concludes that the redemption of the modern world, which he believes Joyce is referring to, is unlikely. "Like the miracle of Georgina Johnson's redemption from her life of sin, this miracle is unlikely, for it requires the reintegration of the disparate elements of Dublin life." [32] This miracle is indeed unlikely, but it is not the miracle that Joyce is talking about. Mr. Lambe of London is Shakespeare, a commercial traveller, and Jesus, all of whom Joyce repeatedly identifies with Bloom. Bloom is then a saviour because he redeems prostitutes.

Literally this is true. Molly is redeemed by Bloom from selling herself. And if Molly is the Earth, this redemption becomes cosmic. But prostitution is also a social metaphor for the selling of the spiritual for the material, which is used again and again by Bernard Shaw and other writers of the late nineteenth and early twentieth centuries. Joyce's dominant metaphor for social corruption — simony — is, in this context, only another name for prostitution.[33] How does Stephen-Bloom-Joyce perform this redemption from prostitution? As a man in his family and as a writer in his books.[34]

Moreover, my conjecture about redemption from prostitution as a major theme in *Ulysses* is corroborated by Joyce's choice of June 16 as Bloomsday. Many critics have speculated on Joyce's reasons for selecting this date, and while I do not believe that my hypothesis is more plausible in itself than Richard Ellmann's suggestion that Joyce met Nora Barnacle on that day [35] or A. M. Klein's ingenious reasoning about the suitability of June 16 for a Black Mass,[36] I do think that it has the advantage of greater relevance to the theme of *Ulysses* and to the great argument of much of Joyce's work. Bloomsday, June 16, is, in the Catholic calendar, the feast day of St. John Francis Regis. Like Stephen and Joyce, John Francis Regis was a student in Jesuit schools. Unlike them, he became a Jesuit, a priest of the Church rather than a priest of art. His special work, however, was the redemption of prostitutes,[37] the equivalent, for a priest, of Joyce's battle as artist-priest against simony — the selling of the spiritual for the material — in his life and in his art.[38]

NOTES

1. Hugh Kenner, *Dublin's Joyce* (Bloomington, Indiana, 1956), p. 262.

2. For example, see Maurice Beebe's "James Joyce: Barnacle Goose and Lapwing," *PMLA*, LXXI (June, 1956), 302–20.

3. Chester G. Anderson, "James Joyce's 'Tilly,'" *PMLA*, LXXIII (June, 1958), p. 295.

4. See *Stephen Hero*, p. 225, and *Ulysses*, pp. 143–48. I have used the Modern Library editions of *Dubliners, A Portrait of the Artist as a Young Man*, and *Ulysses*; the 1955 New Directions edition of *Stephen Hero*; the Viking editions of *Exiles* (1951) and *Finnegans Wake*. All citations of Joyce's works refer to these editions.

5. See Emile Mâle, *Religious Art in France* XIII *Century*, trans. Dora Nussey (London and New York, 1913), pp. 188–93, for an account of the use of this motif in French cathedrals.

6. Stephen, in *A Portrait*, is associated with Jesus, as many Joyce critics have pointed out.

7. See Anderson, p. 296. He compares the stick with which Cranly threatens Temple to the pandybat and cabbage stump used to beat Stephen in *A Portrait*. They are symbols of the appeal of unjust authority to force as the *ultima ratio*.

8. William M. Schutte, *Joyce and Shakespeare* (New Haven, 1957), pp. 126–27 and *passim*.

9. William T. Noon, S.J., *Joyce and Aquinas* (New Haven, 1957), pp. 110, 117, and 125.

10. See Richard Ellmann, "The Limits of Joyce's Naturalism," *Sewanee Review*, LXIII (Autumn, 1955), 567–75. Ellmann goes so far as to make coincidence, "correspondence," the basis of Joyce's art. My own studies are pushing me towards his conclusion. Certainly there can be no doubt that "correspondence" is very important in Joyce's work. All the biographers who knew Joyce are agreed. Joyce's fascination by the fact that James Stephens was also born on Feb. 2, 1882, and his half-serious proposal that Stephens should complete *Finnegans Wake* if he were unable to are persuasive examples of his preoccupation with birthdays.

11. *Dubliners*, p. 10. See Marvin Magalaner in Marvin Magalaner and Richard M. Kain, *Joyce: The Man, the Work, the Reputation* (New York, 1956), pp. 71–75, for an account of the changes Joyce made in the three drafts of "The Sisters." Along with the addition of symbolic content to the story, he added the date 1895 as the time of the story, which identified the boy narrator as approximately Joyce's age. The same boy narrator of "An Encounter" and "Araby" is of course also about Joyce's age.

12. Joyce began writing *Ulysses* in 1914 when he was thirty-two and completed it at the age of thirty-nine in 1921. He had an approximate time schedule of work in mind while he wrote and he could see the author of *Ulysses* as a man in his late thirties. Moreover, the episode in which Bloom's age is emphasized (Ithaca) was written when Joyce was thirty-eight.

13. See Julian B. Kaye, "The Wings of Daedalus: Two Stories in *Dubliners*," MFS, IV (Spring, 1958), pp. 32–34.

14. *Exiles*, notes, pp. 117–18. See also Beebe, pp. 315–17, etc.

15. *Exiles*, notes, p. 113.

16. See *Dublin's Joyce*, pp. 81–82 and 89–90.

17. See Beebe, p. 320.   18. *Exiles*, notes, p. 124.

19. See *Ulysses*, pp. 232, 515–41, and 550–53. See also Frank Budgen, *James Joyce and the Making of* Ulysses (New York, 1934), pp. 241–42.

20. *Exiles*, notes, p. 125.

21. Richard Ellmann, "The Backgrounds of *Ulysses*," *Kenyon Review*, xvi (Summer, 1954), p. 378.

22. J. F. Byrne, *Silent Years* (New York, 1953), pp. 156–57.

23. *Ulysses*, pp. 431, 666, and 705.

24. "The Dead," p. 230.

25. *Ulysses*, p. 666. Joyce was born in Rathgar, a suburb of Dublin.

26. Bloom plans concert tours for his wife; Joyce planned them for John Sullivan. Joyce asked Lucie Noel to see the management of the Metropolitan Opera about Sullivan's singing there again, an almost Bloomian request. See Lucie Noel, *James Joyce and Paul L. Léon: The Story of a Friendship* (New York, *ca.* 1950), p. 21.

27. Herbert Gorman, *James Joyce* (New York, 1948), pp. 272–73.

28. All the biographical accounts of Joyce's friends and acquaintances agree on his enjoyment of middle class comforts and fashionable luxuries. His "sentimentality" is attested by some of the poems in the *Pomes Penyeach* collection, "Ecce Puer," and his fondness for birthday and anniversary celebrations.

29. See *Joyce and Aquinas*, pp. 122–23.

30. *Joyce and Shakespeare*, p. 145.

31. *Ibid.*, p. 151.

32. *Ibid.*, p. 152.

33. See Julian B. Kaye, "Simony, the Three Simons, and Joycean Myth," in *A James Joyce Miscellany*, ed. Marvin Magalaner (New York, 1957), pp. 20–36, for an account of the theme of simony in Joyce.

34. See note 17.

35. See "The Backgrounds of *Ulysses*," p. 386.

36. See A. M. Klein, "The Black Panther — A Study of Joyce," *Accent*, x (Spring, 1950), 154–55.

37. See *The Catholic Encyclopedia*, viii, 464–65, for a short biography of St. John Francis Regis

38. See "Simony, the Three Simons, and Joycean Myth."

6

James Joyce: A First Impression

JAMES STERN

BEFORE speaking of the impression, perhaps I should mention an incident that occurred a couple of years before.

One night, soon after I came to live in Paris, I was invited to a party at a house on the Île St. Louis. The room was candle-lit and filled with people, only one of whom I knew. She was the hostess, an American woman with a fine soprano voice, and she was accompanying herself at the piano. Opposite me, by the fireplace, sat a young man dressed in a dark suit, tightly knotted tie, and white starched collar. Under a rather promi-nent nose he wore a neat, clipped moustache, and the lenses of his spectacles had the thickness of those magnifying glasses that the well-to-do sometimes use as paper weights on their writing tables.

When the hostess's song had come to an end and the ap-plause had died away, a girl approached the young man and began speaking to him in French. Slowly, a little wearily, he answered her in that language — in a voice remarkably rich and deep, a voice charged, even more surprisingly, with the unmistakable accent of Dublin. Before long an elderly gentle-man took the girl's place, and I found myself catching snatches of conversation in Italian — a language which the young man spoke with equal fluency, in that deep bass voice, and with the same brogue.

Presently the old gentleman departed and the young man and I were left alone by the fireside. As he glanced up at me,

93

something, I knew, had to be said. The question was: what?

A stickler for the oblique approach, I sensed he might well be one, too. So: "Ireland's a grand country!" I ventured.

He stared at me, his eyes tremendous behind the lenses.

"They say it is," he boomed. "I've set foot in it only once in the last twenty years."

Flummoxed, I began diffidently to speak of Irish literature, of Yeats and O'Casey, of Stephens and Colum, of the Abbey, and finally of Dublin. But in my casual observations the young man appeared to take little interest. He is undoubtedly in business, said I to myself, a professional linguist, a superior agent for Thomas Cook's, or possibly that rarest of birds — a renegade Irishman of means. I made, nevertheless, one more effort.

"There's only one writer," I declared defiantly, "who really knows Dublin. Did you ever hear of *Ulysses*, by James Joyce?"

"Oh, I did", said he, reaching for his glass. "He's me father."

A few nights later I ran into Robert McAlmon.[1] When I told him of the incident, he grinned. "You should meet the old man," he said. "Remind me to call him one of these days."

Bob had often made this remark. And he had told me many stories of Joyce, whom he had known long before the publication of *Ulysses* — the last chapter of which, at the author's urgent request, Bob had reluctantly agreed to type for the printer. What had happened was this: Molly Bloom's unpunctuated meditations had already been typed by an Englishwoman. Her husband, however, enraged at the "filth" she had been persuaded to put through her machine, tore both her copy and the original script to shreds. As a result, Joyce had to rewrite the famous chapter. And in the process, Molly acquired fresh thoughts. Unfortunately for Bob, who in an unguarded moment had mentioned to Joyce that he was a fast typist, many of these thoughts were not included in the new script. They were marked, instead, by various colored pencillings in the pages of eight notebooks — to be inserted by the typist at places indicated by similar markings in the script. Having taken care on many occasions to remind Bob that he had claimed to be a fast typist, Joyce finally handed him the new script and the bundle of notebooks. "You surely understand, McAlmon," he said, "what I am doing better than that lady typist."

Molly's monologue was typed by Bob in the throes of a thundering hangover. "Even drunk," he once wrote to me, "I knew that my eyes were to be taxed and that he [Joyce] would notice that I had got some of the thoughts out of his mystic order. He detected that, but agreed with me that Molly's thoughts might be irregular anyway."

Though twenty years his junior, Bob always talked of Joyce as a contemporary, with total lack of awe. Awe, for that matter, was a sensation utterly unknown to Bob. On perceiving it in another, he was likely to let out a yell and, should the hour be late, shower the unfortunate with a niagara of American invective. He looked upon Joyce not as a scholar or man of letters, but as a human being, a companion with whom, when the daylight over the city had begun to fade, he would sometimes start to celebrate — celebrations that night continue until or after the dawning of another day. I had seldom if ever heard a worldly, hypercritical writer speak so warmly, so unbitterly of an older and eminent man of the same profession. His stories began, as a rule, in the home. They would be sitting together, waiting, until a hush fell over the apartment. Joyce would then tiptoe to the door, open it an inch, peer through the aperture, tip Bob the wink, and together, like schoolboy conspirators, they would steal down the stairs. They would walk to L'Avenue's, to the Café d'Harcourt, or to Fouquet's on the Champs Élysées, and there, at a marble-topped table, Joyce would order two bottles of his favorite Swiss wine, one for the table, the other for under his chair — in the hope that should his wife suddenly appear, she would be less likely to take it away from him.

How such evenings progressed, how long they lasted and how they ended, Bob himself has related in a racy, uproarious volume of reminiscences [2] too little known — a book, indeed, not even honored with publication in the United States.

Despite Bob's stories and his many suggestions that he would arrange a meeting with Joyce, I never encouraged the idea. A man will meet, I say, whom he deserves and is meant to meet. And those who have earned renown by hard labor I respect as I do the dead. Both, I believe, should be left in peace.

Thus I came to know Joyce only indirectly through Bob. It was Hilaire Hiler, one of Bob's closest friends, who, anxious to make some sketches of the writer's head, made fact of the fancy.

At this time, the fall of that grim year 1934, Norah and James Joyce were living in a furnished apartment on the rue Galilée, a residential district a couple of blocks from the Étoile. In the métro from the Left Bank I remember feeling slightly nervous. The day was cold, sunless, the time the fearful hour of four. What, I kept wondering, could the author of *Ulysses* find to say to me, or I to him, over a cup of tea in the middle of a gloomy autumn afternoon? Hiler, however, that huge man — painter, pianist, teacher, writer, clown, whom Bob has described as "rather like a handsome frog" — appeared even more distracted.

"*Quelle horreur! Quelle idée!*" he groaned, as we emerged from the métro. "Whoever suggested it? James Augustine Aloysius Joyce, he won't want to have us around!"

"Hell, man," exclaimed Bob, "come off it. You said you wanted to draw the old man's head. The idea's okay with him. So all you have to do is go ahead and draw."

"And what," I asked, "could Joyce have to say to me?"

"You'll make him think of Bloom," replied Bob with a grin. "Oh, he'll get something out of you, don't worry. He'll quizz you — — "

"I'm a very 'umble person," clowned Hiler, suddenly the image of Uriah Heep. "All I ask is a 'umble drink!"

"Quizz me!" I exclaimed, "what about?"

"Ireland, of course," replied Bob, leading the way into a *bistro*.

"It's he who knows Ireland," said I, "not me."

"Ah, shucks!" cried Bob, gulping his brandy. "He's not been there in twenty years. He loves to hear of it."

"I don't like the idea," moaned Hiler, ordering another *fine*. "I don't like it at all. In fact," he added, placing his satchel of drawing materials on the bar, "I think I'll stay right here. Maybe I'll come along when I've had a few and sobered up."

"The hell you will!" cried Bob. "Let's get outa here. You're acting like a coupla schoolkids about to be walloped!"

We paid and walked out into the street.

The Joyces' apartment, if I'm not mistaken, was on the fourth floor. At our ring a door opened slowly, and there he stood. At first glance, he struck me as smaller, frailer than I had imagined. Dressed in a peacock-blue velvet jacket and dark trousers, he held himself in the position of the blind — chin raised, head tilted slightly back.

"That you, McAlmon?"

I had heard it said of Joyce that he rarely used first names, addressing women almost always as Mrs. or Miss. Raised barely above a whisper, his voice — that tenor to which as a young man he considered devoting his life — sounded excessively tired, the voice of a sufferer in whose presence, as in hospitals, one feels instinctively all sounds should be muffled. His hand, too, suggested the hand of a recluse, an invalid — bony yet soft to the touch, conveying on the instant a marvellous gentleness. As it lay for a moment in one's own, the silken skin of the fingers softly closing, one forbore to do more than carefully close over them one's own.

In my mind's eye I can see but one book in that dim, depressing, impersonal sitting-room. (I remember wishing that we had brought a flower: must not his sense of smell be unusually acute? Then it occurred to me that maybe this very sense might explain the lack of flowers.) It was to the single book, which lay alone on a grand piano, that he — while Hiler and

I seated ourselves on the sofa, and Bob on a chair — slowly, his hands out, fingering the furniture, soundlessly in slippers, made his way. The volume was large, of many pages, and clearly new, possibly unopened. Joyce leaned over it, touched it with his long fingers, lifted it as though it were beyond price, then laid it down.

"Is that the American edition?" [3] asked Bob, getting up.

Joyce said nothing, simply turned and handed the book to his friend with the faintest, barely perceptible sign of a smile. He then sat down in a chair opposite the sofa, facing the light, so that Hiler, in his corner under the window, had a full view of his features. Now that they were clearly visible, these features resembled so much those of the drawings and photographs I had seen that I had the sensation of having known him — and better than by sight — for years. Only the brow seemed even higher than I had thought, the grey-black hair thicker, the expression of the face in repose more sad.

"A dreadful thing has happened, McAlmon," said Joyce, in that faraway, lovely Livia Plurabelle voice. "I have to be fitted."

"Fitted?"

"Norah insists that I have a new suit. Let us try not to think of it. But I warn you, it can happen — any minute." And he glanced towards the door, as though expecting to hear it burst open and the fitter spring into the room.

"McAlmon tells me, Stern," he suddenly said, "that you were born in Ireland."

Because the eyes behind the round, heavy, loose-lensed spectacles seemed to be directed at a spot a little above my head, it struck me only then that he could not see me. And with the shock came the piercing flash, like jet lightning, of the black world of the blind, the physical realization of what it must be like never to be able to behold the face we are addressing.

"Yes," I answered, "I spent my youth in southern Ireland." And I told him where.

He raised his head, as though chasing a memory, then repeated the name of the place.

"There's an abbey, is there not," he asked, "a Cistercian monastery of that name?"

"There is," I replied, surprised. "It's a ruin, of course — a couple of miles from where we lived."

I was about to ask if he knew its history when he continued his questions: "That's famous hunting country round there, is it not? Were your people hunting people?"

"They were," I told him.

"Did they go in for racing, too?"

"No," I said. "But my brother does. He's a great race rider. Lives in the County Cork."

"Is that a fact?" Joyce remarked with sudden interest.[4] "In what condition would the Irish people be, do you think, without racing?"

"I don't like to think of it," I replied, and I began to feel at ease. "In our part of the world they used to say that the British put an end to the Rebellion by threatening to ban racing throughout the country!"

"Ha!" exclaimed Joyce, almost loud, "I never heard that one! — Tell me, did y'ever know the C. family from round Fermoy way? Their son must be about your age."

"I didn't," I replied. "I've kept up with very few of the younger people in Ireland. My family left after the Troubles. It's the older people I know and remember best."

"What about Sir Francis F. now? He must have lived near your place?"

"Oh, he did," I said. "My people knew him well."

"Tell me of him," said Joyce eagerly, clasping his hands and smiling to himself. "I never met him. Wasn't he a very gruff kind of a man?"

I glanced at Bob, who urged me on with a wink.

"Oh, he was," I began. "A regular tyrant at times. Big, six foot three or four, he was bald and very fat. He ate enormously. Sometimes, after hunting, his wife used to ask us in to tea. Huge as he was, you could see little more than his head above the diningroom table. He didn't sit: he practically lay in his chair. Once, when there were some ten to fifteen guests at the table, an aunt of ours found herself sitting next to him. She made an effort at conversation, but he promptly closed his eyes. Being very hungry, she and most of the other guests readily accepted the suggestion of fried eggs. When the footman brought them in — six plates of them on a silver salver — Francis sniffed, opened his eyes. 'Whatcha got there?' he howled at the footman. 'Eggs, Sir Francis,' answered the man. 'Bring 'em heeah!' bawled Francis. Whereupon he sat up and devoured the lot."

Since I am not, by nature, a story-teller, the silence that greeted this little anecdote made me turn hot with embarrassment. Then I noticed that Joyce, sunk in his chair, his hands up to his mouth, was shaking — with silent laughter.

"And what did Francis do then?" he enquired, recovering.

"He called for jam," I said. "And when the footman brought two pots of jam, Francis howled that when he demanded jam he meant not two bloody pots but twelve bloody pots. So the footman brought twelve pots!"

"Ha!" laughed Joyce, "a terror of a man! Didn't he write a book one time on how to shoot big game?"

"I didn't hear of him ever writing a book," I replied. "But on shooting he might have — for though he was cross-eyed or had a walleye, I forget which, he was a great man with a gun. I remember watching him once when he didn't know it. It was one winter during the Troubles, when all firearms were strictly forbidden. From our house a narrow path ran under great beech trees high above the river. By January the farther bank was always under water and waist-high in rushes. I was wandering along this path one soft afternoon when all of a sudden my eye was caught by something moving on the opposite shore. I saw a kind of mound of rushes rising slowly from the ground. It had risen as high as a man when it stopped, began to keel over. Just as I thought it would fall, from out of the middle of it sprang an object, black, long, thin, and — bang! — a shot, then another, shattered the silence. Before the echoes and reverberations had died away, I heard the splash of a bird hurtling into the water, a thud as another fell on land, then a howl of fury as I saw the cloak of rushes collapse — and there stood Francis, in shirt and breeches, his gun raised above his bald white head, bellowing a stream of curses at his dog."

"That's grand!" exclaimed Joyce, clasping his hands in a soundless clap. "What were they — duck?"

When I told him yes: "Go on, man," he urged, "tell us more! Wasn't he very fond of cricket [he pronounced it 'crickut']?"

"He was," I confirmed, "he even played it in the house."

"Ha?"

"On the billiard table. After dinner he would order all the guests, men and women, into the billiard room. They were obliged to play whether they wanted to or not."

Suddenly the door opened. A woman stood there — tall, grey-haired, dignified. She greeted Bob. Then: "Come on, Jim," she said. "He's here."

Joyce let out a groan. Then he looked up in my direction. "But what did they play with?" he asked.

"Matches," I told him. "Three Swan Vesta's made a wicket, and the ball, I believe, was a piece of cork, cut round and very small."

"Jim," called Norah Joyce, "did ye hear what I'm after sayin'? The tailor's here. Another week, an' ye'll not be fit for the street!"

Groaning, Joyce rose slowly from his chair. "And what about the bat?" he asked.

"Oh, the bat . . ." I began.

But Norah had had enough. "Ah, come on outa that!" she urged, and with his hand in hers she drew him, shuffling, from the room.

In his absence we thumbed through the American edition

of *Ulysses* (Joyce pronounced the word "Oulyssays") and looked at Hiler's sketches — lovely simple things done in a few light, pencilled lines. These drawings, on his return, Joyce — with the charm, the modesty, the deference of another century — asked if he might be allowed to see. Sitting in his chair he raised the paper closer, closer to his face, till it finally touched his nose. He moved the sketch now up, now down, at the same time adjusting the loose lenses of his spectacles as he tried with his one seeing eye to trace the line. At last he surrendered. "I'm not able," he almost whispered, laying it down. "The line's too thin."

Quickly Hiler produced a stick of charcoal and, with a few swift strokes, thickly blackened the outline of another sketch. Again Joyce raised the paper to his eye. Then he licked the tip of a finger and, by smudging the thick lines thicker, traced the features of his face on the paper.

He was still absorbed in this task when the door opened again and Norah announced it was "time" — for what, I cannot recall.

For an instant Joyce seemed to pretend not to hear. Then he slowly raised his head towards her, and, as his thin lips parted in what might have been wonder, annoyance, anxiety — or a combination of all three — I remember how his whole attitude struck me as that of a child.

NOTES

1. Died in California, February, 1956.
2. Robert McAlmon, *Being Geniuses Together* (London, 1938).
3. Of *Ulysses*, whose publication in the United States had recently been permitted by Federal Judge John M. Woolsey. Joyce had just received this, his first copy.
4. Joyce's father, John Stanislaus (1849–1931), was a Corkman and a great hunting enthusiast.

7

The Joyces in the Holloway Diaries

MICHAEL J. O'NEILL

ALTHOUGH Joseph Holloway (1861–1944) is best known as the architect of the Abbey Theatre, he also contributed in a unique way to the Modern Irish Literary movement. For over fifty years he made it his concern to be a ubiquitous observer of Dublin's theatrical and literary life. What he saw and heard he recorded daily in diary form, calling his memoirs "The Impressions of a Dublin Playgoer." As might be expected, the two Joyces, father and son, came within Holloway's orbit and his diaries include not only his own personal recollections of both, but also the comments made to him about the novelist by several of Dublin's literary figures.

One of the characteristics of Joyce's father that caught Holloway's fancy was his choice flow of choleric epithets. Thus he notes, "Joyce is a great man to swear. He gets off a string of swear words and then prays to be forgiven." How like Stephen's father and his similar habit, especially when castigating the idling Stephen!

From the diarist's attendance at various centers of amusement in Dublin he had several opportunities of seeing the elder Joyce in action as an entertainer, as a person who liked to "mix with fine decent fellows able to do something." On March 17, 1896, for example, he reports seeing a performance of the father at the convivial Bohemians whose members met every Tuesday evening at the Dolphin Hotel, then a mecca for sporting bloods. The program that Holloway heard was not

103

to his liking, and his critical comments about the elder Joyce give some point to Stephen's ironic attitude toward his father's style of singing with its "quaint accent and phrasing." "Found a small number present. Mr. Joyce sang a tiresome, never-ending topical rigmarole about 'Erin's Heroes,' written by himself."

Feckless living over the years had undoubtedly brought about this deterioration in his father's abilities. Ever since his days as a medical student at Queen's College, Cork, Joyce Senior was known to have had a flair for dramatics, which prompted him to aid in the revival of the College's moribund Dramatic Society. Indeed, the Cork papers on at least two occasions, March 12 and May 27, 1869, favorably reviewed the roles he enacted in plays presented at Cork's Royal Theatre.

Holloway's first opportunity to see the younger Joyce act was on March 21, 1900, in a production of a prize winning playlet written by Margaret Sheehy entitled *Cupid's Confidante*. She and her brothers were the organizers of an amateur company which staged this piece in a tiny theatre at the rear of the X.L. Cafe on Grafton Street, Dublin, quite close to Joyce's University.

During the performance the audience was given a sample of Joyce's ready wit. The script in one scene called for Joyce, playing the villain, to light a cigarette with proper melodramatic flourish. While trying to do so, Joyce's match broke, but this did not upset his aplomb. He merely ogled the audience and leered, "Damn those Irish matches!" This quip could have boomeranged, because Irish nationalists at this period were somewhat self-conscious about the defects of Irish-made goods. But Joyce's impromptu satire gained their laughing approval.

Holloway indicates that *Cupid's Confidante* was a flimsy work, even though it met with a very cordial reception before a full house: "Its scene is laid in a Palmist's tent at a garden party and tells how a pair of lovers are reunited and an adventurer unmasked. . . . Mr. Sheehy spoke as if he had a pain in his little inside. . . . Mr. J. Joyce, as Geoffrey Fortesque, the adventurer, showed some sense of character in the acting."

Four years later, on June 8, when James Joyce competed at the Feis Ceoil, he apparently must have prepared seriously for the event, in which he barely won the third prize of a bronze medal through some technicality in the rules of the competition. The nature of young Joyce's preparations can be gathered from the remarks of one of Holloway's friends, the noted historian of the Elizabethan theatre, W. J. Lawrence, who lived on Shelbourne Road, near where Joyce had temporary lodgings in 1904. Lawrence, in reminiscing with the diarist, "assumed that Joyce was in training for grand opera, because whenever he passed his house he was always singing operatic songs and his window was wide open. He used to see Joyce, an odd creature with his strange eyes and long hair, walking along their street with huge strides, seven-league-boot style, and his arms waving constantly."

During the spring months of the same year Joyce became active once again in the social gatherings of Dublin's literary circles. He frequently was to be found at the "At Homes" of James Cousins, whose writings for the Irish Literary Movement and whose exotic religious interests he later satirized in *Gas from a Burner*.

Since Holloway was a popular reciter of dramatic poems, he too was invited to these parties, and at several of them, he met Joyce. Two of Holloway's three notes of these occasions are very brief, but each speaks appreciatively of Joyce's spirited renditions of *Dick Turpin, Hero*. The third and fullest of the diarist's impressions of Joyce during this period he made on June 8, subsequent to Joyce's earlier success that day at the Feis Ceoil: "Dropped in for a chat at Cousins's 'At Home,' where I stayed for a couple of hours. . . . Mrs. Cousins played a couple of classical pieces on the piano. Then Mr. J. Joyce, a strangely aloof, silent youth, with weird, penetrating, large eyes, which he frequently shaded with his hand and with

a half-bashful, far-away expression on his face, sang some
dainty old-world ballads most artistically and pleasingly, some
to his own accompaniment. As he sang, he swayed his head
from side to side to add to the soulfulness of his rendering.
Later he sat in a corner and gazed at us all from under his
brows in an uncomfortable way and said little or nothing all
evening. He is a strange boy. I cannot forget him."

Despite Joyce's earlier sharp criticism against the parochial-
ism of the Irish National Literary Society, the diarist's entry
for June 10, 1904 reveals that the novelist retained his interest
in its welfare. The Society that year with the backing of Miss
Horniman's money advanced its cause by taking over the idle
Mechanic's Theatre, the acquisition of which Joyce had pre-
viously suggested to Yeats. Acting as Miss Horniman's agent,
Holloway went to the Society's temporary headquarters on
Camden Street, on the evening of the 10th, to report to the
members about the latest plans for the construction of the
Abbey Theatre.

Present with the group, who were discussing another written attack against them by F. H. O'Donnell, a former Irish
M.P., was Joyce. Upon the diarist's arrival he found "a goodly
gathering. Mr. Synge was present. He had, he said, just completed a new three act play [*The Well of the Saints*] for the
Society. Mr. Joyce put in an appearance. A copy of F. H.
O'Donnell's pamphlet went the rounds of the group's comments. Many questions were put to me in my capacity as architect of the Abbey Theatre about Miss Horniman's visit to
Dublin."

Since Joyce was an infrequent visitor to the Society at their
small rehearsal hall, why did he select that evening to be with
them? Holloway unfortunately gives us no clue. The date,
nonetheless, is of interest: Gorman's biography mentions it
as the day that Joyce "met his wife Nora Barnacle."

Word of Joyce's visit to Dublin in 1909 soon became known
to his former acquaintances. These included D. J. O'Donog-

hue, who had helped Yeats in London to establish the first
home of the Irish Literary Society. In a brief conversation on
August 20, O'Donoghue spoke to his friend, the diarist, about
Joyce's return: "We chatted about James Joyce, who somewhat mysteriously vanished from Dublin some years ago and
got married, it was supposed. O'Donoghue said young Joyce
has been on a visit for some weeks past. He has one of the
little ones with him. O. D. thought him improved in every
way. Arthur Symons once thought a lot of his poems and had
one accepted for the *Saturday Review*, for which Joyce got
three guineas. Joyce once told O. D. he had an idea of touring
the English watering places as a wandering minstrel with a
guitar. But when O. D. said to him what a very strange thing
to do for a person who liked Ireland, Joyce replied it was the
very thing, as the English would not rise above the Negro min-
strels on the strands; his tour would prove that. The ego in
Joyce, O. D. believed, had got the upper hand before he left
Dublin."

Joyce's youthful arrogance was also recalled by George Russell when chatting with Holloway at the home of the hospi-
table Con Curran: "A. E. told me of his first meeting with
James Joyce. One night at 11.45, a knock came to the door.
A. E. opened it and a figure outside asked was he A. E. and
Russell said, 'Yes.' 'I want to see you,' the young man said,
'My name's Joyce. Is it too late to go in?' 'No,' replied A. E.
and in Joyce came. A. E. went to his sofa, where he sat with
his legs crossed and waited for what Joyce had to say. For a
while Joyce seemed confused, but afterwards he thawed and
showed the most utter contempt for everybody and everything. Joyce not only spoke slightingly of Yeats but of all
others. His arrogance was colossal in one so young. Some time
afterwards Joyce read some of his poems to Yeats and to A. E.
But when Yeats expressed an opinion that he liked them,
Joyce condescendingly said, 'Your opinion isn't worth more
than another's. It doesn't matter whether you or he [A. E.]

likes them. Your work will all be forgotten in time.' Joyce also asked Yeats about some of his poems, so Yeats went into an elaborate explanation of their meaning. All Joyce then said was, 'You're past developing — it is a pity we didn't meet early enough for me to be of help to you.' Joyce, at the time, continued A. E., was the condensed essence of studied, insolent conceit."

Joyce had returned to Dublin in 1909, both to see Maunsel's about printing *Dubliners* and to write about the first production of Shaw's controversial *Blanco Posnet* at the Abbey on August 25 for the *Piccola della Sera* of Trieste. On the previous night, at a production of *The Playboy of the Western World*, Holloway met Joyce and talked casually with him about the latest happenings to the Abbey Company; how Yeats's policies had led to the formation of another rival group with Padraic Colum as one of their leaders, and how *The Playboy* riots had caused later productions of it to be toned down: "All this fuss that is being made over the production of Shaw's *Blanco Posnet* tomorrow, drew a big house tonight for the reopening of the Abbey. I had a chat with James Joyce, who had been out of town for five years, and had, he said, never been to the Abbey before. He had received a letter that morning from Synge's brother on the dramatic rights of *Riders to the Sea*, which he had just translated into Italian. I again had a few words with him after *The Playboy*, which he liked in the acting. He admired Synge's work generally but did not like *The Playboy*. He thought the last act taken from *The Master Builder*. He liked the role of Pegeen Mike, and he thought O'Donovan's Christy Mahon the true type intended by the author. But I told him W. J. Fay was a much more realistic and repulsive type when he interpreted it. Moreover, Fay was rehearsed under Synge's own direction. Joyce then asked me how Colum's *The Land* had acted. 'Very well, indeed, when the Fays were in it,' I responded. 'But it is not performed at the Abbey now,' I added, 'owing to some little difference of opinion among the original members of the

Company, and Colum had sided with the seceders.' Joyce said
he had heard all that."

Holloway's notes for his final meeting with Joyce on September 8 (Wednesday) refer to the novelist's promise to
send a copy of his Italian review of Shaw's play to Henderson,
who was the manager of the Abbey and an avid collector of
theatrical mementoes. Joyce seemingly forgot his promise,
but later, in substitution, he sent Henderson a newspaper
clipping signed, "For your collection, J. J." The article was
"Il Capolovaro del Theatro Irlandese," written by Guigliemo
Emmanuel for the Milan *Corrière della Sera* on September
9, 1911.

On Wednesday morning before rehearsal at the Abbey,
Holloway, as his diary mentions, was backstage gossiping with
the Abbey staff when James Joyce was announced: "He came
in with his critique of *The Showing Up of Blanco Posnet*
with him. He hoped, he said, to make the Italians interested
in the Irish theatrical movement. He did not give Henderson
this copy of the paper, but said he would send him one. He
will be leaving Dublin tomorrow; everyday here means a loss
of money to him. He had translated Synge's play for the love
of the thing and had handed his Ms. over to the manager
about to produce it. He told Henderson to communicate directly with the manager, since he did not care to be further
troubled personally about it. I asked Joyce how he liked the
acting of the Company and he said, 'Well.' He then bought
a few postcard scenes of *Riders to the Sea*. He also told me he
chiefly remained in Dublin so long because of a book of short
stories he intended to bring out through Maunsel and Co.;
then leaving his address he left himself."

Later that day, the diarist met O'Donoghue who told him,
"Joyce had spent last evening with Tom Kettle." Joyce had
shown O'Donoghue his article for the *Piccola della Sera*, and
it would be publicized in that evening's edition of the Dublin
Evening Telegraph.

Because Holloway's main interests were confined to local

theatrical activities, Joyce's later cosmopolitan life moved outside the diarist's range. Consequently, except for a description
of Joyce's Volta Cinema at its opening and for some later very
brief and random entries, Holloway did not keep in touch
with the novelist's rise to fame on the international scene.

8

Portraits of James Joyce,
A Preliminary Check-List

RICHARD M. KAIN

I N March, 1926, writing to Miss Harriet Shaw Weaver, James Joyce perpetrated one of his less successful puns on the subject of his portraits. "It never paints but it pours," he exclaimed. Three artists — Jo Davidson, Ivan Oppfer, and an Irish sculptor Knox had shown interest in doing pictures of him and members of his family. Yet he was ironical about his appearance. He recalled with amusement that he had been nicknamed "Herr Satan" in a portrait of 1920, and he insisted that even casual glimpses of his reflection in shop mirrors sent him scurrying along the street. Endlessly repeated images were tiresome to him, though he admitted that in the middle 'twenties he was not quite so dreadful a spectacle as he had been in earlier days of ill health and insufficient nourishment. And though he was later to be proud enough of Patrick Tuohy's portraits of himself and his father to carry photographs of them in his pocketbook, he had first asked the artist whether his interest was in painting the person or the name.

For thirty years now there has been a world-wide interest in both the person and the name. Joyce's features were apparently well defined and dominantly intellectual. His photographs as well as his portraits reveal something of the same uncompromising strength and underlying gentleness which is apparent to sensitive readers of his work, while caricatures, whether Satanic or Dadaist, seem appropriate to one who knew himself to sing, and build the lusty mime.

One is tempted to suggest that the many pictorial images of Joyce reflect his literary facets. The sprightly caricature by Abin, details of which were suggested by Joyce himself, symbolized his irrepressible highjinks. The Satanic Zurich painting has not been located, but the gesture of revolt is apparent in the early Silvestri oil, while the drawing by Stuart Davis, revealing a dark bearded figure seated in a cafe, wearing a greatcoat with upturned collar, perhaps manifests the seriousness with which the avant-garde took the revolutionary Joyce in 1922. It seems to derive from the dark profile photograph of the period, reproduced in the Gorman biography (1939 edition, opposite p. 171). The bold outline of the Wyndham Lewis drawing (1920) shows a scholar and philosopher, head bent in concentration. The Oppfer drawings intensify the strength of the gaze. The features are softened by O'Sullivan into meditative wistfulness, and relaxed into sorrowful resignation by Blanche.

To one who did not know Joyce personally, the popularity of the Davidson and the Augustus John sketches seems merited. They depict an energy controlled by introspection. A final word is in order regarding the toll of disappointment and worry apparent in the deathmask (in Patricia Hutchins, *James Joyce's Dublin* as well as in Carola Giedion-Welcker, *In Memoriam James Joyce*).

In the following list, no attempt has been made to note every appearance of each portrait. Photographs are not included, although special mention here may be made of the fine and familiar Berenice Abbott half-length picture of Joyce in a dark suit, with hat on head, cane in right hand, and left arm draped over the back of the chair. The Man Ray profile with head bowed, forehead resting on right hand, is also deservedly popular. One of the most engaging of youthful pictures is the snapshot of the Joyce of 1904, cap on head, hands in pockets, standing before a greenhouse. The most convenient places to find these portraits are as follows: Abbott, frontispiece of Seon Givens, *James Joyce: Two Decades of Criticism* (1948); Man Ray, frontispiece of Harry Levin, *James Joyce* (1941); and the Curran snapshot, Patricia Hutchins, *James Joyce's Dublin* (1950), p. 18.

The only earlier listing of pictures is in Alan Parker, *James Joyce; A Bibliography* . . . (1948). Parker includes some photographs. In the check-list below, items in Parker are indicated by an asterisk. For the sake of completeness his citations are included, though in many cases later and more convenient sources are added. References to *Letters* are to the recent edition by Stuart Gilbert, *Letters of James Joyce* (1957); the "La Hune" numbering refers to items in the Paris exhibition of 1949 at the La Hune Bookshop, described in *James Joyce, Sa Vie, Son Œuvre, Son Rayonnement* (1949).

No full-dress bibliographical description is made here. The list is by no means definitive. Such an inventory must await the complete cataloguing of the great Joyce collections at Yale, Buffalo, and Cornell. The compiler will welcome additions and corrections, and takes this opportunity to thank the fellow Joyceans who have aided his researches.

*Abin, Cesar. Caricature, body in form of question mark. *transition* # 21, March, 1932. Seon Givens, *James Joyce: Two Decades* . . . (1948), opposite page 3.
  Jean Paris, *James Joyce par lui-même*. Paris [1957], p. 133.
*Baker, Ernest Hamlin. From Abbott photograph. Right arm raised, hand behind head. *Scribners*, October, 1936, p. 67.
Beeson, Fred B. Woodblock. *Manuscripts*, I, 2 (November, 1929), opposite page 75. Not seen; from Joseph Prescott.
Blanche, Jacques Emile. *Letters*, p. 344. See also Blanche, *More Portraits of a Lifetime* (1939), pp. 278–84 for an unfavorable personal impression. Oils, done in 1934.
  Blanche, 1. Seated, half right, facing front. National Portrait Gallery, Dublin. See O. Gogarty, "Ireland's Heroes and Humbugs," *Art News*, October, 1950. In John Harvey, *Dublin* (1949), opposite page 76.
  Blanche, 2. Full length, leaning back against table. National Portrait Gallery, London. In Alfred C. Ward, *Illustrated*

History of English Literature (1955), III, between pages
256 and 257. Frontispiece, J. I. M. Stewart, *James Joyce*
(1957).

Blanche, 3. Seated, facing right. In Maria Jolas, *A James
Joyce Yearbook* (1949), opposite page 33, "Courtesy the
owners, M. and Mme. André Noufflard."

Blanche, 3a. Almost identical to 3, darker tones. La Hune,
109.

Blanche, 4. Standing in a park, panama hat, *profil perdu*. In
New York Times Book Review, March 2, 1947, p. 1.

Brancusi, Constantin. *Letters*, 279, 284, and 312.

*Brancusi, 1. Abstract whirl. Frontispiece, *Tales Told of Shem
and Shaun* (1929). In La Hune catalogue, after item 346.
Jean Paris, *James Joyce* [1957], p. 100.

Brancusi, 2. Outline profile, facing right. Frontispiece, James
Joyce, *Epiphanies* (1956).

Budgen, Frank. *Letters, passim.*

Budgen, 1. Seated on sofa, right knee raised. Frontispiece,
Budgen, *James Joyce* (1934).

Budgen, 2. Seated on sofa, with right fore-arm on arm of
sofa, looking over right shoulder. Collection of Dr. H. K.
Croessmann, now at Southern Illinois University.

Budgen, 3. Similar to Budgen, 2. Collection of Mr. Feinberg,
Detroit. Note from Dr. H. K. Croessmann.

Cotton, W. Caricature in color, exaggerated nose, *Ulysses* in
hand. *Vanity Fair*, March, 1934.

*Davidson, Jo. *Letters*, 240. Davidson, *Between Sittings* (1951),
pp. 241–43.

*Davidson, 1. Bust. Frontispiece, Herbert Gorman, *James
Joyce* (1940). La Hune # 108.

*Davidson, 2. Pencil sketch, head facing right. Frontispiece,
Pastimes of James Joyce (1941). Cover design, Folkways
Records, "Meeting of James Joyce Society on October 23,
1951/ Finnegans Wake."

*Davis, Stuart. Pen drawing. *Dial*, LXXII (June, 1922), p. 222.

D'Hoffmeister. Thirteen caricatures. La Hune, # 100.

Elgin, Jill. Drawing. Head facing right. Cover and frontispiece,
A.D. 1951, II (# 3, Autumn).

Gentilini, Franco. Caricature. Head and shoulders. Facing front,
pipe in mouth. Jean Paris, *James Joyce* [1957], p. 120.

Gimmi, Wilhelm. Posthumous. Three-quarters length, dark coat
and hat. Maria Jolas, *James Joyce Yearbook* (1949), opposite
page 112.

Harmsworth, Desmond. Outline drawing of head facing right. Dust jacket, Charles Duff, *James Joyce and the Plain Reader* (1932).

John, Augustus. *Letters*, 340. See also Augustus John, *Chiaroscuro* (1952), pp. 216–17 for the artist's reminiscences.

*John, 1. Head only, three-quarters left. The most popular of the John portraits. Frontispiece, James Joyce, *Collected Poems* (1936). La Hune # 107.

John, 1a. similar to John, 1, but with less shading (possibly a retouched engraving). Arland Ussher, *Three Great Irishmen* (1953), opposite page 115.

*John, 2. Head and shoulders, three-quarters left. Wearing hat. Collection of Mrs. Murray Crane. Frontispiece, James Joyce, *Stephen Hero* (both 1944 and 1955 editions).

*John, 3. Half length, turned left. Frontispiece, *The Joyce Book* (1933). National Gallery, Dublin.

John, 3a. Similar to John, 3, but with less shading. Collection of Mrs. V. I. Hamilton. In Augustus John, *Drawings*, edited by Lillian Browse [1914]; also Augustus John, Rainbird Ltd. edition (1957). Frontispiece, Herbert Gorman, *James Joyce* (London, 1941).

John, 4. Head and shoulders, three-quarters left, chin in right hand. *Horizon*, III, 14 (February, 1941), facing page 104.

John, 4a. Similar to John, 4, with right hand slightly different. Treatment of lapels and tie more sketchy. *Apollo*, XV (March, 1932), 117.

John, 5. Similar to John, 3, with head more erect. *London Studio*, IV (August, 1932), p. 119.

Joyce, Lucia. 1. Head, facing front, red crayon. La Hune catalogue facing first (unnumbered) page. La Hune # 130.

Joyce, 2. Another sketch, in the Buffalo collection. From Dr. H. K. Croessmann.

*Kristian, Roald. Woodcut. *Egoist*, IV (February, 1917), p. 22.

Le Gallienne, Gwen. Painting, shoulder-length, facing slightly right. New York *Herald Tribune*, January 21, 1934.

*Lewis, Wyndham. Frontispiece, Hugh Kenner, *Dublin's Joyce* (1956). La Hune, # 87.

Loy, Mina. Profile left. *Vanity Fair*, April, 1922.

Opffer, Ivan. *Letters*, 240, "Opfer."

*Opffer, 1. Crayon, half length, one-quarter left. *Bookman*, LIX (July, 1924), 519.

Opffer, 2. Crayon, head and shoulders, one-quarter right. Cover portrait, Alan M. Cohn (ed.), *James Joyce: An*

Exhibition from the Collection of Dr. H. K. Croessmann
(Southern Illinois University Library, Carbondale, Ill.,
1957). Now at Southern Illinois University.
O'Sullivan, Sean. *Letters*, 384, n. 1.
   O'Sullivan, 1. National Gallery, Dublin. Frontispiece, Marvin
   Magalaner and Richard M. Kain, *Joyce: The Man, The
   Work, The Reputation* (1956).
   O'Sullivan, 2. National Library, Dublin.
   O'Sullivan, 3. John L. Burke, in Eugene Sheehy, *May It
   Please the Court.*
   O'Sullivan, 4. Harry Barnardo. O'Sullivan 2, 3, and 4 are last
   minute additions contributed by Dr. H. K. Croessmann
   and not seen by the compiler.
Salazar, Tono. Cartoon with mechanistic detail (flat-top head,
   wheel-like glasses). In F. B. Snyder and R. G. Martin,
   A Book of English Literature, fourth edition (1943), II,
   931.
*Sava, Arnastas Botzaris, 1. Bronze head. *London Mercury and
   Bookman*, xxxv (April, 1937), 556.
   Sava, 2. Drawing. Head and collar, facing slightly right. *London Studio*, 115:156.
Scheel. Woodcut cartoon, half length, with right arm raised and
   right hand bent downward towards puppet figure of Greek
   warrior. In Harvey Wickham, *The Impuritans* (1929), op-
   posite page 236.
Silvestri, Tullio. Oil, facing forward, head slightly tilted, with
   chin in left hand. Trieste, 1914. La Hune # 60.
*Spicer-Simon, Theodore. Portrait medallion in Spicer-Simon,
   Men of Letters (1924), p. 94.
*Stern, Arthur. Woodcut. *Washington Square College Review*,
   III (February, 1939), p. 10.
Taylor, Richard. Cartoon, with bandanna around head, seated
   in study with word chart on wall. *Ringmaster*, July, 1936.
Tuohy, Patrick. *Letters*, 214–17, 228, 254, and 257.
   Tuohy, 1. Oil. Half-length, seated, white jacket, dark trou-
   sers, facing front, relaxed pose, thumbs in belt. Patricia
   Hutchins, *James Joyce's World* (1957), opposite page 149.
   Tuohy, 2. Similar, darker background. La Hune # 106.
Unnamed artist. Line drawing published with Alcantara Sil-
   veira's "Una Sentencio Judicial Sobre 'Ulyses,' " *Universidad
   de Antioquia* (Medellin, Colombia), Tomo xxx, No. 117,
   Mayo, Junio, Julio, 1954, p. 265. Not seen; from Dr. H. K.
   Croessmann.

Zurich, painter in? Unidentified portrait, half finished in February, 1920, nicknamed "Herr Satan." *Letters*, 137. Probably Budgen, who wrote Dr. Croessmann in 1950, "During the Zurich (or Ulysses) period I am fairly certain he never sat to anybody but me."

9

Joyce and the Strabismal Apologia

RUTH VON PHUL

I T is hardly possible to overestimate the autobiographical element in Joyce's work. It is not always literal reportage, but with the possible exception of a few of the stories in *Dubliners* everything is an essentially true continuing narrative of his interior life. Evidence accumulates that episodes which the reader might assume to be inventions are instead based on actual events.

Of crucial importance is the historicity of the episode recounted on the second page of *A Portrait*. It seems to have been of the profoundest significance to Joyce, not merely for his purposes as a writer, but because of its personal, emotional impact. In this scene Stephen ". . . hid under the table," and his mother said, " — O, Stephen will apologise." Dante threatened "O, if not, the eagles will come and pull out his eyes." The six-year-old culprit makes the ominous jingle: "Pull out his eyes,/ Apologise. . . ." [1]

Marvin Magalaner comments: "Thus, even in early childhood, Stephen is revealed as guilty of an unspecified crime possibly related to sex ('. . . he was going to marry Eileen') or to religion (Eileen is a Protestant) or simply to disobedience to constituted authority." Citing Hugh Kenner's remark that in the motifs found in the first pages of *A Portrait* are the germ of all Joyce's later work, Magalaner continues: "In this first reference to the motif, as Kenner mentions, Prometheus is undoubtedly suggested: first, because of his awful torment at the hand of the authority he had defied (Stephen's eyes are more vulnerable than his liver . . .); second, because in stealing fire from the gods, Prometheus performs literally Stephen-Joyce's later act of taking creative inspiration from its mysterious source." [2]

This succinct scene might appear to be an invention that Joyce, the perpetual allegorist, shaped to show forth his theme. Instead, it is an almost exact transcription of objective fact. The pristine material appears in the collection of epiphanies: "Mr. Vance [Eileen's father] — (*comes in with a stick*) . . . O, you know, he'll have to apologise, Mrs. Joyce." The mother says: "O, yes . . . Do you hear that, Jim?" but it is Vance, not Dante, who voices the threat of the eagles. The account continues: "Joyce — (*under the table, to himself*) — Pull out his eyes,/ Apologise. . . ." [3]

Joyce's emendations of this literal reporting are slight but significant. He transposed the stage direction "*under the table*" to a point where it equivocally suggests both the attempt to evade discovery and the nature of the offense. And he placed the threat in the mouth of Dante, who represents the Church or its priesthood, earthly spokesman for the Deity, as the mother stands for the Virgin, heavenly monitrix and intercessor with divine authority.

The occurrence gave Joyce a ready-made playing out of his most important persistent theme, but it also seems to have been to him personally a deeply traumatic event. The childish naughtiness is only a figure for a greater guilt, but the threatened punishment of blindness Joyce feared literally.

The offenses of Prometheus and Adam are of course identical. Each defied deity to seize creative power. The creativity that the Greeks symbolized, in the Hebrew telling is explicitly promised by the serpent: "Ye shall be as gods, knowing of good and evil." Even in a narrowly sexual reading the myth of Adam suggests that the fruit of the tree gave him a power, procreation, incomparably greater than the dominion over the beasts that had been assigned to him.

Having announced the theme of disobedience and prying with its condign punishment of blindness as early as the first pages of his first novel, during the remainder of A *Portrait* Joyce virtually abandons this linking of the specific crime and appropriate punishment. The minatory sermon [4] deals with both original and personal sin, but sin is said to be a "turning away" from God — and the Church — and is elaborated only as "base consent to the promptings of our corrupt nature" — hardly a Promethean offense. And the retribution is not blindness in this life but the torments of an eternal hereafter. In *Ulysses*, however, Joyce returns to the original paired themes, the impious snatching of divine secrets and the fitting punishment of blindness, but he does so obliquely. Stephen makes an elliptic reference to the early transgression: "Sixteen years ago I twenty-two tumbled." A few minutes earlier he had said: "Must get glasses. Broke them yesterday. Sixteen years ago. Distance. The eye sees all flat." [5]

The theme, nevertheless, is found throughout *Ulysses*, but Joyce obscured it by one of his characteristic devices, the use of minor as well as major characters as surrogates for himself. These proxies differ from the frankly autobiographical major portrayals of the total self: Stephen, Richard Rowan, Jerry-Shem. Instead, they seem to embody internal conflicts: temptations to Joyce to conform, or rebukes by the super-ego that he rejects while half-acknowledging that they may have a certain validity. In some of his aspects Shaun acts as such a gadfly. Robert Hand is a creation of a like process: he is Joyce as he might have been had he remained in Ireland, yielding to its standards, relinquishing his freedom to write untrammeled. Magalaner has pointed out [6] that Mr. Duffy in A *Painful Case* is a similar projection of the possible; he is Joyce relegating intellectual pursuits to the status of a hobby, and in his personal life carrying his egocentric isolation to a sterile and dangerous extreme. J. Mitchell Morse finds other partial surrogates in *Ulysses:* the blind stripling and McHugh, the "professor" who holds forth from a chair in the newspaper office.[7]

All such surrogates represent an exploration of the realm of possibles: extrapolations of what Joyce might have been, or might yet become. (Perhaps the daft, hypersensitive, litigious Breen is a sardonic admonition from Joyce to Joyce.) And it seems possible that one of the enigmas of *Ulysses*, the man in the macintosh, is Mr. Duffy, now irretrievably withdrawn from reality, a mental patient, an eater of dry crusts.[8]

A like personification of unrealized but still menacing possibles seems to be found in the elusive Penrose. Instead of offering us, like Duffy, a parable of the penalty for rejecting life and love, Penrose combines with the blind youth to show us the other horn of a dilemma, the perils of snatching the interdicted secrets of life. They are not two separate surrogates of Joyce as Adam and Prometheus, but are so curiously linked that they seem to be a single decomposed surrogate.

Penrose is seen only through the memories of Leopold and Molly. Bloom, musing on the "stream of life," thinks of him in the morning. At first he cannot recall more of his name than that it began with "Pen," but remembers him as a "priestylooking chap was always squinting in when he passed? Weak eyes, woman," [9] who was a neighbor ten years before. The full name returns to Bloom only when he is helping the blind youth across the street. The stripling's thewless body and "bloodless pious face like a fellow going in to be a priest" [10] brings back the name with its adumbration of Icarus. For Penrose is more than a writing implement and a flower, no matter how symbolic; it is also a pinion that soared. Bloom's impression is augmented by Molly's more pungent addendum: "Penrose nearly caught me washing through the window only for I snapped up the towel to my face that was his studenting." [11] Penrose's physical attributes, like the blind man's, suggest a thumbnail sketch of Stephen-Joyce; his deeds reveal him to be like the adult Stephen, a student seeking to penetrate intellectual and metaphysical arcana, and like the peeping child, as a voyeur who pries into the secrets of sex.

The actual presence of the blind youth is always announced

by the tapping of his stick, but he is heralded earlier in
Ulysses, although we are not yet aware of it, by Stephen's
consideration of blindness on Sandymount strand. Here, half
mocking his own Idealism, Stephen tests the objective reality
of the physical world, the ineluctable modality of the visible,
by shutting his eyes and assuming the role of a blind man.[12]
But there is emotional as well as intellectual content: "If I
fell over a cliff that beetles o'er his base" — the quotation had
been spoken earlier by the usurper Haines, and Stephen's recall of it now, evoking the mad, blind Lear who had preferred
empty words to the wordless message of the heart, brings up
the whole constellation of his self-identification with Shakespeare and Hamlet, his dramatization of his position as a
fatherless son, an alienated and displaced victim of usurpa-
tion, wandering in spiritual and emotional darkness.

Yet he refuses to seek safety by opening his eyes, either
physically or spiritually: "I am getting on nicely in the dark.
My ash sword hangs at my side. Tap with it: they do. My two
feet in his boots are at the end of his legs." And later: "Has all
vanished since? If I open and am forever in the black adiaphane." The boots are in fact and in figure those of the chief
usurper, Mulligan, a scoffer more insouciant and more blas-
phemous, and so blinder than Stephen, but they are also imagined as the boots of one who is physically sightless. Stephen
is consciously terrified by the spiritual blackness, yet he is
equally fearful, although it may be subliminally, of the literal
bodily blindness.

When the blind piano-tuner himself appears, Bloom shows
us his resemblance to Penrose and we recognize the likeness
to Stephen-Joyce. To the Ormond barmaids his playing seems
masterly.[13] We do not hear the music Miss Douce extols; we
hear only the eternally tapping stick and the stripling's curse
on the deranged Farrell (perhaps another partial surrogate)
who innocently brushes against him: "You're blinder nor I
am, you bitch's bastard." [14] We witness his reluctant acceptance of Bloom's help, and the sour silence with which he re-

ceives Bloom's small tender of conversation foreshadows
Stephen's failure of response, as the aid he accepts toward
crossing the way and turning a corner suggests the much
greater help in finding a new direction which Stephen — and
Joyce — will take from Bloom.

To J. M. Morse [15] the stripling's tuning fork represents an
"absolute standard of an aesthetic rightness, not made by man
but inherent in the nature of things." (But the fork itself is
man-made, a soulless, mechanical instrument by which those
not granted the sense of absolute pitch — direct personal experience — are forced to gauge eternal verities. Possibly more
than aesthetic standards is suggested.) When the fork is forgotten at the Ormond, the youth is "wandering functionless";
it is during this wandering that he invokes "God's curse" on
Farrell, his fellow in affliction. Morse points out also that the
blind man is like Maimonides and Averroes, those "dark men"
who denied the light and whom Stephen thinks of as "flashing
in their mocking mirrors the obscure soul of the world, a darkness shining in brightness which brightness could not com-
prehend." [16]

There is another linking of the surrogates and their principal. Just before Bloom first consciously becomes aware of the
blind youth who is tapping his way close by, he sees in a shop
window the book *Why I Left the Church of Rome* and is reminded of the potato conversions of his grandfather's day that
seduced Jews as well as Catholics from their faith.[17] In "Circe"
Grandfather Virag announces: "I am the Virag who disclosed
the sex secrets of monks and maidens. Why I left the Church
of Rome. Read the Priest, the Woman and the Confessional.
Penrose." [18] Here Bloom's clairvoyant subconscious has tied
together the blind youth, Penrose, and — by synopsizing *A
Portrait* — Stephen and Joyce.

It would appear then that Joyce is showing us a multiple
image of himself. As Penrose he is the culprit, as the stripling
he pays the penalty with a double loss of vision, spiritual — or
emotional — and physical. In a passage which again demon-

strates the kinship of Stephen and the blind lad, we are sharply reminded how much Stephen had to learn from his unrecognized father after the spirit, the wise and compassionate Bloom. To explore blindness Stephen attempted to play a role, but he took for his model only abstract, undifferentiated blind men: *they* tap. The would-be novelist had yet to master an indispensable element of his craft, one that the young critic Joyce recognized in theory if he could not yet apply it in practice: "a principle of all patient and perfect art which bids him express his fable in terms of his characters." [19]

It is Bloom who has the heart to sympathize, the insight to empathize, who shows us blindness in terms of an individual. It is Bloom, whose absurd literary aspirations would inevitably be expressed in the curdled syntax and clotted clichés of "Eumaeus," who nevertheless possesses the all-important talisman of the writer, which Stephen, with all his word hoard, still lacks. For Bloom, with concrete detail, can reconstruct for himself, and for us, the plight of this particular blind fellow man: "Poor young fellow! How on earth did he know that van was there? Must have felt it. See things in their foreheads perhaps. . . . Queer idea of Dublin he must have, tapping his way round by the stones." He continues: "And with a woman, for instance. . . . Must be strange not to see her. Kind of a form in his mind's eye. . . ." and concludes: "Really terrible. What dreams would he have, not seeing. Life a dream for him." [20]

Surely Joyce nowhere surpassed the multilevel irony of this passage; nowhere did he set down a more acid criticism of his younger self than Bloom's innocent reflections with their unintended application to Stephen: his nightmare detachment from reality; his "feeling" useful only to perceive a dyeworks van; his vision constricted to the exiguity of cerebration; his benighted view of a Dublin whose people, under the blows of his stick — a Nothung that is only a wooden sword — are to him mere stones; his concept of woman as "form" — delicious ambiguity — a body to be used, an Idea to be philosophized over, but not yet seen as human, all too human, as Joyce was someday to see Molly, Molly who hid her face from Penrose.

In *Finnegans Wake* man's first disobedience is an explicit theme explicitly equated with the human peccadillo of voyeurism; HCE spying on the girls in the Park is Adam in the Garden. But the erring HCE is himself the target of various indignities perpetrated by numerous strangers: the three soldiers, the cad, Hosty, the author of the scurrilous rann, a tramp, a "seeboy." As I have pointed out elsewhere,[21] all their offenses against HCE have a common factor: all peep, spy, inform on him, expose him to obloquy; he is both agent and victim of the same misdeed. And all these strangers are disguises for the dreamer — all strangers in a dream, says Freud, are surrogates for the dreamer. The dreamer is not HCE but his son Jerry Earwicker, a mellowed, middle-aged Stephen, and in his dream he is explicitly identified with Noah's guilty son Ham who saw and exposed his father's nakedness.

All the episodes of spying and exposure by the scapegoat assailants are constructs of the censor to veil an event finally revealed in a scene realistically presented almost at the end of the dream. It seems to be a reminiscence of very early childhood: Jerry dreams of himself as a child even younger than the little peeping Stephen, who wakes from a terrifying nightmare of his father. When the parents come to his bedside to comfort him, he sees his father naked and sexually aroused.

If the episode is not as factual as the early scene in *A Portrait*, it is equally true psychologically in the fable of Jerry Earwicker who is Stephen-Joyce. Some such event would be the original trauma screened by the memory of the subsequent threat of the eagles. But the guilt of Jerry is a figure for the guilt of the adult Joyce. Twice he portrayed his father as Simon Dedalus, a contumelious picture, and showed him rejected and replaced by Bloom. But it was not only the human father who was exposed and rejected in the earlier works. Stephen's *non serviam* refused service to a hangman god but neither Stephen nor Joyce denied the god's existence. In

Finnegans Wake the son at last seeks atonement: through confession, through identification of Bloom, the substitute father, with HCE, the "actual" father, and above all through the identification of the son himself with the father image, a father who is all fathers in one. HCE comprises in himself all men, he is the Hegelian synthesis of Shem and Shaun, and he is also the Absolute, a mystical body embracing his creation as truly as the Mystical Body of Christ embraces the faithful of the Church. He is to be feared, he is inscrutable, in his unity are comprehended both the evil and the good, but the father image is no longer a purely malign divinity nor a merely contemptible human parent as Stephen-Joyce had proclaimed.

Taking on himself anew the guilt of Adam and Prometheus, but showing himself at one with the offended deity as well as with the defiant culprit, Joyce completes his great trilogy of alienation and atonement. But there seem to be motivations that transcend the aesthetic and philosophical. Jerry, like Joyce, is "a poor acheseyeld from Ailing" [22] but in *Finnegans Wake* the menace of blindness as retribution, and the metonymy that equates spiritual and emotional blindness with literal sightlessness, seem to have disappeared. That the threat had vanished from Joyce's psyche seems unlikely, and here we may find a clue as to why the last book is, as a work of art, such a regression from *Ulysses*.

Endlessly and needlessly tautological, unstructured and chaotic, the book is often mechanical in its elaboration, as in the jejune piling up of river names. Unless mere copiousness is a virtue, *Finnegans Wake* is in every way inferior to *Ulysses* and its obscurity seems to conceal other aesthetic transgressions: reflections of private resentments, rehearsals of old conversations that Joyce could not expect his readers, or even certain of his colloquists, to decipher. Too often we feel the author is talking to himself while we eavesdrop on matters of purely personal interest, neither transmuted by Joyce nor transmutable by us into suggestions of the universal.

Why should Joyce have spent seventeen years, even allowing for the handicaps of impaired sight and recurrent illness, expanding and re-embroidering the fabric of *Finnegans Wake?* Why did he abandon the economy and control which in the many pages of *Ulysses* permitted never a superfluous word? It is possible that the control abandoned him, that he was truly obsessed, under compulsion, unable to lay down the work. An hypothesis can be framed to explain these defects and the compulsion that caused or permitted them.

Mystical, fey, superstitious almost to the point of animism, an admitted mass of fears, Joyce may have indeed attempted to propitiate an offended deity by examination of conscience, contrition, confession, penance, all the prerequisites of absolution, although it was an empty confessional he entered, rejecting the doctrines that would authorize a priestly confessor to absolve him. To the guiltridden the twentieth century has made available a new confessional, the couch. Joyce derided dynamic psychology and its high priests but there is no doubt that he valued their findings. The dream of *Finnegans Wake* conforms in detail to Freud's dicta on dream construction and dream wit. Myron Nutting, who during the years of his friendship with Joyce in Paris underwent a short analysis with Otto Rank, writes: "Jung and Freud were sore points with JJ. He did not seem much interested in discussing them with me anyway. . . . JJ showed not only great familiarity with their theories, but also it seemed to me skill in some of their applications. I used to tell him my dreams and his immediate comments and analytic remarks went straight to the point. . . . He would point out elements in the dream stemming from things that I had forgotten which he happened to know, or remembered." [23]

Just as he rejected dogmatic theology but held to certain truths which he discerned underlying it, Joyce selected what suited him from the new dogma psychoanalysis, that compound of science, intuition, and art. He could hardly have failed to appreciate the hysteric's symbolical conversion of escape or punishment into symptoms. No matter that his eye troubles were actual somatic ailments and that psychosomatic medicine, in his time still embryonic, claims only that psychic distress works pathological changes on a "vulnerable" organ (and rather begs the question why, in the absence of hereditary causes, one organ is more vulnerable than another). Whatever the cause, Joyce's eyes were weak from childhood.[24] Thomas Mann, in *The Magic Mountain*, had anticipated discoveries still to be made in boldly positing a psychosomatic etiology for some cases of tuberculosis. Joyce was no less bold, no less ready to claim equal prerogatives for the prescience in which he had such profound belief. We are conscious that in all his writing he sought to assuage the wound that Edmund Wilson speaks of. Rather, perhaps, he sought to smooth layer after iridescent layer about the irritant that lies at the core of the pearl. But in *Finnegans Wake* the product is a flawed baroque monstrosity, and indeed, Joyce tells us, the secretions that form it are a "corrosive sublimation." [25] In choosing the dream form, surely he was conscious of choosing the fittest instrument to explore and perhaps rid himself of his guilt and its poisons. He rejected the ministrations of an analyst as he would have those of a priest: "I can psoakoonaloose myself anytime I want . . . without your interferences or any other pigeonstealer," [26] but he sought by his own efforts to achieve a deeper self-analysis, a more complete and therapeutic katharsis than any he had reached earlier.

At best, psychoanalysis is notoriously long drawn out, but certain patients try to prolong it interminably and, from the analyst's viewpoint, needlessly; they persistently make a "sinistrogyric return to one peculiar sore point in the past," [27] endlessly elaborating and contaminating certain dream material that especially appeals to them. Here may lie an explanation of the inordinate repetitiousness of *Finnegans Wake*. When Yawn lies in trance — or under psychoanalysis — his inquisitors mock him: "Happily you were not quite so successful in the process verbal whereby you would sublimate your blepharospasmockical suppressions . . . ?" [28] (Ble-

pharospasm is pathological blinking; as a conversion symptom
its utility would be obvious.) And of *Finnegans Wake* the
dreamer remarks: "We must grope on . . . like pou owl
giaours as we are would we salve aught of moments for our
aysore today." [29] It can be argued that Joyce sought more than
anodyne for the neurosis of the artist, that he hoped to salve
the sore eyes, the physical counterpart of the psychic wound.
But he lost control of the process and of his skill, obsessed
with the need to go on and on with his "strabismal apologia" [30]
lest the outraged god or the gnawing inwit permit the eagles
to complete their work and take from him the last vestiges of
his sight.

NOTES

1. James Joyce, *A Portrait of the Artist as a Young Man* (New
York: The Modern Library, 1928), p. 2.

2. Marvin Magalaner and Richard M. Kain, *Joyce: The Man,
The Work, The Reputation* (New York, 1956), pp. 112–13.
(The Kenner comment cited is from "The Portrait in Perspec-
tive," in *James Joyce: Two Decades of Criticism*, ed. Seon
Givens [New York, 1948].)

3. James Joyce, *Epiphanies* (Buffalo, 1956), p. 6.

4. *A Portrait*, pp. 123–55. If the preacher had drawn on St.
Augustine's views of the nature of sin, he might have included
intellectual curiosity. J. Mitchell Morse discusses Joyce's in-
debtedness to St. Augustine on this point in "Augustine, *Ayenbite*, and *Ulysses*," *PMLA*, LXX (December, 1955), 1143–59.

5. James Joyce, *Ulysses* (New York: The Modern Library,
1934), pp. 549 and 546. It appears that "tumbled" is equivocal.
It refers to the child's fall from grace, but in the episode of the
pandybat Stephen "tumbled" to the insensate injustice of divine
authority represented by Father Dolan.

6. Marvin Magalaner, "Joyce, Nietzsche, and Hauptmann in
James Joyce's 'A Painful Case'," *PMLA*, LXVIII (March, 1953),
95–102.

7. J. Mitchell Morse, "Joyce and the Blind Stripling," *Modern Language Notes*, LXXI (November, 1956), 497–501.

8. "M'Intosh," who "loves a lady who is dead," first appears in the cemetery where Mrs. Sinico lies, on the eight-month anniversary of the day before her burial, perhaps to commemorate the evening when the news of her death gave Duffy the shattering revelation of his own death in life. It may be the seven-month anniversary; in "A Painful Case," Mrs. Sinico's death occurred in November, but Bloom attended her funeral on October 17, 1903. (*Ulysses*, p. 695.)

9. *Ulysses*, p. 153. 10. *Ibid.*, pp. 178–79.
11. *Ibid.*, p. 739. 12. *Ibid.*, p. 38.

13. *Ibid.*, p. 259. But his playing, applauded by menials, is subordinate to his real function which is, as it were, a menial service to music. This may be a comment on Joyce's rejection of the singing career urged by Nora, the career Shaun adopts: the interpreter of other men's music has a role inferior to the creative role Joyce — and Shem — elected.

14. *Ibid.*, p. 246.

15. "Joyce and the Blind Stripling," p. 500.

16. *Ulysses*, p. 29. The Jewish sages of course bring in Bloom who denies not merely Christ but the Godhead, yet who is enlightened in his compassionate heart. There is also a foreshadowing of the boy Shem, Glugg in the "Children's Games," the dark brother who cannot speak the required answer "heliotrope" — the sunwise turn — but thrice garbles it: "O theoperil! Ethiaop lore, the poor lie." (*Finnegans Wake* [New York: The Viking Press, 1947], p. 223.)

17. *Ulysses*, p. 178. 18. *Ibid.*, p. 508.

19. James Joyce, "Catilina," a review of Ibsen's play in *The Early Joyce: The Book Reviews, 1902–1903*, ed. Stanislaus Joyce and Ellsworth Mason (Colorado Springs: The Mamalujo Press, 1955), p. 18.

20. *Ulysses*, pp. 178–79, *passim*.

21. Ruth von Phul, "Who Sleeps at Finnegans Wake?" *The James Joyce Review*, 1 (June 16, 1957), 27–38.

22. *Finnegans Wake*, p. 148.

23. In a personal communication to me, dated June 11, 1957.

24. The available data on Joyce's clinical history are strikingly suggestive in a number of points and on a variety of illnesses.

132   VON PHUL

25. *Finnegans Wake*, p. 185.   26. *Ibid.*, p. 522.

27. *Ibid.*, p. 120.   28. *Ibid.*, p. 515.

29. *Ibid.*, p. 107. Since a giaour is an unbeliever, it is possible that "pou owl" points to Paul — throughout the book identified with Jerry-Shem — here shown blinded by divine light, on the road to Damascus.

30. *Ibid.*, p. 189.

10

The Man in the Macintosh

J O H N   O .   L Y O N S

T H E most shadowy and mysterious figure in James Joyce's *Ulysses* is undoubtedly the recurring man in the macintosh. By comparison the anonymous Citizen of the Cyclops episode is perfectly obvious, and Blazes Boylan whom we hear much of but see only fleetingly is a perfectly flat character. Of these two the reader knows as much as he needs or even cares to know. But the man in the macintosh is as teasingly enigmatic to the reader as he is to Bloom. When Bloom first sees him at Paddy Dignam's burial in Glasnevin Cemetery he wonders who he can be (108).[1] There are many characters who are introduced in as shadowy a fashion as the man in the macintosh, but they are usually pinned down for the reader before the day is over. This is not the case with "M'Intosh," and shortly before Bloom retires he again asks himself who he can be.

> What selfinvolved enigma did Bloom risen going, gathering multicoloured multiform multitudinous garments, voluntarily apprehending, not comprehend?
> Who was M'Intosh? [714]

This question has not been answered, although the reader is led to suspect that he at least knows what the man in the macintosh represents. When Bloom first sees him at Dignam's burial he counts those present and the man in the macintosh makes the thirteenth mourner. "Death's number," muses Bloom, and every subsequent time that "M'Intosh" appears or is mentioned it is in connection with death. To know this is to know something. And yet it might further be asked why Joyce makes his Grim Reaper appear as a "lankylooking ga-loot" in a brown macintosh, and why Bloom partially iden-tifies himself on several occasions with "M'Intosh."

I suspect that there are good reasons for thinking that the man in the macintosh is Mr. James Duffy of the short story "A Painful Case" in *Dubliners*. I think that this identification answers both why Death wears a brown macintosh and why Bloom is sometimes identified with "M'Intosh."

Joyce was not wasteful of his characterizations. Many of the characters in *Dubliners* appear in *Ulysses*; Corley and Lenehan of "Two Gallants," Bantam Lyons of "The Boarding House," O'Madden Burke of "A Mother," and Messrs. Cun-ningham, Power, and M'Coy of "Grace," to name just a few. Joyce uses Dublin at the turn of the century as his Yoknapa-tawpha County and lets characters survive from one narrative to the next. James Duffy survives in this way. And yet he does not survive wholly as these others, for after his painful case — his arid courtship of Mrs. Sinico, estrangement from her and then remorse at her disgrace and suicide — he is a shell of humanity and "outcast from life's feast" (146).[2] James Duffy is perhaps Joyce's most severe illustration of the hated brown Irish paralysis. He pushes the characterization to an extreme, and seems bent on showing Duffy's gnawing remorse at the consequences of his sterile righteousness. In "A Painful Case" Duffy comes to a realization about himself and about life, but it seems too late to change his drab existence. From the very first he epitomizes Dublin's drabness.

His face, which carried the entire tale of his years, was of the brown tint of Dublin streets. On his long and rather large head grew dry black hair and a tawny moustache did not quite cover an unamiable mouth. His cheekbones also gave his face a harsh character; but there was no harshness in the eyes which, looking at the world from under their tawny eyebrows, gave the impression of a man ever alert to greet a redeeming instinct in others but often disappointed. [134]

After the experience of Mrs. Sinico's suicide Duffy is perfectly alone, and the long brown face which is the tint of Dublin streets belongs to a "lankylooking galoot" who is a shadowy wanderer and courter of a dead woman.

There are more reasons than this for thinking that the man in the macintosh is James Duffy. Bloom mentions that the man in the macintosh was not in the chapel, and if he is simply the figure of Death there is no reason why he should not have been (108). A little later we hear that Bloom has last been to Glasnevin to the funeral of Mrs. Sinico (and so he remembers his father who was also a suicide) (113). But another reason for mentioning Mrs. Sinico's burial the previous fall would be that it would explain why "M'Intosh"-Duffy would be at Glasnevin but not specifically an attendant at Dignam's burial.[3] Also, there is no reason why Bloom should know Duffy if both of them knew Mrs. Sinico, for Bloom seems not adverse to attending the funerals of slight acquaintances, and Duffy's relationship with Mrs. Sinico had been broken off four years before her suicide. Yet there may be a glimmer of memory of a tale for Bloom because his thoughts on the aloneness of "M'Intosh" are appropriate to the life of Duffy. "A fellow could live on his lonesome all his life. Yes, he could. Still he'd have to get someone to sod him after he died though he could dig his own grave"(108).

There is a further connection made between Mrs. Sinico, Bloom's father, and the man in the macintosh when in the Circe episode Bloom appears in the form of Lipoti Virag (a combination of Bloom and his father Rudolph Virag) (500). He wears a brown macintosh. There is no reason why he should, except that the suicides of Mrs. Sinico and Virag are joined in Bloom's mind by the figure of the man in the macintosh at Glasnevin Cemetery. But an even more gratuitous comment about the man in the macintosh occurs in Bloom's catalog of love relationships in the Cyclops episode. There he muses, "The man in the brown macintosh loves a lady who

is dead" (327). Here it would seem that Bloom is on the
verge of remembering who the man in the macintosh actually
is, or Joyce is coyly tossing us a clue to his identity. Certainly
if the man in the macintosh is simply the figure of Death it
would be odd to say that he loves a lady who is dead. Tradi-
tionally Death would love only his mistress and mother Sin,
and she is anything but dead. "M'Intosh" is then not so much
a figure of Death as he is a characterization of the results of
the Joycean concept of the peculiarly paralyzed and sterile
Irish kind of death.

In the Nausicaa episode of *Ulysses* Bloom repairs his ego
after the battle with the Citizen-Cyclops. In his imaginings
he becomes a suave and mysterious lover of the beautiful princess on the beach. When Gerty MacDowell, the princess,
turns out to be lame, Bloom soothes himself with thoughts of
his other imaginary accomplishments. He fancies himself a
man of letters — the author of and hero of *"The Mystery
Man on the Beach*, prize titbit story by Mr Leopold Bloom"
(369). And then for no reason but that the man in the macintosh has appeared to him also to be a wanderer and mystery
man he thinks, "And that fellow today at the graveside in the
brown macintosh" (369). If "M'Intosh" is James Duffy, however, the connection is based on more than that both are essentially lonely wanderers. For James Duffy is also a man of
unrealized literary projects. "In the desk lay a manuscript
translation of Hauptmann's *Michael Kramer*" (134). Indeed,
it seems impossible that Joyce could not have thought of
Duffy when he gives us the contents of Bloom's library and
desk drawers in the Ithaca episode. The opening pages of "A
Painful Case" abbreviate that later catalog by giving simply
the beginning and the end of Duffy's collection — Words-
worth and the *Maynooth Catechism* — and by mentioning
some of the trivia of Duffy's possession — including the advertisement for *Bile Beans*, which seems a kind of prototype for
the Wonderworker prospectus in the Bloom desk drawer
(706). This kind of identification between Bloom and

"M'Intosh" comes to a head in the Circe episode when the man in the macintosh interrupts Bloom's hallucinatory swearing-in as Lord Mayor of Dublin. At the height of the adulation of Bloom by the populace the man in the macintosh appears and says, pointing an elongated finger at Bloom, "Don't you believe a word he says. That man is Leopold M'Intosh, the notorious fireraiser. His real name is Higgins" (475). Bloom is of course not a fireraiser. On the contrary, he is a man of socially acceptable ambitions and actually very innocuous. The linking of "Leopold M'Intosh" is based on other things. Both of them, at least in Bloom's mind, are men of mystery. Yet their pseudonyms are accidental. The man in the macintosh is of course not "M'Intosh." And Bloom really isn't Bloom or Higgins — nor is he "L. Boom" as he appears with "M'Intosh" in the newspaper account of Dignam's funeral (632).

I suspect that the connection between Bloom and "M'Intosh"-Duffy goes deeper than this and that this connection is very good reason why Bloom should be disqualified for political office. There are obvious differences between the ascetic James Duffy and the sensually imaginative Bloom. Yet both are lonely wanderers and "outcasts at life's feast." When James Duffy realizes this he gnaws at "the rectitude of his life" (146). Bloom, on the other hand, is an outcast because of his Jewishness and pompous defences against injury on this score. Bloom often prefers his own little mental and corporeal microcosm to risking injury at life's feast. Joyce seems to be saying that it is this holding back from life which is a death in life. Bloom is a person who works hard at engagement in life (how much he looks forward to having the lost son Stephen living in the room upstairs), and so it would be hard for him to recognize in himself this love of disengagement. Perhaps this is why he is unable to identify "M'Intosh," and yet is so curious about his identity. For Joyce the major sin seems to be this brown paralysis of the spirit. In this light Bloom is often a passive sinner — a sinner by omission. But the history of James Duffy illustrates the consequences of a willful and complete paralysis and disengagement from life. It is appropriate that Bloom dismissed the figure of the man in the macintosh just before the affirmation of climbing into a warm bed.

NOTES

1. All references are to the Modern Library edition of *Ulysses* (New York: Random House, 1934).

2. All references are to the Modern Library edition of *Dubliners* (New York: Random House, [n.d.]).

3. There is a discrepancy in the date of the death of Mrs. Sinico. In "A Painful Case" the suicide is in November, but no year is mentioned (140). In *Ulysses* her death is dated "14 October 1903" (680), which establishes it as the previous fall.

11

Molly Bloom Revisited *

J . MITCHELL MORSE

P E R H A P S because of the researches of mythologists, perhaps because of the light-hearted naughtiness of certain movie
heroines or the motherly kindness of certain fictional prostitutes, perhaps by way of reaction against puritanism or Vic-
torianism, perhaps merely from inexperience — however it
may be, our gallant critics have a tendency to regard any sexually indiscriminate woman as a fertility symbol. It is a cliché
among them that Molly Bloom is an earth-goddess, a nature-
goddess, a mother-goddess, a symbol of the irrational but fertile, the witless but somehow creative, the amoral but somehow good, force of nature. She is spontaneity, they tell us; she
is *élan vital*, she is Gea-Tellus, she is Isadora Duncan, she is
Madame Dionne, she is the great *Lebensbejahung* of modern
letters. They ask us to admire her; they ask us to believe that
Joyce considered stupidity a necessary concomitant of fertility,
creativity, freedom, kindness, and honesty.

Though I hope I am as gallant, unpuritanical, un-Victorian
and inexperienced as anybody, I see no evidence in the text

* Erwin R. Steinberg's article, "A Book with a Molly in It,"
which appeared in the Autumn, 1958 number of *The James
Joyce Review*, raises many of the points discussed here by
J. Mitchell Morse. Written at approximately the same time as
Mr. Steinberg's piece, Mr. Morse's goes beyond refutation of
the conventional interpretation of Molly to offer an alternate
view.

for the prevailing view. Molly is not honest, she is not kind,
she is not creative, she is not free, she hasn't enough *élan vital*
to get dressed before three P.M., and her fertility is subnormal.
Though she lies "in the attitude of Gea-Tellus, fulfilled, re-
cumbent, big with seed" (721),[1] she is not Gea-Tellus: she is
not big with seed (754) but only fat from drinking too much
stout (735), and nowhere is it indicated that she is fulfilled
or that she fulfills anyone in any way. She blames her husband
for "a limitation of fertility" in herself (720), but if anyone's
fertility has been limited by their marriage it is his: she has
had a long series of lovers, but has borne no child by any of
them. They do not worship her as men have worshipped Isis,
Ashtaroth, Aphrodite, Cybele, and (if we follow Robert
Graves and Henry Adams) the Virgin Mary. They do not take
her seriously as a woman. She is a dirty joke. No one regards
her as anything but a whore.

Whatever else may be said of Joyce, he was not an anti-
intellectual; he was not one to set the mind at odds with all
that is desirable or to equate brainlessness with vitality. If anyone has ever known, he knew that creative spontaneity is not a
gift of nature but a development of art: that the intuitions of
genius do not come to the untrained. A virtuoso violinist,
swimmer, or mathematician can express himself with spontaneity proportionate to his skill; a beginner can only scrape or
flounder or imitate, and express nothing: he does not take
liberties with the medium, the medium takes liberties with
him. This is true for any form of intelligence. What intuitions
come to Molly Bloom? None of any freshness, truth, or value.
What does she express? Hardly more than Gerty MacDowell.
Her view of life is essentially that of a reader of confession
magazines, who both salaciously enjoys and virtuously disapproves. Her attitude is anything but a hearty acceptance of
everything that is; it is rather "the lethargy of nescient matter" (719). But the Aristotelian state of pure potentiality is
hardly admirable. Molly's first utterance of the day is "Mn" —
a sleepy soft equivocal grunt which Bloom interprets as "No"

(56) but which is really an expression of indifference. If any one word could indicate her temper, surely "Mn" would be more likely than the famous "Yes" — which, as we shall see, can also be interpreted as an expression of indifference. We need not follow the romantic reading of Siobhan McKenna, beautiful though it is.

Bloom is the one whose *élan vital* encompasses a pork kidney for breakfast; Molly can't manage anything but tea and four thin slices of bread; he is all activity, deft and cheerful: he shops, cooks, feeds the cat, greets a neighbor, eyes a woman, brings in the mail, serves his wife, and even does a bit of reading before setting out for the day; if all these things are trivial dissipations of energy, at least they are more vital and complex than Molly's greatest effort, which is to sit up in bed. She does ask Bloom about metempsychosis, but pays no attention to his explanation; he asks questions solicitous for her comfort, and she doesn't even bother to answer. Her underwear is soiled; the soles of her stockings are shiny with dirt; she holds the teacup as if it had no handle (a universal plebeian habit), wipes her fingers on the blanket, uses a hairpin to follow the lines of a pornographic novel, and says, "It must have fell down" (63–64). Her furniture is covered with dust, the keys of her unused piano are dirty (766), her complexion is "a bit washy" (734), and at age thirty-two she is beginning to worry about growing old (736). This is not life, this is death; this is the center of paralysis.

At three p.m. or shortly afterwards she expresses her soul in a "gay sweet chirping whistling" and flings a coin to a crippled sailor; these actions are quite within the range of ordinary people at ordinary times; they cannot be taken as signs of superabundant vitality or overflowing generosity; and she is only just getting dressed (222, 732). At four or shortly afterwards she is back in bed again, with Blazes Boylan; we see and hear Boylan on his way to the encounter (265, 267), we observe the simultaneous motion of the barmaid's hand on the beer-pull (281), but we do not witness the encounter itself.

Bloom's imagination of it excites him (270), but though they have intercourse "3 or 4 times," or possibly (who counts?) "5 or 6 times handrunning," Molly permits it to run its natural course only once, and then takes measures against conception. She can achieve orgasm only by masturbation or by the friction of her partner's finger (725, 727, 739, and 765). She is afraid to have another child; she scorns the fecund Mrs. Purefoy (727). This is all very well for a prudent woman, but since when does an earth-goddess sneer at fecundity and practice coitus interruptus? Like nescient matter, Molly is indeed "fertilisable," as Joyce said in one of his letters; but she resists fertilization — not fiercely, as certain female animals do, but corruptly, in the manner of a sentimentalist, *who would enjoy without incurring the immense debtorship for a thing done*" (197). And she doesn't even enjoy it very much. For her, sex is hardly more than what Plato called it, the scratching of a troublesome itch.

Her attitude toward most of the other activities of life is equally corrupt: it is the attitude of a tourist, sentimental or disdainful as occasion may suggest, not of a participant. This is not to say that she is detached; she lives rather in the limbo of passive souls, neither detached nor engaged but irresponsibly and vulgarly censorious. She scorns Mrs. Riordan's political fervor and Miss Stack's charitable nursing; she hates to tend her husband when he is sick (723); she dislikes cooking and housekeeping (725); she deplores the way women's bodies are made (727); she doesn't appreciate men's bodies either (738); she says she would rather die twenty times over than marry again (729); she disapproves of young girls' showing their legs (731, 735); she calls Bloom's interest in national affairs "trash and nonsense" (733); she dislikes lying under a man of Boylan's size, weight, and hairiness; she admires nothing about him but his clothes and his success in business (734); she has little confidence in her own sex appeal; she doesn't respond to Rabelais (736); and so on and so on — we could turn through all the pages of her soliloquy to the end, turning up such examples.

As far as the evidence goes, Molly's reputation as an earth-goddess rests on nothing more than a romantic appreciation of nature (766–67), a fondness for fruit and flowers (765), and a child's or tourist's enjoyment of such things as riding in trains and carriages (733), watching parades and military exercises, shopping in new cities (734), and sightseeing in foreign countries (767–68). Her sexual appetite is certainly indiscriminate (765), but lack of taste can hardly be equated with vigor — such abject sprawling lust is in fact most often a result of lack of self-confidence. There has never been any love in her heart. She married Bloom because he was so gentle and understanding that she knew she "could always get around him" (767). She even gave him her virginity before marriage with a mixture of indifference and calculation: when he asked her to lie with him, she remembers, "I thought well as well him as another"; "his heart was going like mad," but she was evidently calm enough: "I asked him with my eyes to ask again," and then "I put my arms around him yes and drew him down to me so he could feel my breasts all perfume" (768). A person blind with passion would hardly think so coolly. At that stage certainly no words would have been necessary if she had been really passionate; she felt a need to say "yes I will Yes" (note the capital) because she was consciously dramatizing a situation in which she was not emotionally involved. If the man had been D. H. Lawrence instead of Bloom, he would have found her annoyingly loquacious.

In view of these facts about Molly's character, a major question arises as to her role in the novel. What is Joyce's purpose in making one of his chief characters a woman who lacks sufficient energy to be effective in the ordinary tasks of daily life, whose health is declining, whose fertility is below par, whose capacity for sexual enjoyment is questionable, who considers the sexual act dirty and in fact makes it dirty, whose heart is cold, and whose attitude is generally negative and censorious? Who is Molly, what is she, that most of our critics adore her?

The anthropological interpretation of literature as mythography has degenerated into a fatuous ritual; overlooking the obvious in their fond search for occult meanings, our fable-minded critics often myth the point. One hesitates to play such a game. Joyce, however, was consciously a mythographer: he "put in the symbols" as deliberately as Mary McCarthy's college student, and the question "Who is Molly?" can be answered in terms of myth more concretely than we have hitherto suspected. With her striped petticoat (62), with her face veiled by the sheet (83) and by the window shade (222), she is pretty clearly the Penelope of pre-Homeric tradition, goddess of the dawn, seduced by Hermes-Boylan and by all the suitors.[2] This is perhaps the saddest of all Joyce's contrasts with heroic times; for not only is no Pan born of their embraces, but the dawn-goddess herself lies sluggishly abed, and the sun-god, be he Hermes or Odysseus, is up before her. Her birds don't chirp and whistle until mid-afternoon. Molly is thus not only a faithless figure of faith but also a force of nature that doesn't function: in Dublin even nature is awry, perverse, and moribund.

And by implication in the whole modern world. Joyce grew up in the romantic tradition as in the Catholic Church, and renounced the one as he renounced the other, with almost equal need to keep resisting their visceral attraction. He continued to attack the Catholic Church — by way of fighting off its seductiveness — for the rest of his life; with regard to romanticism, however, he seems to have relented in *Finnegans Wake*. In *Dubliners* he attacks every aspect of romanticism: exoticism in "Araby," the desire for adventure in "An Encounter," and the romantic attitude toward various things in the other stories: toward religion in "The Sisters" and "Grace," toward filial affection in "Eveline," toward maternal

affection in "The Boarding House," toward married love and
Don Juanism alike in "A Little Cloud," toward Don Juanism
and the lower classes in "Two Gallants," toward political action in "Ivy Day in the Committee Room," toward the past in
"The Dead," and so on. In the *Portrait* Stephen's romantic
ecstasy on the strand is expressed in the ripest manner of *A
House of Pomegranates*: "Her bosom was as a bird's, soft and
slight, slight and soft as the breast of some dark-plumaged
dove. But her long fair hair was girlish: and girlish, and
touched with the wonder of mortal beauty, her face" (199).
The ironic tone is heavily emphasized by the seemingly natural introduction of an inappropriate element — "the white
fringes of her drawers were like feathering of soft white down"
— a device Joyce was to use repeatedly in the Cyclops and
Oxen of the Sun episodes of *Ulysses* and throughout *Finnegans Wake*.

In *Ulysses* also Stephen walks on the strand: but it is a
different strand, since it is seen through the eyes of a different
Stephen. In his walk in the *Portrait*, Stephen thinks roman-
tically and tends to romanticize his experience, however un-
romantic the external facts may be; the facts that cannot be
transformed he simply overlooks. In the *Portrait* the strand is
free of débris, detritus, death, and life: there are no rusty boot,
no dead dog, no warren of weasel rats, no porterbottle stogged
in sand, no broken hoops, no fishermen's nets, no chalk-
scrawled backdoors, no dryingline with two crucified shirts
(*Ulysses*, 38 and 42). As far as Stephen's awareness goes, these
things do not exist. The girl he sees far out in the shallows is a
silent figure of romance or dream. There is no life in her to
compare with that in the crucified shirts. Joyce's description
of the strand in the *Portrait* is thus as much a parody of intellectual emptiness as is the speech of the priest at the beginning of the retreat in honor of Saint Francis Xavier (123–26).
But in *Ulysses* Stephen opens his eyes and sees that "the black
adiaphane," the world of concrete facts through which we

cannot see and beyond whose influence we cannot fly except by delusion, was "there all the time" without his apprehending it (38).

This is not to say that in *Ulysses* Joyce limits himself to opaque and unintelligible particulars; he is too well acquainted with Aristotle for that. But, like Aristotle, he generalizes only from particulars; he does not, like Plato, exalt the general to Heaven and deny the essential reality of the particular. The Platonizing disposition leads to romanticism and mysticism; Stephen explicitly rejects Plato along with Hermes Trismegistus and Æ, and Joyce makes the fatuous John Eglinton Plato's chief defender. "Hold to the now, the here," says Stephen, "through which all future plunges to the past" (183–84). This is out of Aristotle by way of the Neo-Platonic Saint Augustine.[3] Holding to the now, the here, Joyce ridicules Ireland's romantic view of its past heroes by equating them with an actual hero of the present, the Citizen (291), and their palaces with Kiernan's pub (289). The last extreme of romantic fatuity he presents in the confrontation of Bloom and Gerty MacDowell, where drab and degenerate reality shows all too clearly through the sickly prose of magazines purveying romayunce to the semiliterate (342 ff.).

But the romantic sensibility, if it is not permitted to run away with our intelligence, can serve us well. The problem is to be sufficiently aware of its nature to control and use it, without destroying it in ourselves through the process of achieving awareness. The youthful Joyce who wrote "Ibsen's New Drama" knew the value as well as the dangers of romanticism; the youthful Stephen of the *Portrait*, who when asked to name the greatest poet said, "Byron, of course," was pathetic but not ridiculous or undignified (90); and at the age of forty-eight Joyce could still call Byron "a great poet."[4] In *Finnegans Wake*, though continuing his parodies, he finally learned to manage the impulse without treating it as a joke. Here for the first time we have straight romanticism: for example in the passage from Edgar Quinet on page 281:

Aujourd'hui comme aux temps de Pline et de Columelle la jacinthe se plaît dans les Gaules, la pervenche en Illyrie, la marguerite sur les ruines de Numance et pendant qu'autour d'elles les villes ont changé de maîtres et de noms, que plusieurs sont entrées dans le néant, que les civilisations se sont choquées et brisées, leurs paisibles générations ont traversé les âges et sont arrivées jusqu'à nous, fraîches et riantes comme aux jours des batailles.

This passage — the only one quoted straight at such length in *Finnegans Wake* — is echoed unmistakably on pages 14–15, 236, and 615, and more faintly on pages 255, 271, 354, and 604. The impudent Issy in a footnote calls it "gaswind" (281), but Joyce himself frankly called it "a beautiful sentence." [5] Why? Though well constructed, it is not structurally so remarkable as to be called beautiful on that account by such a connoisseur as Joyce; neither is its content so fresh as to be intellectually beautiful, as some sentences of Pascal or of Paul Valéry may be called beautiful. It is beautiful for a reason Stephen thought little of in the *Portrait* (193–94), for its imagery of flowers and ruins, its evocation of the past — of old, unhappy, far-off things, and battles long ago — and its sentimental attribution of peace and joy to the flowers. Flowers laugh only in romantic poetry: this is romantic poetry of the purest kind, fully expressing the pathetic fallacy, and Joyce was willingly seduced by it. "Margaritomancy!" he wrote, comparing himself to Faust saved from the devil by love (281).

In *Finnegans Wake* we have also for the first time a romantic portrait of a woman which is not a caricature. Anna Livia Plurabelle is as natural as Molly is perverse, and as attractive as Molly is repulsive. Harry Levin points out a similarity, "for what it is worth," between her last name and *Pia et pura bella*, "Vico's catch phrase for holy wars," [6] which Joyce quotes on page 178. The similarity turns out to be worth a great deal, for on page 280, just before the passage from Quinet, Joyce construes the phrase as singular and feminine — "Pious and pure fair one" — and on page 518 exclaims, "O

bella! O pia! O pura!", thus assimilating war to lovely woman
— the eternal Kate, goddess of battles, to the eternal ALP.
Joyce doubtless recognized in himself something that is perhaps in all of us, a childish tendency to romanticize war; he
suppressed it in his life more rigorously than most of us do, but
in *Finnegans Wake* acknowledged its existence. His personification of war as a woman was of course not new; its chief interest for us is the romantic character of the woman, the new
Joycean woman, who, whether she brings life or death, is always desirable. Even in old age she is attractive: "Grampupus
is fallen down but grinny sprids the boord" (7, 58).

All the women in *Finnegans Wake* are in their various ways
attractive: ALP, Isabel, Lily, the Prankquean, the Maggies,
the Jinnies, the Leapyear Girls, the Rainbow Girls, the two old
washwomen at the ford, even Kate the Slop. They are in sharp
contrast with the women of *Ulysses*, who with three exceptions are unattractive. Some — the old milkwoman, Milly
Bloom, Mrs. Dignam and Mrs. Breen — are merely pitiful;
some — Gerty MacDowell, Cissy Caffrey and Edy Boardman
— are tiresomely vulgar; and some — Molly Bloom, Martha
Clifford, the whore of the lane, and Bella Cohen and her girls
— are figures of sterility, perversion, disease, and death. The
only exceptions are the midwife, her companion, and Mrs.
Purefoy, pure faith, whose achievement in giving birth is the
basis of the only joyful episode in the book; and though Joyce
congratulates her in Dickens' most unfortunate manner
(413–14), and her husband in Carlyle's (416), that is only by
way of indicating how inadequate are all our celebrations of
the *élan vital*. Joyce does nothing gratuitously or by hazard. It
is therefore significant that the only person who deplores the
birth is Molly (727).

Joyce never mocked fertility or creativity or love or the joy
of life; he mocked instead the ways in which they are falsified
and perverted, including the cheap, sentimental, vulgar ways
in which they are often celebrated — ways as mechanical and
perfunctory as the performance of a sideshow chorus girl, a

cynical priest or an anti-intellectual professor of literature. But a more deadly weapon than mockery is accurate quotation. Molly's soliloquy is the bitterest and deadliest thing Joyce ever wrote. Without exhorting or haranguing his readers, observing strictly his own canon of reticence, he let Molly damn herself as the very center of paralysis.

NOTES

1. The numbers in parentheses refer to pages in the Modern Library editions of *Ulysses* and *A Portrait of the Artist as a Young Man*, and the Viking Press edition of *Finnegans Wake*.

2. See Robert Graves, *The Greek Myths* (London and Baltimore: Penguin Books, 1955), §§ 26 b, 2; 160.10; 171 l, 2. Also see F. Max Müller, *Contributions to the Science of Mythology* (London, 1897), II, 682–83.

3. For details and citations see "Augustine, *Ayenbite*, and *Ulysses*," PMLA, LXX (December, 1955), 1158.

4. *Letters of James Joyce*, ed. Stuart Gilbert (New York, 1957), p. 296.

5. *Ibid.*, p. 295.

6. *James Joyce: A Critical Introduction* (Norfolk, Conn., 1941), p. 149.

12

Joyce and the Three Ages of Charles Stewart Parnell

ADALINE GLASHEEN

I T is tolerably well-known that in *Dubliners*, *A Portrait of the Artist*, *Ulysses*, and *Finnegans Wake* Joyce "uses" Ireland's lost leader, Parnell. He does not use him as a dramatic character, although Parnell was a fascinating man, quite unlike anybody else: instead, Joyce's Parnell is a power, no longer present, that pervades men's minds like Stendhal's Napoleon and Shakespeare's King Hamlet.

Certainly, Parnell pervaded Joyce's mind and in very much the way that the head of King Charles I pervades the mind of Mr. Dick. "That's his allegorical way of expressing it," Miss Betsy says. "He connects his illness with great disturbance and agitation, naturally, and that's the figure, or the simile, or whatever it's called, which he chooses to use." Joyce naturally connected Parnell with the spiritual sickness of Ireland, a sickness that Joyce fled, as from a plague-spot. He fled, he was safe — theoretically — but nothing was ever so vivid to him again. By the time he wrote *Finnegans Wake* he had come to see that spiritual sickness is not localized or Irish, but common to all men everywhere.

At the start, however, Parnell was the great man who did not manage to flee, but fell victim of all that young Joyce feared in Ireland, victim of Irish nationalism, of Irish Catholicism, of Ireland's excess of sexual purity. With Parnell, Joyce could scourge the Irish conscience; with Parnell, he could contrast a paralyzed present with a lively, heroic past; with Parnell, he could show that the propensity to make myths did not die out with the glory of Greece and Rome. All this was extraordinarily useful to so didactic a writer as Joyce.

PARNELL AS HERO IN *A PORTRAIT OF THE ARTIST AS A YOUNG MAN*

From September 1, 1888, to December 29, 1891, Mrs. Riordan, a widow of independent means, lives in Bray with the Simon Dedalus family,[1] who presumably hope (as Leopold Bloom was later to hope) that she would leave them money; but after a political argument with her host, she takes umbrage in a hotel.

Little Stephen Dedalus calls her "Dante," a childish corruption of Aunty, and is impressed by her brushes which stand for the Irish national cause, then flushed with success. "The brush with the maroon velvet back was for Michael Davitt and the brush with the green velvet back was for Parnell." (PORTRAIT, 2). Stephen doesn't know it then, but the brushes also stand for the illusory nature of Mrs. Riordan's political involvement. She is a bigoted Catholic and yet she enshrines Davitt — an anticlerical and a Henry George socialist — and Parnell — a Protestant and an adulterer. Stephen falls into illusions of his own when he associates the brushes with maroon clouds and green earth in a geography book (PORTRAIT, 11). With Joyce, association is identification, and Parnell (who had a superstitious horror of anything green) thus becomes the green and fertile earth.

When Parnell dies, hopeful green is whelmed by destructive elements, water and fire — tears of the Irish, fire of their anger, rising and falling in concert with the Chief. Stephen is sick at Clongowes. He imagines himself beautifully dead and lying on a "catafalque." Then he imagines Parnell's death and links it to his own by that splendid word, "catafalque."

The fire rose and fell on the wall. It was like waves. . . . Or the waves were talking among themselves as they rose and fell.

He saw the sea of waves, long dark waves rising and falling, dark under the moonless night. A tiny light twinkled at the pierhead where the ship was entering: and he saw a multitude of people gathered by the waters' edge to see the ship that was entering their harbour. A tall man stood on the deck, looking out towards the flat dark land. . . .
He saw him lift his hand towards the people and heard him say in a loud voice of sorrow over the waters:
— He is dead. We saw him lying upon the catafalque.
A wail of sorrow went up from the people.
— Parnell! Parnell! He is dead!
They fell upon their knees, moaning in sorrow. [PORTRAIT, 25–26]

This vision recalls Plutarch's story of the end of the great god Pan; [2] Homerically, I suppose, it corresponds to the moment when Ithaca heard that Ulysses was dead. Stephen, of course, does not actually witness the arrival of Parnell's body in Ireland, for Clongowes is far from the sea. Unconsciously, the boy is myth-making, aping his elders who had made a myth of Parnell with a deal of rhyme and very little reason.

Recollections of the period show a people flown right out of reason in a spasm of hate and love. Here is a typical account of Parnell's death by Mrs. Leamy, whose husband was a devoted Parnellite. Less economical than Joyce, she conveys the same sense of exalted hysteria.

Parnell's last journey home began on Saturday night, October 10, 1891. It was a wild night at sea. My husband . . . often spoke of the agony of the crossing of the Irish Channel. How the winds sobbed and wailed, rising and falling with a Banshee's wail. . . .
When the boat train arrived at Westland Row Station, Dublin, this deal box was removed from the coffin and cast aside. Immediately the great crowd which had gathered seized it, and with their naked hands broke it up and divided it to keep as souvenirs in memory of the beloved Leader, chips of wood to be handed down as rich heritage to their children — wood that had touched Parnell's coffin. The bands played a funeral dirge, and a great sob arose from the hearts of the people.

.   .   .   .

On every side as we slowly passed along, a wail went up from the multitude, it passed like a great sigh — Oh, Parnell! Parnell! Especially noticeable was the grief of the poor women. They abandoned themselves to sorrow in a way that was almost terrifying to behold.

.   .   .   .

   The shades of the autumn night were closing in when he was laid to rest. . . . Then, suddenly a great light shone. The sky seemed to open and forth burst a fiery globe which sped across the heavens with incredible swiftness, down, down, down — it disappeared into the grave and left the gloom more intense for its momentary brightness. A symbol surely of our fallen Star — as at the death of Caesar! [3]

Thus the worshippers, and how Joyce must have blessed the luck that sent him to Ireland in time for this myth-making! The enemies? Dante rips the green velvet off of her brush and joins the "clerical" party in making a devilish Parnell myth, as high-flung and unreal as the myth of the worshippers. In his vision, Stephen sees:

. . . Dante in a maroon velvet dress and with a green velvet mantle hanging from her shoulders walking proudly and silently past the people who knelt by the waters' edge.[4] [PORTRAIT, 26]

But the vision lied, for Dante is not a proud and silent woman.

   On Christmas, 1891, the fire does not rise and fall but "banked high and red, flamed in the grate and under the ivy twined branches of the chandelier the Christmas table was spread" (PORTRAIT, 26). Ivy is the badge of the dead Parnell and its use here is bacchanal — Euripides lies behind the scene. Chewed, the ivy frenzies Parnellite and anti-Parnellite till they tear off the habiliments of decency and rage like fire unsheathed.

   "For pity sake and for pity sake let us have no political discussion on this day of all days in the year," says Mrs. Dedalus, meaning that on the birthday of the Prince of Peace there ought to be peace at the consumption of prime turkey.[5] But the champions are pitiless and "political discussion" a ludicrous meiosis. It is Christmas day and flaming anger has driven Christ out of Irish heart and head.

Early in the fight, Simon Dedalus glances at the vexing question: "Were we to desert him at the bidding of the English people?" [6] (PORTRAIT, 32). But it settles down to a purely Irish brawl between Dante and John Casey, emblems of perverted Catholicism and perverted Nationalism.

John Casey is apparently a Fenian, a member of the Irish Republican Brotherhood, a semisecret society, founded in the 1850's and pledged to free Ireland by armed violence, illdefined. His badge of membership is the three cramped fingers that he got making "a birthday present for Queen Victoria." I take this to mean that Casey was one of the Fenian "dynamitards" who were always just failing to blow up London Bridge or Windsor Palace. Until the Home Rule movement of the seventies, the Fenians were the only coherent body of Irish nationalists, but, for all their fire and devotion, they accomplished very little. Sir Winston Churchill said:

The Fenian societies . . . had long been hampered in practical action by the purity of their principles. Armed insurrection for the sake of national independence is a spirited and uncompromising creed, but the opportunities in which it can be carried into actual practice must necessarily be rare. . . . The most blood-curdling oaths and sentiments tend to degenerate into ritual. They may preserve in all their vivid squalor the hateful memories of the past; but they cannot be said to exert much influence on the politics of the present.[7]

And Michael Davitt (originally a Fenian himself) said that by the seventies the Irish were "stirred only or mainly to a semblance of political life by the release of a political prisoner one day, or his commemorative funeral the next." [8]

John Casey's political hand has lost its cunning, for he never, after all, succeeded in blowing up Queen Victoria or any significant portion of her domain. Little is left to him but to wallow in the vivid squalor of the Irish past where hate of England is a feeble thing by the hate of Irish for Irish.

— Didn't the bishops of Ireland betray us in the time of the union when Bishop Lanigan presented an address of loyalty to the Marquess Cornwallis? Didn't the bishops and priests sell the aspirations of their country in 1829 in return for catholic emancipation? Didn't they denounce the fenian movement from the pulpit and in the confession box? And didn't they dishonour the ashes of Terence Bellew Mac-Manus? [PORTRAIT, 39]

As far as I can make out, they did all these things, but the indictment is fragmentary as a Mississippian's account of Sherman's march to the sea; Casey ignores historical circumstance and the provocation offered by his own side.

Take the ashes of Terence Bellew MacManus, which one might suppose the Irish clergy spat on, trampled, and flung to the four winds. T. B. MacManus was a noted Fenian who died in California in 1862; at what must have been enormous trouble and expense, the Fenians had his body shipped back to Ireland for one of those commemorative funerals of theirs. They wanted the corpse to rest in a Catholic church in Dublin and Cardinal Cullen refused to permit this because the Church did not countenance secret societies — and for good reason. There is no doubt that the Fenians wanted to stir up political feeling over MacManus's much-travelled corpse and Cardinal Cullen, a combative, tactless man, helped them stir. It was all, we may say, unfortunate, loud, and shrill and very much like Casey and Dante at the Christmas dinner table.

Parnell was remarkable among the Irish in knowing next to nothing about the Irish past. In Davitt's words, Parnell was "a beautiful fighter" and his peculiar achievement was to give the Irish something to do to their real enemies in the living present. "Keep a firm grip on your homesteads," he said to the peasantry, who whooped with joy and fortified their mud huts against eviction. "Don't send men to parliament who can make good speeches," he said to the electorate. "Send men who will vote right." Intolerant of sentiment and rhetoric,

Parnell went to playing skilled poker with English politicians. He scared them.

Parnell thought that armed rebellion against the England of his time was lunacy and the Fenian extremists fools. They gave him endless bother, almost brought him to political disaster, as may be seen from the minutes of the Parnell Commission; up to Parnell's divorce and the party split, the Fenians were a drag on him as the Church never was. Until the last year of his life the Fenian extremists had nothing official or public to do with Parnell; but in his last mad fight, Parnell rounded on his own moderation and held out his hands to "fenians and hillside men" (the phrase is Davitt's). Then the Fenians gave Parnell passionate support, for he was being attacked by their long-time enemies, the Church and England. An old Fenian leader said to Barry O'Brien: "When the Grand Old Man interfered, that gave a new aspect to the affair. It then became a question of submitting to the dictation of an Englishman, and for the first time I resolved to support Parnell." [9] Thus — and as usual — Joyce has Irish history in perfect trim. John Casey, the ultramontane Fenian, stood with Parnell when Parnell was a lost cause — "a cold bitter day, not long before the chief died" (PORTRAIT, 36).

Casey says that "the priests and the priests' pawns broke Parnell's heart and hounded him into his grave" (PORTRAIT, 34). How true is the charge? It is, I think, all rather like the ashes of Terence Bellew MacManus. Parnell's conduct was by no means above reproach. His dalliance with Mrs. O'Shea had more than once made him neglect his duty to Ireland and led him to commit certain political acts that were unforgivable. After the divorce scandal, he flouted common sense and the good of Ireland when he did not retire from politics, at least temporarily. But tell a man that he is a king — and Ireland had been telling him for years — and he will begin to believe it.[10] Parnell's last fight was doomed, was plain wrongheaded; he acted just like a hero, like Achilles, standing on his

sulky honor against Agamemnon, like Marc Antony before
Actium: "I'll fight by sea!" His heroics plunged Ireland into
distracted decades of backbiting that figure in *Ulysses* as the
Trojan war.

With Parnell's wrongness securely in mind, it must still be
said that his enemies behaved badly. " 'Twas Irish humour,
wet and dry,/ Flung quicklime into Parnell's eye." Yes, that
happened, and they pursued him with virulence and inde-
cency, taunting him with the petticoats of Kitty O'Shea.
There are a legion of scare stories that involve the clergy — a
priest at the altar — a priest in a polling booth — a priest re-
fusing absolution to a Parnellite — a woman removed from a
sodality. I will give one reading from the anti-Parnellites and
have done.

The following is taken from an article, probably by Tim
Healy, that appeared in the *National Press*, a newspaper said
to have been partly owned by the clergy. It deals with some of
those "Paris Funds" that the old harridan in Arklow screams
about (PORTRAIT, 37), funds for the national cause that had
been banked in Paris to keep them safe from the English.
Parnell was a slatternly man with money, but no one seriously
thought he had been dipping his hand into the Paris till, and
Healy, in his book of memoirs, does not repeat the accusation.

STOP THIEF

On his native heath at Wicklow yesterday, Mr. Parnell
shirked in the most cowardly and hang-dog fashion the terrible dictment of Archbishop Croke. . . . As to the damning
discourtesy with which the burrowing adulterer treated the
Metropolitan of Munster, no answer is attempted.

.   .   .   .

A wily thief is Mr. Fox. . . . This charge, if he fails to
face it, has come to stay. It will haunt Mr. Parnell on platform, in Parliament, at bed and board, for the remainder of
his career. We will force him to face it, or amidst the contempt of his own supporters, 'lash the rascal naked through
the world. . . .'

If Mr. Parnell debauched Mrs. O'Shea, one of the commandments delivered to us by Moses called that 'adultery.' If he appropriated the money left in trust with him — and we are prepared to prove he did — the same old-fashioned law-giver called that 'theft.' [11]

There are phrases here that betray a hate which is patholog-ical, like Dante's maenad triumph: "We crushed him to death! Fiend!" (PORTRAIT, 41).

The violence of the clerical party has its explanations. The Irish had long been known for their "domestic virtue," i.e., their sexual coldness which in our own day has been blamed for contributing to the depopulation of Eire.[12] At the same time, the Irish often ran after leaders who were notoriously loose in their sexual lives — O'Connell, Biggar, Butt, Parnell spring to mind. Joyce points up this paradox by having Dante keep a lamp alight before a statue of the Immaculate Concep-tion at the same time she keeps a green brush dedicated to Parnell (ULYSSES, 665). The Irish Catholic clergy had the right to try to dispel this moral confusion and condemn Par-nell's leadership of their people, but the timing of the con-demnation was most unfortunate and made it possible to accuse the Church of hypocrisy and kowtowing to Gladstone. From 1886, when the O'Shea affair was an election issue in Galway, Parnell's adultery must have been known to the Irish clergy who seem to have put patriotic before moral considera-tions. There is good evidence to show that they did not speak out against Parnell immediately after the divorce because they hoped he would resign quietly. Conscious of their too long forbearance, they were the bitterer when they ceased to for-bear.

What was almost worse, the Vatican had been telling them all along that they were wrong. Prodded by the English gov-ernment, which wanted to damp-down Irish nationalism,[13] the Pope had taken a consistent line since the late Seventies, and in 1883 had made a strong attempt to break the hold that the Protestant Parnell had on Catholic Ireland. It was in the matter of the Parnell Tribute, a fund that was being raised in

Ireland to pay off the mortgage on Avondale, Parnell's Wicklow estate.

The Pope had never looked with favour on the Land
League agitation. Indeed, he regarded it as nothing more or
less than a revolt against the lawfully constituted authorities,
which in truth it was. And now the Catholic bishops and
priests and people of Ireland were uniting to place the Protestant leader of the revolt on a pedestal of glory. There were
not wanting, it is said, English agents in Rome who readily
used the Parnellite tribute as a lever to move the Pope
against the agitators. The Irish were losing the faith; even
their religious guides had been led astray, and nothing but
the interference of the Pontiff could avert the dangers which
imperiled the very salvation of the people. So it was whispered and believed at the Vatican. [Barry O'Brien, II, 23]

The Irish clergy were told to give no countenance to the Tribute, and they obeyed, but the Tribute promptly swelled from
£12,000 to nearly £40,000. After the divorce case Gladstone
said with satisfaction, "Now the Pope will have one of the ten
commandments on his side." (Morley, III, 449).

All the same, the whisperers in Rome whispered something
like truth. Parnell was no mere political leader, he was a hero-
king, divinely hedged like Henry V or Arthur, and the adora-
tion he roused could not but seduce from the Faith. We have
seen how they scrambled for chips of wood that had touched
his coffin. Irish hop-pickers in an English field caught sight of
him and gave cry: "The Chief!" and jostled wildly to kiss his
hands. Here is how he struck his Irish election agent:

When he ascended the platform they cheered him again and
again. What a king he looked . . . so handsome, so quiet,
so self-possessed, so dignified. People thought of looking
at no one but him. He dwarfed all around him. There was
a majesty about the man which fascinated and awed you.

.   .   .   .

Yet with all his self-deprecation, modesty, and gentleness,
you always felt you were in the presence of a master. [Barry
O'Brien, II, 40]

And here is an Irish poetess:

. . . everywhere around there was a sea of passionate faces, loving, admiring, almost worshipping that silent, pale man. The cheering broke out again and again; there was no quelling it. Mr. Parnell bowed from side to side, sweeping the assemblage with his eagle glance. The people were fairly mad with excitement. I don't think anyone outside Ireland can understand what a charm Mr. Parnell has for the Irish heart; that wonderful personality of his, the distinction of look which marks him . . . All these are irresistible to the artistic Irish. [O'Connor, ii, 284]

The history of nations, pagan and Christian, shows that now and again people give their hearts to living heroes, forsaking the unseen gods. The practical Greeks turned their heroes into demi-gods; the Irish Church — for a little — seemed almost to give a tacit and unofficial support to the Protestant Parnell. But whether the hero is Oedipus or Parnell, he lives in danger, for if he is revealed a sinner, he will not be taken as a human sinner, rather as a force, still powerful, but now malignant. When the Irish saw that Parnell was the golden calf, whose tinsel glitter had seduced them from the Faith that lies beyond change, they turned to rend him. Dante, no less than Casey, bleeds from a wounded heart, for her love had been wrongly given.

They are well-matched, he and she, matched in brutality and darkness, alike unable to bring peace to Ireland. Dante joys in having crushed Parnell, Casey joys in having spit in an old woman's eye; he would have joyed in blowing up Queen Victoria. He is openly unchristian –"No God for Ireland!"– because he will have no other God than Parnell. Dante, in her hatred, ignorance and bigotry, is as profoundly unchristian as he. She has the local bitterness, the relish for hell-fire that mark her great namesake, but oh the difference of intellect and spiritual capacity! What worse could be said of Irish Catholicism than that Mrs. Riordan dared speak for it?

The Christmas dinner scene is Joyce's own hell-fire sermon, an attempt to forge the conscience of his race by exhibiting the perverse, futile extremes of degraded Nationalism and

degraded Catholicism, nets to catch the Irish soul. On this
Christmas a net catches the little soul of Stephen Dedalus,
who has followed the brawl attentively and at last chooses
sides, snared by the spell of Casey's "silver noise," his vain-
glorious rhetoric.

— Didn't the bishops of Ireland . . . Didn't the bishops
and priests . . . Didn't they . . . And didn't they . . .
    His face was glowing with anger and Stephen felt the glow
rise to his own cheek as the spoken words thrilled him. [POR-
TRAIT, 39–40]

He thrills to anger, allies himself with Simon Dedalus and
Casey on the side of manhood. In Joyce's mind, Irish Catholicism is always guarded by weakly-potent women who are not
feminine but antimasculine, wanting to tear at male courage
and turn men into mice.[14] Here, for the first time, but not the
last, the women frighten Stephen — manhood can be broken.

At the door Dante turned round violently and shouted down
the room, her cheeks flushed and quivering with rage:
— Devil out of hell! We won! We crushed him to death!
Fiend!
    The door slammed behind her.
    Mr Casey . . . suddenly bowed his head on his hands
with a sob of pain.
— Poor Parnell! he cried loudly. My dead king!
He sobbed loudly and bitterly.
    Stephen, raising his terrorstricken face, saw that his father's
eyes were full of tears. [PORTRAIT, 41]

Parnell left behind him a story that he would return, and a
good deal is made of this in Ulysses, but there is not a whisper
of return in A Portrait of the Artist. The king is dead, usurpers hold the island, and Stephen-Telemachus is too weak to
dislodge them. Instead, he drifts into fantasies of power: he
will be a dark avenger like Monte Cristo or Satan. Parnell is
scarcely mentioned throughout the rest of the book, but by
the time he reaches young manhood Stephen has persuaded
himself that Parnell's enemies — Church and national cause
and sexual morality — are his enemies, too. His *non serviam*

to Irish nationalism shows that he has not flown its net. Bitter, emotional, breathing past wrongs in the Casey manner, he says in unmanly unchristian cowardice, "I will not serve you because you will betray me."

— No honourable and sincere man — said Stephen — has given up to you his life and his youth and his affections from the days of Tone to those of Parnell but you sold him to the enemy or failed him in need or reviled him and left him for another. And you invite me to be one of you. I'd see you damned first.[15] [PORTRAIT, 237–38]

PARNELL AS GOD IN "IVY DAY IN THE COMMITTEE ROOM"

But for the lost "Et Tu, Healy," [16] this story in *Dubliners* is Joyce's first published work on Parnell. I take it up here in its historical order, as I think Joyce meant it to be taken; for in *Ulysses* the theme of Parnell as hero is glanced at in the Nestor section and the theme of Parnell as god follows in the Hades section.

"Ivy Day" takes place on October 6, 1902, anniversary of Parnell's death.[17] A Dublin city election is in limp progress. The scene is a bare committee room (election headquarters) of Richard Tierney, publican of the Black Eagle, who doesn't belong to "any party good, bad, or indifferent." Tierney is what the Irish call a *shoneen* or a flunky, one who curries favor with the English in hopes of a government job. Parnell had frowned on *shoneen* candidates.

Election workers drift in and out of the cold room, seedy and hard-up like Ireland — "look at all the factories down by the quay there idle"; they go up to the fire and find it gives no heat, is a sickly thing, nothing like the grand blaze of Christmas, 1891.[18] For all their perversity, Dante and Casey were alive and these men are not. They take no interest in the election, they are weakly cynical, languidly suspicious of "Tricky Dicky" Tierney who may be trickster or dupe just as long as he sends them drink and the promise of pay.

A healthy country does not let men go to waste like this. Ireland is sick and barren. When Parnell was "crushed to death" a political blight took his place. Irish nationalism splintered and resplintered into snarling cliques; a second Home Rule bill was defeated and another was not even promised until just before the 1914 war. In 1895 Mr. Gladstone summed it up in conversation with Barry O'Brien:

"Parnell was the most remarkable man I ever met. I do not say the ablest man; I say the most remarkable man, the most interesting. . . . He was unlike anyone I had ever met. He did things and said things unlike other men. His ascendency over his party was extraordinary. . . . He succeeded in surrounding himself with very clever men, with men exactly suited to his purpose. They have changed since, I don't know why. Everything seems to have changed. . . ." [Barry O'Brien, II, 357]

Everything seems to have changed. Yes, for Parnell was not just a politician, he was a king on whose health the nation's fertility depended.

It is easy enough to turn Parnell into a "slain god" for as head of the Land League he brought a very literal fertility to the Irish earth, and he was "slain" — who he was slain by depends on what myth one is pursuing: (1) he was slain by Judas (Tim Healy), the priests, and his own countrymen, in which case the myth is Christian or (2) he was slain by the foreign Dalilah, Kitty O'Shea, and her people. (In *Finnegans Wake* Joyce plays with the second possibility.) Parnell left behind a story that he would come again.

Whatever the details of the myth, "they have waved the green boughs over him, they have torn him limb from lamb." Entering the committee room, Joe Hynes says, "What are you doing in the dark?" They are doing nothing in the dark but embody the paralysis that is Ireland. The only green thing in the dank room is the ivy leaf that a couple of the men wear in Parnell's memory, badge too, of the slain gods, Attis and Osiris. Ivy no longer maddens, scarcely reminds them that once they were living men. Ivy alone calls up the words "life" and "alive."

The old man began to rake more cinders together. Mr. Hynes took off his hat, shook it and then turned down the collar of his coat, displaying, as he did so, an ivy leaf in the lapel.

"If this man was alive," he said, pointing to the leaf, "we'd have no talk of an address of welcome."

"That's true," said Mr. O'Connor.

"Musha, God be with them times!" said the old man. "There was some life in it then." [DUBLINERS, 153]

Of those in the committee room, only Joe Hynes stuck to Parnell "like a man"; Joe is a "decent skin" (Joyce's Parnellites are always decent skins), but here and in *Ulysses* he has no distinct character, just a dog's faithfulness, acts by rote, by rote when he defends the working man, by rote when he opposes an address being made to Edward VII, by rote when he repeats his poem about Parnell. His manhood has been crushed, just like all their manhoods.

Is Dublin to welcome or not to welcome the English king — this mild and politically futile question rouses the company to thin animation.

"But look here, John," said Mr. O'Connor. "Why should we welcome the King of England? Didn't Parnell himself. . . ."

"Parnell," said Mr. Henchy, "is dead. . . . Here's this chap come to the throne after his old mother keeping him out of it till the man was grey. . . . He's a jolly fine decent fellow, if you ask me, and no damn nonsense about him. He just says to himself: 'The old one never went to see these wild Irish. By Christ, I'll go myself and see what they're like. . . .'" [DUBLINERS, 166]

This is one of the few places where Joyce deliberately rearranges history to suit his theme. Victoria *had* come to see the wild Irish only two years before in April, 1900. Joyce and the men of the committee room knew this, of course, but Joyce wanted Edward VII to be the first king to come after the death of Ireland's true king, Parnell. The men of the committee room, like the men of the old black tower, watch for the alien banners that

> . . . come to bribe or threaten,
> Or whisper that a man's a fool
> Who, when his own right king's forgotten,
> Cares what king sets up his rule.

As Mr. O'Connor was going to say, Parnell had told the Irish not to make an address of welcome to Edward when he was a prince and came to Ireland in 1885; they met him with placards reading: "We'll have no King but Charlie!" Now Parnell is dead, and Mr. Henchy goes on to advance the pathetic hope that Edward will bring prosperity to Ireland, set the idle factories to work; the more he talks, however, the more Mr. Henchy reveals Edward as unkingly — "an ordinary knockabout like you and me," a man kept out of power by an old woman through all the years of his strength. Nor is Edward sexually immaculate: "Do you think now after what he did Parnell was a fit man to lead us? And why, then, would we do it for Edward the Seventh?" (DUBLINERS, 167). Divinity does hedge Parnell, rough-hew him how they will, but it does not hedge Edward VII, that knockabout of a monarch.

The argument, never virile, dies away. They solemnly agree that, now he is dead, everybody respects Parnell — Parnell thought they would say that. And since they all respect him, and all passion's spent, they permit the faithful Hynes to recite the poem that he wrote when Parnell died, a poem that Mr. Kenner has called "the right sort of bad rhetoric without cynicism."

> He is dead. Our Uncrowned King is dead.
> O, Erin, mourn with grief and woe
> For he lies dead whom the fell gang
> Of modern hypocrites laid low.
>
> He lies slain by the coward hounds
> He raised to glory from the mire:
> And Erin's hopes and Erin's dreams
> Perish upon her monarch's pyre.

. . . .

> Shame on the coward, caitiff hands
>   That smote their Lord or with a kiss
> Betrayed him to the rabble-rout
> Of fawning priests — no friends of his.

.   .   .   .

> They had their way: they laid him low.
>   But Erin, list, his spirit may
> Rise, like the Phoenix from the flames,
>   When breaks the dawning of the day . . .
>   [DUBLINERS, 169–70]

What is more touching than deeply-felt bad verse? This bad verse is a genre piece, a perfect imitation of the hundreds of gauche laments that snowed over Ireland when Parnell died.[19] Like most of them, Joe Hynes's poem sees Parnell as more than man, vaguely a surrogate for Christ, but it does not press the Christ theme because Parnell is, after all, the nonsectarian slain god of Ireland. The resurrection theme is pagan and looks to *Finnegans Wake* (see 472–73). But whatever its future extensions, the poem shows that by 1902 the fire of anger and life is nearly out. Read on Christmas, 1891, the poem would have brought men to each other's throats. Now Joe holds his grief within himself, and his political enemy, Mr. Crofton, allows that it was "a very fine piece of writing." The most blood-curdling sentiments do turn into ritual — Sir Winston was right — for ritual is rhetoric, just some very fine piece of writing.

PARNELL AS HUMAN IN *ULYSSES*

Parnell as hero, god, and man is likely to suggest Vico and his cycling ages — divine, heroic, human — ages created by mass imagination (Jung's collective unconscious?) and acted out by societies which are sure that their play is reality itself. Certainly, Joyce is at great pains to show us that Parnell as hero and as god is a creation in the minds of the beholders. I cannot feel, however, that "Ivy Day" is Viconian; the men of the committee room have nothing in common with the fathers of Vico's divine age for whom "every hollow holds a hallow." The movement of Parnell from hero in A *Portrait of the Artist* to god in "Ivy Day" follows the classic process of myth-making whereby Hercules or Adonis lives into hero and dies into god.

A *Portrait of the Artist* and *Ulysses* are, however, Viconian, and we very much need to have somebody tell us how and why. Here I can only brush the subject with uncertain fingertip. I think that A *Portrait* is Joyce's heroic book (as its original title suggests), *Ulysses* his human, *Finnegans Wake* his divine book, but the cycles turn within each book.

Parnell's death as the great god Pan marks the end of a divine Viconian age. Stephen grows up and becomes a Viconian hero which means that his peculiar status is that of son and never father. In the gap between A *Portrait* and *Ulysses* Stephen's fall into the sea marks the end of a heroic Viconian age. At the start of *Ulysses* Stephen Hero is dead and Stephen Human powerless to be born. *Ulysses* traces Stephen's progress to humanity, his rebirth as the child of Mrs. Pure Faith, his initiation into manhood and consubstantiality with Bloom. Heroic tension rises intolerably in "Circe" and then lets go into the calm, comic innocence of "Eumaeus," where the linguistic basis is the Irish bull and where human disguises are transparent and child-like. Consubstantial with Bloom, Stephen enters the human age, for Bloom perfectly fulfills Vico's formula for the human: "intelligent, modest, benign, reasonable, recognizing for laws conscience, reason, and duty." [20]

As Parnell is not the highest sort of god and Stephen not the highest sort of hero, so Bloom is not the highest sort of human being; his human world generates its own tensions and ugliness, his house is not a House Beautiful. Stephen will not stay in it long, but, become the creator-like-to-God-the-Father, go cycling on to meet his fate in the divine age of *Finnegans Wake*. For the moment, however, there in the cabman's shelter, the human age has the queer innocence and mercy of early morning, and in that mercy, Bloom makes Parnell into a human sinner, loves him, and lets him be reborn with Stephen into life.

It is, of course, impossible that Parnell should go from hero and god to man all in a single rush. The transition is not elaborate, but Joyce makes a workman-like job of it. In *Ulysses* he restates the themes of hero and god, but in less exalted keys. The heroic theme is restated in "Nestor" when Mr. Deasy, fanatic as John Casey, though at the opposite political pole [21] gets into a rhetorical rehash of the ugly past, when Ulster was always right.

. . . I saw three generations since O'Connell's time. I remember the famine. Do you know that the orange lodges agitated for repeal of the union twenty years before O'Connell did or before the prelates of your communion denounced him as a demagogue? You fenians forget some things. [ULYSSES, 32]

Stephen is as yet so little free from the net of nationalism and the vivid past that his mind leaps instantly to a bitter retort about Orange slaughter of Catholics. Then, as Casey had warned Stephen against the priests, Deasy warns him against other scapegoats — Jews and women.

A woman brought sin into the world. For a woman who was no better than she should be, Helen, the runaway wife of Menelaus, ten years the Greeks made war on Troy. . . . A woman too brought Parnell low. [ULYSSES, 35]

This is the first time in Joyce's books that any but the "priests and the priests' pawns" have brought Parnell low. Deasy is a true Nestor — as well as silly — for if a woman brought Parnell low, Parnell is not Christ or even Caesar; and he is not such a very great hero after all if he is coupled with Paris, the one lover whom the world has not somehow loved.

The "Ivy Day" or god theme is restated in the Hades section and strongly altered toward humanity. Paddy Dignam's mourners are not the zombies of the committee room because they are seen through Bloom's merciful eyes. Perhaps they dwell in a Waste Land, but they are shored up by a certain human self-consequence and this narrows the gap between them and Parnell. Joe Hynes is there to suggest a visit to the Chief's grave.

They turned to the right, following their slow thoughts. With awe Mr Power's blank voice spoke:
— Some say he is not in that grave at all. That the coffin was filled with stones. That one day he will come again.
Hynes shook his head.
— Parnell will never come again, he said. He's there, all that was mortal of him. Peace to his ashes. [ULYSSES, 111]

The glowing fire of Christmas, 1891, sank to the cindery thing of October 6, 1902; now on June 16, 1904, it is ashes. Mr. Power speaks of Parnell's resurrection in human terms, no mystery, but a wily trick, something Ulysses might think of. Joe Hynes denies his faith in Parnell as Phoenix — ashes to ashes, not ashes to the fiery bird reborn.

Bloom does not go along with the other men to the Chief's grave. As we see later on, he has the most amiable feelings for Parnell, but political hysteria and the heroic Irish past have no hold on his very human mind.

For instance, when the evicted tenants' question, then at its first inception, bulked largely in people's minds though, it goes without saying, not contributing a copper or pinning his faith absolutely to its dictums, some of which wouldn't exactly hold water, he at the outset in principle, at all events, was in thorough sympathy. [ULYSSES, 641]

There's Bloom for you — sympathetic, but he does not pin faith, does not lay out money for causes to which the fevered Irish patriot gave, or felt he gave, his heart's blood.

It is Bloom who has no faith, and Hynes who denies his faith in Parnell, who play Cleopas and his companion, failing to recognize the returned god on the road to Emmaus.[22] The man in the macintosh, the mysterious thirteenth mourner, is Christ or Parnell, the slain god come back to a world not ready to receive him, a theme which Bloom expounds in "Eumaeus" and to which Joyce returns in *Finnegans Wake* (24–29). Here at the funeral Bloom does not know what he says when he says, "Good Lord, what became of him?" (ULYSSES, 110).

Parnell the hero becomes Paris the adulterer, Parnell the Phoenix returns as a man in a macintosh. Very little more is made of him — save for a passing identification with King Hamlet — until he is entirely humanized in the cabman's shelter, which belongs perhaps to Skin-the-goat who drove the getaway car for the Phoenix Park murderers.

It is altogether fitting and proper that in this shelter Bloom should cleanse the Irish past, for there was no more wicked act in that past than the murders in Phoenix Park, brutal, senseless murders, the sort of regrettable thing that always takes place on the fringes of revolution, the sort of thing that Dante and Casey, in their violence, are morally responsible for.

Discussion begins in the shelter with the yarn about the coffin-full-of-stones, brought up by a cabby who looks like Parnell's private secretary, Henry Campbell. These stones and Parnell's hiding out as De Wet, the Boer general, were so firmly folk-beliefs in Ireland that when Michael Davitt was in the Transvaal he made a special trip to take a look at De Wet, who was not, it proved, Parnell.

Bloom takes hold of Stephen's fantasy of the avenger who will return and concludes that after "twenty odd years" (the period of Ulysses's absence, not Parnell's), return would be "highly inadvisable." Return and a bloody shambles of one's enemies have no charm for Bloom.

. . . you were a lucky dog if they didn't set the terrier at you directly you got back. Then a lot of shillyshally usually followed. Tom for and Dick and Harry against. . . . A more prudent course, Mr. Bloom said to the not over effusive. [Stephen], in fact like the distinguished personage under discussion beside him, would have been to sound the lie of the land first. [ULYSSES, 634]

Remade in Bloom's mundane image, the missing father — call him Ulysses or Parnell — has not much of the god or hero

about him; and just as Stephen's mother was not murdered,
but died of cancer, so Bloom is quite right in stating that
Parnell had "feet of clay" and

. . . owed his death to his having neglected to change his
boots and clothes after a wetting when a cold resulted and
failing to consult a specialist he being confined to his room
till he eventually died of it amid widespread regret.[23] [ULYS-
SES, 633]

There is something healing and sanitary in Bloom's anti-
rhetoric, and Stephen, in his heroic anguish, has desperate
need of it; but the passing identification of Parnell-Ulysses
with Bloom-Ulysses cannot hold up for long. Bloom is too
humble to play that proud man; he notes Stephen's resemblance to Parnell, and, while the talk veers to the O'Shea
affair, Bloom gives up the role of Parnell to Stephen, accepts
the thankless role of Captain O'Shea, and sets about making
it a role that he can bear to play.

Whereas the simple fact of the case was it was simply a case
of the husband not being up to the scratch with nothing in
common between them beyond the name and then a real
man arriving on the scene, strong to the verge of weakness,
falling a victim to her siren charms and forgetting home ties.
[ULYSSES, 635]

He says to Stephen — what wasn't so — that Katharine
O'Shea was half Spanish like Mrs. Molly Bloom, and accepts
seriously Stephen's tag about Mrs. O'Shea being the King of
Spain's daughter.[24] So now Molly is identified with Kitty
O'Shea, and hence with Helen, who, like Penelope, had troublesome suitors and was rid of them by Ulysses. Roles break
down, melt, and reform at the end of *Ulysses*, just as they do
in *Finnegans Wake*. That's what makes Joyce so exciting —
he has the strongest sense of the mysterious possibilities of
people — they can turn out to be anybody at all. It is thinking
makes it so.

In his humility, Bloom gives up the role of Parnell to

Stephen, but his reading of the role is very different from Casey's or Joe Hynes's or Stephen's fantasy of a dark avenger. Stephen-Parnell is to be the living lover, not the hero or the god, and who should he love but Molly Bloom? I have always found this one of the most touching acts in literature. Bloom loves Stephen, he has proffered him his worldly wisdom, his religious and political opinions — and they mean nothing to Stephen. Now he makes — or means to make — Stephen a present of Molly, his only valuable, the only possession for which men envy him. In effect, he plans the slaughter of the suitors. He had spoken his philosophy in Barney Kieran's bar, now he acts upon it.

— But it's no use, says he. Force, hatred, history, all that. That's not life for men and women, insult and hatred. And everybody knows that it's the very opposite of that that is really life.
— What? says Alf.
— Love, says Bloom. I mean the opposite of hatred. [ULYSSES, 327]

Christ taught this, and, as we know, it can be interpreted in a thousand different ways. Bloom's interpretation is literal and low. By the standards of the Church, it is sinful; by the standards of good breeding, graceless; but given Bloom's limitations, it is an act of goodness. To force, hatred, history, to Dante and John Casey,[25] Bloom opposes love. He shows Stephen Molly's photo with all its "symmetry of heaving *embonpoint*," and when Stephen allows that Molly is handsome, Bloom goes on in his mind to cover the projected adultery with his usual charitable resignation: "And why not? An awful lot of makebelieve went on about that sort of thing." (ULYSSES, 638).

John Casey's exploit on Parnell's behalf was to spit in a woman's eye, Bloom's was to return a fallen hat to "Erin's uncrowned king in the flesh," on the occasion of the to-do over *United Ireland*.[26] Parnell, "knowing what good form was came out at once because he turned round to the donor and thanked him with perfect *aplomb,* saying: *Thank you, sir.*" (ULYSSES, 639).

Where are the priests and the priests' pawns now? Where the image of Christ or the Phoenix from the flames? Bloom's common sense seems to have blown them away like so many bubbles, and for the moment there is relief in their going. But common sense is itself an illusion. Parnell the man is just as much an imaginative creation as Parnell the god, or Parnell the hero. Bloom's incapacity for the divine and the heroic is his defect, not his merit. Vico and Joyce would say that gods and heroes are no more and no less real than men, and that they will come again in one way or another. The last word of *Ulysses* belongs to the earth goddess, Molly Bloom.

NOTES

1. *Ulysses,* p. 664. Citations from Joyce in my text are to the Modern Library editions of *Dubliners, A Portrait of the Artist as a Young Man, Ulysses,* and to the Viking edition of *Finnegans Wake.*

2. *De orac. defectu,* 17. Off the isle of Paxi, a pilot was commanded to carry news of Pan's death to Palodes. When he proclaimed the tiding across the water to Palodes, those on shore fell into wail and lament. As the event coincided with the birth (or crucifixion) of Christ, it was taken to herald the death of the old world and the beginning of the new. "Pan," *Encyclopædia Britannica* (11th ed.).

3. Margaret Leamy, *Parnell's Faithful Few* (New York, 1936), pp. 97–101.

4. Cf. "Purgatorio," xxx, 32–33: *donna m'apparve, sotto verde manto,/ vestita di color di fiamma viva.* Joyce would have us remember that Dante Alighieri took part in the Florentine quarrel of Guelph and Ghibelline. I do not know whether Mrs. Riordan signifies Dante or Beatrice or both.

5. Even the turkey is an unsafe bird, for part of it is called

"the pope's nose" and Simon Dedalus, of the anticlerical party, eats it. *Portrait*, 31–33.

6. There is more truth in this than you might think. After pending for a year, the decree was given in the O'Shea divorce case on November 17, 1890. The evidence of adultery between Parnell and Mrs. O'Shea was partly perjured but no one doubted its essential truth. From November 17 to November 24 nearly all prominent Irish nationalists passed fulsome resolutions of confidence and urged Parnell not to retire from leadership of the Irish parliamentary party. The party re-elected him chairman on November 24.

On November 24 Gladstone, in response to nonconformist opinion, wrote a public letter, stating that he could not remain leader of the Liberal party if Parnell remained leader of the Irish party.

The Irish party was in alliance with the Liberals and expected another Home Rule bill from Gladstone should the Liberals (as was likely) win the next general election. At this point, Parnell's parliamentary followers began to rat on him, and, after bickering in Committee Room 15 until December 6, about two-thirds of them followed Justin McCarthy (*Ulysses*, 583) into opposition to Parnell, thus acknowledging Gladstone's mastery.

The Irish hierarchy spoke out against Parnell on December 3.

7. Winston Churchill, *Lord Randolph Churchill* (New York, 1907), p. 140. These words ring hollow and quaint today, but in 1907 they were uttered as a matter-of-course.

8. Michael Davitt, *The Fall of Feudalism in Ireland* (New York, 1904), p. 114.

9. R. Barry O'Brien, *The Life of Charles Stewart Parnell* (New York, 1898), II, 253.

10. In 1880 Tim Healy called Parnell "the Uncrowned King of Ireland." That the kingly sense gained on Parnell may be guessed from his letters to Mrs. O'Shea, whom he calls his "dearest queen" and (unhappily) "Queenie," and he signs himself "Your Own King." In *Charles Stewart Parnell: His Love Story and Political Life* (New York, 1914), I, 173, Mrs. O'Shea tells of wanting Parnell to apologize for a broken political en-

gagement. He said: "You do not understand the ethics of king-
ship, Queenie. Never explain, never apologize. I could never
keep my rabble together if I were not above the human weakness of apology."

11. Quoted in T. P. O'Connor, *Memoirs of an Old Parlia-
mentarian* (New York, 1929), II, 274–75. "Mr. Fox" was
one of the aliases under which Parnell carried on with Mrs.
O'Shea.

12. William Edward Hartpole Lecky, *A History of England
in the Eighteenth Century* (New York, 1891), VIII, 90, and
John A. O'Brien (ed.), *The Vanishing Irish* (New York, 1953),
55, 69, 117, 120–21, etc.

13. Davitt, *Fall of Feudalism*, "Rome and Ireland"; Barry
O'Brien, II, 24–25; John Morley, *The Life of William Ewart
Gladstone* (New York, 1903), III, 63.

14. Cf. *Ulysses*, 204–5 where Stephen denounces the Ma-
donna and asserts the masculinity of the Church.

15. The Irish failed Wolfe Tone and Robert Emmet at need;
they sold Parnell to the enemy; they reviled Isaac Butt and left
him for Parnell. All these statements are made in a purely Mac-
Manian sense.

16. Every Parnellite who did not compare Healy to Judas
compared him to Brutus. If "Et Tu, Healy" was indeed a poem,
it may be that Joyce recast it for "Ivy Day."

17. The year is 1902 because Dublin expects a visit from
Edward VII which was paid in July, 1903. The Dublin corpora-
tion did not present an address of welcome to Edward.

18. Fire and light-dark are the running themes of the story.

19. The following are printed in Mrs. Leamy's *Parnell's Faithful Few*, pp. 175–97.

From "The Dead Chief" by Katherine Tynan:

> They drove you to your death through a long passion
>   Of agony and pain,
> The cup you drank was brimmed of your own Nation,
>   And who shall cleanse the stain?
>
> .   .   .   .
>
> Seed of the Scribes and Pharisees reviled you
>   With a self-righteous prayer;

The tongues of foulness that had fain defile you
   But showed how great you were.

.   .   .   .

Say now to Emmet and Wolfe Tone moreover,
   Who hold their hands to you,
That never your Ireland had a better lover
   Than you your Ireland slew.

From "A Lament, October 11th, 1891" by U. Ashworth Taylor:

He is not dead, he cannot die,
Remember it, brothers, early and late
Our king is buried, but not his heart . . .
He leads us onward to slay the foe.
      His voice is our battle cry
      And our bugle call
From among the dead, where over all
      He standeth tall.

From "The Dead Chief" by Ethna Carbery:

We made of our heart's love a mantle
   That a monarch of men might have worn.
And we knew not the brave brows were bleeding
   'Neath the torture of man a thorn.

Woe to the stranger who prompted
   The sons of our land to disgrace —
Woe to the hypocrite whining
   That flaunted its creed in your face —
Woe to the false friend, the Judas,
   Who smote you to death in your place.

20. Giambattista Vico, *The New Science*, trans. T. G. Bergin and M. H. Fisch (Cornell, 1948), section 918.

21. Mistaking a reference to Haines for a reference to Deasy (*Ulysses*, 31), Richard M. Kain in his *Fabulous Voyager* (Chicago, 1947) on page 178 comes to the amazing conclusion that Deasy is English.

22. If I seem to have strayed into the wrong modern classic, I would remind the reader that *Ulysses* is the great mother of "The Waste Land."

23. Parnell's wet and dry feet are discussed exhaustively in Mrs. O'Shea's book. He did consult a specialist in his last illness. Joyce's mature opinion seems to be that Parnell died a natural death, see *Finnegans Wake*, p. 291, note 8.

24. Mrs. O'Shea was the daughter of an English clergyman and his English wife. Two things could have made Bloom think her Spanish: (1) she and Captain O'Shea lived for a time in Spain and he had business interests there; (2) although Mrs. O'Shea says she had golden hair, her photographs (except that of the miniature that Parnell always carried) make her look a Spanish soubrette type. They make her look exactly like my idea of Molly Bloom.

25. The single mention of Casey in *Ulysses* occurs, as you would expect, in "Eumaeus," p. 608. Bloom recalls "poor John Casey" and how he used to declaim the poem about Caoc O'Leary, a poem about an aged piper who has outlived his time.

26. *United Ireland* was Parnell's paper, edited by William O'Brien. (In his political indifference, Bloom confuses it for a moment with the *Insuppressible* which was an anti-Parnellite paper.) After the party split *United Ireland* came out against Parnell. With his followers, he recaptured it on December 10, 1890; during the night the enemy took it back again; Parnell and his forces recaptured it on December 11. There are many accounts of the thing, but none that I have seen mentions smashing of type. A stirring eye-witness account of the recapture is given in Barry O'Brien's book, II, 294 ff., which does mention Parnell as being hatless after a scuffle, but, unlucky as ever, Bloom was not seen restoring the hat.

13

The Joycean Comedy: Wilde, Jonson, and Others

W H A T does Joyce gain in *Ulysses* from the obsolete spelling "rere"? He is not consistent in his preference for it; he admits "rear admiral" and "rear up"; but he uses it eight times alone, and additionally in such combinations as "rerewards," and it appears first in a context where it is bound to be noticed; in the poised, deliberately tranquil, father-heralding paragraph that closes the Telemachia and points to Bloom's book. Apparently Joyce introduces a variation from the norm because that is precisely what he wants to suggest. "Rere" prepares the eye to interpret Bloom's stammered confession of a pinnacle secret. "What was the most revolting piece of obscenity in all your career of crime?" says Bello (choosing the cliché "career" for its homophone). Bloom squirms but has to answer, gurgling, "I rererepugnosed in rerererepugnant." (526). All the earlier signalling of the spelling "rere," supported by such passages as Bloom's memory of the poor girl who could only say "arks," tells us what he means, and Molly's soliloquy eventually confirms it. Lest doubt remain, Joyce settles the matter in *Finnegans Wake*, by repeating — — as he repeats so many of the gambits of *Ulysses* — the same joke with the syllables of the affectionate German word for rere: "I popopossess the ripest littlums wifukie around the globelettes globes." (532). The omission of this give-away was one of the losses in the *Skeleton Key* abridgement.

The popopossession passage incorporates, a few words later, a Levantine allusion which is Joyce's habitual sign for delighted sensuosity. Among his other acts of transformation of current Irish literary themes, he had transformed the theme of purdah. A slightly older generation of commentators on the nation's troubles had observed that Irish women were, effectively, in purdah: George Moore, echoing the indignant voice of the late nineteenth-century English novelists, had said it in A *Drama in Muslin*; Susan Mitchell had admitted it in her book on Moore and had moderately approved his tilt for freedom. Joyce did better. Ridiculing the nationalist thesis of Irish chastity, describing its failure in Dublin, he showed that though women do not offer the exclusivity of the harem they bountifully offer its favorite "plump mellow yellow smellow" pleasures. Just as Joyce made a celebration of pleasure out of his suffering of 1909 and the conservative, restrictive impulses related to it, so he changed that Irish narrowness, and the seaminess that went with it, into a vessel of pleasure.

One of the drives of Joyce's life, as we know from *Araby* and the essay on Mangan, was towards the preservation and consolidation of what began as a brilliant but isolated and destructible intuition of the east. East and west, he said, had met in Mangan. He planned his own work to realize the interpenetration of the rational and the voluptuous, and to do it on a bigger scale and for a bigger audience than Mangan could. The scheme of *Ulysses*, its Greek-Jewish-Irish constellation, was an answer to the problem that he had set himself. Among several images that affirm the sensuous pleasure of the east, the yashmak, the hammam, the Turkish prostitute in the graveyard, the liveliest is the melon image for Molly's rere. It is, however, not a simple image of pleasure. It is complicated by the guilt which makes Bloom, in the delirium of the brothel, project it as his most intimate confession to the tribunal. It is a part of Bloom's neurosis; its function is ambivalent: it is an expression of the incompleteness of his relations with Molly since the loss of their son, yet it is also the living tissue which still connects him physically with her; at that point alone their relations have not died, and can be rebuilt; and when, in bed with her in Ithaca, he has thought his way through the labyrinth of jealousy, his act of reconciliation is his kiss "on each plump melonous hemisphere, in their mellow yellow furrow." (719).

Joyce's curiosity concerning human conduct is almost all a song of himself. Despite recent controversy on the point, I think we must take it that he is of the great writers one of the most decisively autobiographical. When Budgen reported Joyce's comments on the cannibal king, he probably assumed that the story would echo in our minds when we read *Ulysses*, and Joyce, who must have foreseen the association, was willing to let it enter the tradition. That king chose his wife by comparing the candidates' posteriors. An "enlightened monarch" was Joyce's view. Enjoying their rude exchanges and confidences, men like Joyce and Budgen only select from their problems, seldom expose the whole complex; but they do give expression to important issues on which their imagination is actively engaged, and in fact they hope to quicken the work of the imagination, to understand and modify themselves in the act of mutual entertainment. If we correlate some of the *Dubliners* stories, notably, "An Encounter," with *Ulysses, Finnegans Wake,* and the Budgen anecdote, do we not see the outlines of a problem beautifully faced and solved at the imaginative level over the course of Joyce's writing? The successful outcome is due to the coalescence of his drive towards the east and its pleasures with an entirely different drive to a struggle with his father's image and the acceptance and integration of male energy. There was a period of his life when he could not think of his father without a sense of the steadfast "bodily shame" entailed, it seemed to him, in all father-son relationships. When, with his capacity for looking at the painful potentialities of his make-up, he concentrated on that sense of shame, an image of male union stirred. He succeeded — as Byron may have succeeded — in naturalizing that unattractive image as a voluptuous feminine image. It was a psychological triumph. His love of Mangan's and Molly's east helped him. I also believe that at the early stage when he first confronted his feelings for his father he was helped in the formation of his terrible but necessary images by the impact on his consciousness of an event of 1895 — an event which made an equal impact on all the creative young men of the nineties: Oscar Wilde's libel action, trial, and imprisonment.

Criticism has not yet properly described the effects of the Wilde fracas. It released a rigorously suppressed Victorian secret and altered the complexion of literature in the century to follow; its consequences coruscate in Gide and through current writers. It set in motion the modern exploration of the homosexual sensibility and of the social veto on homosexuality. What we need at the moment or soon, in order to see this movement and our contemporaries in perspective, is a documentation of reactions recorded in the fifteen years following 1895. Much of the material is available, already published, only awaiting co-ordination. Striking passages can be found in — to give one example — Charles Ricketts' *Self Portrait*, as compiled from his letters and journals by T. Sturge Moore, edited by Cecil Lewis, and published in London in 1939. Gordon Bottomley's memory of the downfall is there:

When the crash came I could not tell how it could be or why he had been hunted. I had just been brought to live in this faery country that is like Schubert's music; the dreadful news sent me climbing in helpless rebellion and dumb torment, unable to bear my own thoughts or anyone else's speech, high in the dense precipitous woods behind my home. That brought on the worst haemorrhages I ever had: I bled every day for weeks and was light-headed with the loss of blood. I was told afterwards that I had done nothing but talk of Wilde all the time, which of course made me bleed anew. I had been brought up in a strait, dissenting household and knew nothing of the ways of life; I only knew

what fineness and rareness his books had shown me, and
though I was bewildered by the debacle I did not believe
he was different because of it, and I was sure he could not
be less than what he had done for me. [page 298 and follow-
ing]
Ricketts reports the news of Wilde's death in 1900, "Michael
Field" sobbing on the telephone; then the gradual growth of
Wilde in his memory in the succeeding years:

> Oscar was always better than he thought he was, and no
> one in his lifetime was able to see it, including my clairvoyant
> self. It is astonishing that I viewed him as the most genial,
> kindly and civilized of men, but it never entered my head
> that his personality was the most remarkable one that I
> should ever meet, that in intellect and humanity he is the
> largest type I have come across. Other greater men of my
> time were great in some one thing, not large in their very
> texture. [124]

It is possible to speculate whether Wilde would have seemed
anything quite as important if he had not been prosecuted.
It is clear that he was considerable; otherwise the public
would not have victimized him. But he became more considerable in the memory of the arts because he had been victimized. At the outset of this century it was obligatory for a
young man who had dedicated himself, as Joyce had, to the
heroism of art and defiance of the rabblement, to investigate
Wilde's offence with a keenness near to sympathy.

Stephen's rue Monsieur-le-Prince reminiscence suggests
that during the first stay in Paris, a lonely, introspective time,
when he first saw his family in perspective because detached
from them, Joyce meditated on Wilde's problem simultaneously with his father problem. In every man's mind there
are figures to which he recurs, always inquiring and sometimes
adding to his understanding of them; and Wilde was to be
such a figure for Joyce. Joyce kept in touch with the literature
of the scandal as it appeared. I suspect, though I have not
been able to check, that he studied the Christopher Millard
record of the trial in 1912. He was never to express himself on

Wilde without reservations — for reasons which I will attempt to state in a moment. But at least one phrase in the harsh, depressing record of the prosecution had mobilized both his sympathy and his creative curiosity. In Wilde's initial libel action the defending lawyer, Carson, had exploited the number of the Oxford little magazine, *The Chameleon*, which contained, among other significant contributions, the poem by Lord Alfred Douglas, the debate of "Two Loves":

> ". . . I am true Love, I fill
> The hearts of boy and girl with mutual flame."
> Then sighing said the other, "Have thy will,
> I am the Love that dare not speak its name."

There is rather more than competence in the last line, and Joyce, responsive to the pull of poetry, retained it in his memory; and he also retained and probed the exposition of it which Wilde gave from the dock at his trial. Wilde had evidently foreseen, after the experience of the libel action, that he would be challenged on the verse, and had considered his reply and shaped it as an exculpation:

> The 'Love that dare not speak its name' in this century is such a great affection of an elder for a younger man as there was between David and Jonathan. . . . It is that deep, spiritual affection that is as pure as it is perfect. . . . There is nothing unnatural about it. It is intellectual, and it repeatedly exists between an elder and a younger man, when the elder man has intellect, and the younger man has all the joy, hope and glamour of life before him."

Three repetitions of "love that dare not speak its name" sound in *Ulysses*, touched with nostalgia, compassion, and the artist's rage with the inhibiting mob in whose image the law is made. Wilde's commentary is implicit in the story too. There is an obvious sense in which it describes the Bloom-Stephen relationship, but with the Joycean ironic twist that the younger man has the intellect and the older man, after much tragedy, still the joy and hope. It also describes the relationship in another sense: Wilde's exculpation had beauty and isolated the idealism of love, but was a half-truth, since he was also acquainted with the practice of love. Bloom might have applauded the David and Jonathan comparison and judged it right for his feeling for Stephen, but, Joyce implies in the use of the crucial quotation, his feeling similarly was capable of a physical counterpart.

Now let us look at the reservations — the complications and corrections of the sympathy which the rebel Joyce was otherwise ready to extend to Wilde, and did extend in a *Piccolo della Sera* article. Three factors deterred him from a simple position of defence. The first factor was his fear of sentimentality. He feared and rebuked sentimentality because he had a proclivity for it. In other contexts besides this he often took precautions not to slip into the sentiment on the edge of which his most deliberately beautiful passages are precariously poised. His natural safeguard was "the importunate devil within him" (whose presence he had recorded, without yet understanding, in his early autobiography) — "the importunate devil within him whose appetite was on edge for the farcical" and which gave him his comedy. On the threshold of his creative life he had divided the world into the beautiful and the contaminatingly despicable. Alike the Irish situation which tempted every man to become a politician of one kind or another, and the example of Ibsen with his missionary status, forced him to that uneasy, world-changing orientation. His first step away from it was through the discovery that the despicable is interesting; the secret of the epiphany is not what we attribute to it when we intone the word with a church fervor, but that it afforded Joyce an impressive doctrine on the waftage of which to pass beyond contempt for the marketplace and into a vigorous commingling with the marketers. The Buffalo *Epiphanies* disclose Joyce eavesdropping on the common world and finding surprise and beauty in the grit. Then, subordinating the epiphany till it became one among other devices, he mastered the writing of comedy, but first Jonsonian comedy, thus still con-

cerning himself with a mode which is based on a distinction
between the acceptable and the unacceptable and seeks to
expel the latter. Then the next step was taken in the same
way: putting Jonson's techniques among his equipment to
draw on when necessary, he passed out of the Jonsonian orbit
into comedy which treats everything as simultaneously ridiculous and beautiful. In *Ulysses* the predominant effect, more
and more surely hit as the book proceeds, is a mated comic
beauty. But, and this is crucially important for the total effect
of the book and the criticism of it, the comic beauty is interspersed with residua of early styles. There are passages written
from the Jonsonian position, still satirical and reformist; there
are also passages of beauty for which Joyce has cared so much
that he has abstained from protecting them against sentiment.

Among the residua are the Wilde references. Joyce would
have preferred to catch the comedy of male love, but in this
novel never quite could. Where he tries, the comedy smoul-
ders or crackles as satire. The hoots at Wilde's imitators and
at consciously ephebic posturing are Jonsonian satire. Mulligan's bawdy "O, Kinch, thou art in peril. Get thee a breechpad," (215) is bounced back on him by Stephen's angry inner
comment, "Manner of Oxenford" — a Chaucerian-sounding
but actually Jonsonian accusation by the Irish Joyce that the
upper-class British educational system, of which Wilde and
Mulligan had some of the benefits, had corrupted them with
its ingrained homosexuality, and, worse, had doubly corrupted
Mulligan with its parallel growth, the habit of a horselaugh at
homosexuality. In fact the breechpad paragraph is intricate
for what the superficially bright and truly mediocre Mulligan
cannot treat with compassion may be, ipso facto, worthy of
Stephen's profounder scrutiny. Toward the end of the book,
when Bloom and Stephen are urinating together in the dark,
there is a record of their thoughts which hazards pain, almost
touches beauty, but falls short of comic beauty. Perhaps we
can roughly sum up on the first factor of the Wilde nexus as

follows: Joyce has at moments a rebel's intuition of a possible beauty in Wilde's predicament; he catches it in a phrase so nostalgic that it is nearly sentimental; he would like to develop the intuition to the level of his harder comic beauty; but on this particular issue *Ulysses* never quite mates comedy and beauty, and the comedy is usually arrested at the point where it is satire.

In that sequence the second factor is also involved. Oscar Wilde was an Irish master of the generation immediately preceding Joyce's, and that made Joyce view him and treat him as a rival. All the Irish writers from the nineties onwards bore each other a fearful jealousy. Never has a movement been so riven by mutual slander. Each man wanted to write the Sacred Book for which Ireland was waiting, the book that had been discussed o'nights at Ely Place: "Home Rule will be of no avail unless somebody comes with it, like Fox or like Bunyan, bringing the Bible or writing a book like the *Pilgrim's Progress*." Each was afraid the other might be first. Each had an infantile (but for literature highly fertile) conviction that he could diminish the public interest in the other by belittling him. This was of course half a generation before Joyce. Yes, but Joyce, who criticized the Irish Literary Movement and separated himself from it and saw it with a magnificent objectivity, also was a product of its thinking, worked on its assumptions even if he transformed them in the working. He too was determined to write the Sacred Book, and, oddly enough, did. And among the entertaining features of his paradoxical make-up is that he satirized the older men of the movement as keenly and maliciously as they satirized each other. *Ulysses* and *Finnegans Wake* reverberate with derision of Moore, Yeats, Lady Gregory, Synge, AE. (Do not the Four in some of their more debile phases become these seniors, with AE — *pace* Mrs. Ruth von Phul — as the donkey?) Moore got most ridicule because like Joyce he was Catholic, like Joyce had attacked his country as unwashed, like Joyce had a taste for literary genitalia — all of which, because it made him *mon semblable,* made him the most dangerous rival, whom it was most urgent to debunk. But Wilde, although Mulligan says in ironic imitation of Stephen, "We have grown out of Wilde and paradoxes," was dangerous too. He had demonstrated the use of intellect and comedy. He had been downed by the Pall Mall mob, and that gave him the status of martyr, a very good status for the bearer of a Sacred Book. Joyce had to recognize it as possible, even if remotely possible, that history might choose Wilde as the pre-eminent Irishman. That is an extra reason, then, for the cockshies at Wilde's followers in *Ulysses,* and it is the reason why he is used in *Finnegans Wake* not only for heroic purposes but also as one in the gallery of aunt-sallies. I suspect that not only all the rivals but all the rival Irish sacred books (as well as the world's obviously sacred books, whose presence J. S. Atherton and others have displayed) can be traced in *Finnegans Wake.* For example, isn't one function of the Euclid diagrams to guy the pseudo mathematics in Yeats's *A Vision?* Joyce informs history — if the information be necessary — that *A Vision* is an impostor. Doesn't Shaun in the convent include a bray at Yeats's "Among Schoolchildren"? In addition to rivals, of course, Joyce found a place in *Finnegans Wake* for his more interesting critics, and Wilde qualified, posthumously, for inclusion and a crack or two in that capacity. When Miss Sylvia Beach drew attention to Mrs. Travers Smith's *Oscar Wilde from Purgatory,* psychic messages from the dead writer which included a censure of *Ulysses,* Joyce promptly incorporated the criticisms. (Note, incidentally, that though this story is told in *The Letters of James Joyce,* the name of Wilde is not to be found in the index to that book. Is this symptomatic of a blind spot in Joyce criticism? Or merely of the bad indexing of our age?)

The pleasantness of the Irish Literary Movement is that everything in it, the nonsense as well as the perceptions, contributed to its bright humane force, and, as part of that process, that each man in farcifying the other to knock him out of history actually commended him to history and helped to perpetuate him. I have some doubt whether we may ascribe the result to intention. But perhaps in the last years, when he felt secure as a master, Joyce recognized that that result had accrued, and was willing and happy to let it stand and to perfect it in his final revisions of *Finnegans Wake*. *Finnegans Wake* aureoles the men it ridicules, just as it is both the uttermost howl of derision against Ireland yet also a catalogue of Irish achievement: many kinds of Irish achievement, literature among the many.

But now we come to the third factor, the most powerful factor, which made Joyce's exploration of the Wilde motif necessary, and yet blocked it. It is a datum of Joyce criticism that the mutual relationship of father and son is the axis of *Ulysses*. That can be extended: in all Joyce's work can be seen the silhouette of his struggle with his father's image. His early writing and *Ulysses* represented a denial of his father, whom he categorically excluded from salvation ("my father who will never be in heaven"). He quested for a spiritual father in substitute. He eventually knew that the story he made out of the quest was, for all the superb realism of its setting, a fairy-story. He found, like Julien Sorel, that we draw our sustenance from our father in the flesh or not at all. But there had lain an enormous advantage in the protective web of unreality provided by the Stephen-Bloom fairy-story: it had enabled him to imagine, in the astonishing diagrammatic way which William Empson uncovered in *The Kenyon Review*, Winter, 1956, a physical encounter with his father. When he thought directly about carnal male relationships, his conservative feelings prevailed; he shrank, as his notes for *Exiles* state, from the "dissatisfaction and degradation" involved in the meeting. So he developed the image of a shadow-knowledge between men, a supposition of each other made possible by their alternate presence in the same naturally attractive woman. But when he had invented this solution, he had the courage to apply it only in a grouping where the son en-

countered his *spiritual* father in Molly's body. There is one
hint — and I fancy that Joyce jumped at his own audacity, as
the reader at the first contact jumps at it — that Stephen also
met his real father in Molly: that is the paragraph where his
father's name is called in the roll of her previous lovers. Even
there he protects himself from an idea dangerous to his psyche
at that stage of his development: he includes in the same
catalogue (Leporello's catalogue-song) lovers who, the text
has already made clear, never possessed Molly by more than
a tweak at her rere in the press of a theater-crowd. So perhaps
that cohabitation on which there is an antique taboo — and
which, for example, a Jacobean prostitute refused to permit
when Sir Walter Ralegh's son came to the door soon after
him — never occurred in Dublin. Joyce closed the possibility
as quickly as he had opened it, having dared enough, for the
time being, with the spiritual ancestor.

When Joyce drafted *Finnegans Wake* he was a stronger
man. The accomplishment of *Ulysses* had strengthened him;
the fact that he was paying the penalty of superiority by blindness and suffering authorized him to enjoy the privileges of
superiority. Abandoning fairy-tale sanctions, he confronted
his father four-square. He made John Joyce one of the epic
villain-hero protagonists. The death of his father while the
work was in progress released emotions that had been battened
down and half-understood till then, and fortified his plan.
One among several resultant splendors is that the sodomite
theme is more energetically treated in *Finnegans Wake* than
has been possible before. The other factors are still in adverse
operation against the fullest enquiry into "love that dare not
speak its name," but this factor which has been fiercest, embarrassment in the face of the father, is largely resolved.

The most obvious and important function of Wilde in
Finnegans Wake is of course to provide an outstanding case
of the Fall of Man. The *Wake,* for all that Joyce had volun-
teered to re-tell the *Paradise Lost* story, which must be the
Fall of the Average Man, tends to slide towards the artist's

and politician's special problem of the Fall of the Great Man. That shift of emphasis was inevitable. Joyce not only wanted to emulate Milton's *Paradise Lost* but — after he had read the description of the "Metempsychosis" in Jonson's conversations with Drummond, and, later, the challenging correction in Grierson — to fulfil Donne's original design for *The Progress of the Soul*, examining the great spirits who have troubled and yet quickened the world. He considered himself a great spirit of the heretical procession "from Cain to Arius and from Mahomet to Elizabeth" and onwards. And while the fall of the average man is a religious myth, it was an observable fact in the nineties that greatness falls. Parnell and Wilde proved it. Greatness nourishes in itself an essential concomitant of its rebellion against mediocrity: a spot offensive to, and vulnerable to, mediocrity. At that spot it will be fatally damaged. Writing the story of Parnell and Wilde and Ja'far the Barmecide into *Finnegans Wake* Joyce dramatized the fate of the intellect transfixed on the cross of the flesh and caught the farce and beauty of human foibles. He pursued the Wilde legend into all the byways of pederasty. In the handling, the dilemma of Buckley when the Russian General turns the other cheek to his muzzle, becomes a correlative for the human predicament, but it begins as a meditation, droll yet profound, on sodomy. It is supported by a ratter-tatter of verbal associations with the male skills. Peter the Great, a version of the Russian General, is mutated into Peder the Greste; five pages later we have "pedarrests"; three pages after that "homosodalism"; five pages after that Wilde's friend (and almost fellow-sufferer in the 1895 crisis, when he had to run for it) "Mr. Aubeyron Birdslay. Chubgoodchop, arsoncheep and wellwillworth a triat!" Later, since Joyce evidently read Mark Twain as Leslie Fiedler does, we have Tom, Sid, and Huck as "pedestriasts." The Four Annalists of course become the Four Analists — of course, since it is one of the defects of Joyce's wit, as of Shakespeare's, that once we have seen his method in action we can see the next trick a mile off;

but perhaps this is really because of the well-known limitation
of love, that the will is infinite and the execution confined.
Those who know *Finnegans Wake* better than I do will probably agree that I am not straining to pick these examples,
certainly not taking a fine tooth-comb through the text for
them; I am mentioning those that are obvious, and I expect
there are many which have escaped me. It is clear that Joyce
has set out to include Wilde's love in the Sacred Book of
Ireland, which is synchronously the Sacred Secular Book of
Human Behaviour. He has decided that it is time this love
spoke its name, its lineage, and its domicile; and I will say
here that the simplest of the several things that the Wilde
scandal did was guide Joyce's attention (and his generation's)
to the anatomical domicile of that love. Thus it brought Joyce
to Molly's many-sidedness, with its promise of total pleasure,
and to the Russian General in his posture of, at once, submis-
sion and vigor.

Two apocalyptic transformations are the reward for Joyce's
effort in celebrating his father and exploring male relationships. He stares at the General's rere; in accordance with the
simultaneous negative positive of *Finnegans Wake* he both
holds his fire in deference to humanity and shoots in fulfilment of aggression (and we must understand the shot not
only as the murder of his father but as a symbol of physical
integration with his father); and then he sees a vision that
he has never seen before, or never so piercingly. He himself,
after all, is the Russian General as well as Buckley, in the
sense that he is his father as well as his father's son, and now
in privacy, relieving himself like the General, he has his
intimation of the author of nature and is "enlivened" towards
him "by the natural sins liggen gobelimned theirs before me."
The other miracle is the miracle of the dung. Joyce allegorizes
his life's work as the delivery of dung and the alchemistic act
of creation from it. His exposure of himself is the initial step
in the process of creation.

In the *Wake* as in *Ulysses* there are still, despite Joyce's

domination of his material, residual elements that have not
been tamed to his over-all intention, though they are perhaps
fewer than in *Ulysses*. We are not, however, to take it for
granted that, because Joyce worked towards a reconciled
beauty and largely arrived at it, it necessarily follows that
his sublime reconciled beauty is the best of his work. It may
be that the interspersed unreconciled sections of both his great
books are more interesting and durable than the reconciled elements and the whole. There is a pleasure in discovering
Joyce's total intention and the contribution of the details
towards it; and in regard to *Finnegans Wake* this is the great
pleasure of 1958, this wonderful period in which point after
point of the comic epic is opened up and a current of excitement runs between readers; but it is a pleasure different from
that of a later day when the writer will have his tradition
and the pleasure must come from the literary texture itself.
There are obvious short-run superiorities in what is least
sublime in Joyce; some of his presublime work meant more
to Ireland when it was written and published, and still speaks
more nakedly and poignantly to all of us. Even in the long
run it may continue to be more human and more moving.
Joyce moved in his late phase into literature's greatest danger:
the danger of the illimitable, the loss of the particular in all.
Cocteau, scribbling the preliminary notes to *Les Mariés de la
Tour Eiffel* at the date when Joyce meditated the first sketch
of the *Wake*, drew attention to the tedium of the sublime
(though he added a footnote to sanction the volte-face he has
since made). Joyce, I think, knew the peril, and, though he
had to follow the line of evolution on which he had started,
believed he could find a way past it, and relied for help on
the compensatory effects of the residua which he left in his
complex structures. I have a quarrel with critics who fail to
let the corrective factors function, instead translating actual
words into the illimitability against which he needed protection and which his actual words often sidestep. C. E. Magny,
for example, an otherwise captivating writer, admires Gerty

MacDowell and Molly because they can be "stripped of their temporal attributes." The fact is, that without their temporal attributes they would be dead to literature. There is no surer way of frustrating literature than distilling abstractions from it and begging us watch the play of forces. If we are to have philosophy, the philosophers will give us more exercise and interest than the poets and novelists can. If we are to have Vico, we can find him in Vico and, according to our capacity, enjoy him there. Joyce can delight a reader with his transpositions of Vico, but the pleasure lies in the art of the transposition, not in the substance for its own sake; and the glory of Joyce is not his representation of Vico but of Molly and Earwicker. He does not give us the play of forces but of Molly's rere and the General's. Shall we not do best if we can think at least one-tenth as often as Bloom and Joyce did of melons, shylight windows, the goat on Howth Head; and if we can think of Bloom's and Joyce's thoughts on them as petty, temporal, individual — the proper business of literature? The point at which art is interesting is the point at which it fails to be superhuman. And it is fortunate and significant that though Joyce could not resist attempting a superhuman book for the culmination of his work, he took as his material men interesting because they lived at a nearly superhuman, nearly divine pitch and then at last their Troysirs fell and showed their illexpressibles and humanity — Parnell, Wilde, and one or two other gentlemen whom he thought similar, notably himself.

14

Hardest Crux Ever

HENRY MORTON ROBINSON

T O an extent unmatched in any other piece of world literature, a character familiarly known as Humphrey Chimpden
Earwicker, Haroun Childeric Eggeberth, and He'll Cheat
E'erawan, permeates the Book of Double-Ends Jyned. Every
Joycean prattler knows all about the stuttering innkeeper of
Chapelizod, who, delving in his garden one sabbath afternoon, gained the agnomen and "sigla H.C.E." Sometime
thereafter he acquired a wife; became the father of three
identifiable children; kept a house of fairly decent repute;
ran for public office and was defeated by voters who had
gotten wind of his unsavory, though never quite specific,
activities in Phoenix Park.

Ecce homo! Behold the man as he is — *h*umile, *c*ommune,
and *e*nsectuous (29, line 30); or, if you please, *h*uman, *e*rring,
and *c*ondonable (58, line 19). What commentator in possess-
sion of these demonstrable facts would choose to dig deeper,
when in the course of such digging, he is bound to strike
the hitherto-uncracked strata of meaning embedded in
"hardest crux ever" (623, line 33)?

As understood by scholars and critics "crux" is any word
or passage that presents special difficulties of explanation.
In Latin, *crux* means "cross," the instrument of crucifixion
— usually a stake with a transverse bar on which criminals
and martyrs were nailed to suffer ignominious death. The
title of my present paper subsumes both meanings: (1) the

uncounted martyrdoms and deaths that occur in the *Wake*; and (2) the number of occasions and variety of meanings that Joyce assigns to words beginning with h.c.e.

The crux is indeed hard, and Joyce clews it together with such diabolic cunning that he can afford (or is compulsively driven) to scatter a few hundred clues over the scene of the crime. Having collected a random fistful of clues indelibly stamped with "initials majuscule," H.C.E., I am now in a position to ask: Why H.C.E.? Why not B.G.O., X.T.U., or any other combination of two consonants and a vowel to designate the male character dominating the *Wake?*

Until these questions are answered — until the identity of H.C.E. and the source of his initials are indisputably established — it seems to me that commentators on *Finnegans Wake* labor in vain.

Compilation is by no means the highest activity of the mind; indeed I would not stoop to it unless the cumulative effect of my compilation were far greater than the sum of its separate parts. The following list of 216 h.c.e.'s (admittedly incomplete) should be regarded as the elements of an incalculably huge metonomy which becomes, at last, the *Wake* itself. On a more obvious level the list may serve to indicate both the frequency and variety of uses to which Joyce puts his h.c.e.'s. Meanwhile the reader is invited to observe the mutations, inversions, and increasingly difficult counterpoint employed in combining, separating, echoing, and re-echoing the H.C.E. motif. Each letter, word and passage, deserves — and should receive — as much philologic scrutiny as the reader can bring to it. Joyce's advice: "Wipe your glosses with what you know" was never more applicable than here and now. I regret that limitations of space and time have prevented me from supplying even the minimal gloss (now in preparation) that might enable the reader to recognize the protean shiftings of Joyce's elusive hero who finally coalesces into a "certain stable somebody."

Without further comment let the following catalog of
H.C.E.'s cognomens, agnomens, sobriquets, and subterfuges
be placed upon the record.[1]

Howth Castle and Environs   (3:3)
Helviticus committed deuteronomy   (4:21)
hod, cement and edifices   (4:26)
Haroun Childeric Eggeberth   (4:32)
Hic cubat edilis   (7:22)
How Copenhagen ended   (10:21)
happinest childher everywere   (11:15–16)
Hush! Caution! Echoland!   (13:5)
How charmingly exquisite!   (13:6)
till heathersmoke and cloudweed Eire's ile sall pall   (13:22)
Hither, craching eastuards   (17:25)
hence, cool at ebb   (17:26)
When Head-in-Clouds walked the earth   (18:23)
A hatch, a celt, an earshare   (18:30)
here, creakish from age and all now epsilene   (19:10)
Hark, the corne entreats!   (21:3)
Humme the Cheapner, Esc,   (29:18–19)
humile, commune and ensectuous   (29:30)
he is ee and no counter   (29:34)
hubbub caused in Edenborough   (29:35)
Hag Chivychas Eve   (30:14)
bear the sigla H.C.E.   (32:14)
Habituels conspicuously emergent   (33:12)
H.C. Earwicker   (33:30)
Hesitency was clearly to be evitated.   (35:20)
Sayings Attributive of H.C. Earwicker   (36:12)
Hence my nonation wide hotel and creamery establishments
   (36:22)
a hundred and eleven others in her usual curtesy   (38:13)
He'll Cheat E'erawan   (46:1)
the average human cloudyphiz [Phonetic substitution of "y"
   for "e."]   (51:1)

that fishabed ghoatstory of the *h*aardly *c*reditable *e*dventyres
    (51:14)
the *H*aberdasher, the *C*urchies and the three *E*nkelchums
    (51:14)
the *h*en and *c*rusader *e*verintermutuomergent   (55:11)
an *e*xcivily (out of the *c*ustom *h*uts)   (55:13)
*h*aughty, *c*acuminal, *e*rubescent   (55:29)
*h*uman, *e*rring and *c*ondonable   (58:19)
*H*umpheres *C*heops *E*xarchas   (62:21)
*H*aveyoucaught-*e*merod's temperance gateway   (63:18)
*h*uge *c*hain *e*nvelope   (66:13)
*H*yde and *C*heek, *E*denberry, *D*ubblenn   (66:17)
*h*ence these *c*amelback *e*xcesses   (67:29)
*H*ouri of the *c*oast of *e*merald   (68:11)
*H*ouse, son of *C*lod, to come out, you jewbeggar, to be *E*xe-
    cuted   (70:34)
*H*atches *C*ocks' *E*ggs   (71:27)
up *h*ill and down *c*oombe and on *e*olithostroton   (73:30)
*h*aught *c*rested *e*lmer   (74:1)
*h*e *c*onscious of *e*nemies   (75:15)
(*h*ypnos *c*hilia *e*nonion!)   (72:3)
And we are not trespassing on *h*is *c*orns *e*ither   (81:2)
*h*e would *c*hallenge their *h*emispheres to *e*xterminate them
    (81:25)
*h*esitency *c*arried to *e*xcelcism)   (82:30)
a *h*ighly *c*ommendable *e*xercise   (85:12)
*h*igh *c*hief *e*vervirens   (88:2)
(for was not just this in *e*ffect which has just *c*aused that the
    *e*ffect of that which it *h*as *c*aused to occur?)   (92:33)
$H_2C E_3$ (95:12)
our *h*agious *c*urious *e*ncestor   (96:34)
*H*e had fled again . . . this *c*ountry of *e*xile   (98:4)
An infamous private ailment (vulgovarioveneral) had *c*laimed
    endright, closed his vicious circle, snap.   (98:19)
*H*owforhim *c*hirrupeth *e*vereachbird!   (98:36)
*H*omo *C*apite *E*rectus   (101:13)

after *h*iding the crumbends of his enormousness (102:6)
Handiman the Chomp, Esquoro (102:16)
He Can Explain (105:14)
Howke Cotchme Eye (106:24)
the *h*ardily curiosing entomophilust (107:12)
(*H*ear! Calls! Everywhair!) (108:23)
*h*idmost coignings of the earth (118:36)
like a *h*eptagon crystal emprisoms trues and fauss for us
    (127:3)
*h*idal, in carucates he is enumerated (128:5)
*h*ock is leading, cocoa comes next, emery tries for the flat
    (128:24)
was *h*atched at Cellbridge but ejoculated abroad (129:9)
*h*oveth chieftains evrywehr (131:7)
Hwang Chang evelytime (130:35)
*h*ereditatis columna erecta, (131:30)
*h*agion chiton eraphon (131:30)
*h*allucination, cauchman, ectoplasm (133:24)
Dear Hewitt Costello, Equerry (135:29)
*h*ears cricket on the earth (138:26)
*h*as come through all the eras of livsadventure (138:30)
If hot Hammurabi, or cowld Clesiastes, could espy her prank-
    lings (139:25)
I can easily believe heartily (150:36)
like all tomtompions *h*aunting crevices for a deadbeat escupe-
    ment (151:18)
clement, urban, eugenious and clestian in the formose of
    good grogory *h*umours (154:20)
though the heavenly one with his constellatria and *h*is emana-
    tions stood between (154:18)
Heliogobbleus and Commodus and Enobarbarus (158:26)
East Comma Hillock (160:12)
Mr. Humhum, whom *h*istory, climate and entertainment
    made the first of his sept and always up to debt (173:23)
Henressy Crump Expolled (176:6)
the *h*uge chesthouse of *h*is elders (179:18)

on account of his smell which all cookmaids eminently objected to   (181:10)

How elster is he a called at all?   (197:7)

Huges Caput Earlyfouler.   (197:8)

H.C.E.   (198:8)

has a codfisck ee   (198:9)

Score Her Chff Exsquire!   (205:22)

Hircus Civis Eblanensis!   (215:27)

for he can eyespy through them   (239:3)

He, by bletchendmacht of the golls, proforhim penance and
come off enternatural.   (240:13)

So she not swop her eckcot hjem for Howarden's Castle,
Englandwales.   (242:32)

Hulker's cieclest elbownunsense.   (245:21)

Housefather calls enthreateningly.   (246:6)

ancients link with presents as the human chain extends
(254:9)

is hued and cried of each's colour   (256:10)

Now have they children entered into their habitations.
(258:27)

old Herod with the Cormwell's eczema   (260: footnote 1)

Hispan-Cathayan-Euxine   (263:12)

Haud certo ergo.   (263:28)

Honour commercio's energy   (264:1)

Harbourer-cum-Enheritance.   (264:1)

It's haunted. The chamber. Of errings.   (272:19)

With its tricuspidal hauberkhelm coverchaf emblem on.
(273:28)

Show that the median, hce che ech, intersecting at royde angles the parilegs of a given obtuse one biscuts both the arcs
that are in curveachord behind. [HCE and ALP]   (284:1)

Hoop! As round as the calf of an egg!   (294:1)

Hengler's Circus Entertainment   (307:8)

Harbour craft emittences   (309:20)

This harmonic condenser enginium   (310:1)

with a howdrocephalous enlargement   (310:6)

hummer, enville and cstorrap (310:19–20)

So *he* sought with the lobestir claw of his propencil the clue
    of the wickser in his ear. (311:10)

Howe cools Eavybrolly! (315:20)

Hircups Empytbolly! (321:14)

They *h*ailed him cheeringly, their encient, the murrainer
    (324:8)

Heave, coves, emptybloddy! (324:11)

*h*ero chief explunderer of the clansakiltic (326:8)

bings Heri the Concorant Erho (328:25)

Horuse to crihumph over his enemy, (328:32)

H*olophullopopulace is a shote of excramation! E*mancipator,
    the Creman hunter (Major Hermyn C. Entwhistle)
    (342:18)

His Cumbulent Embulence (352:32)

*h*ow comes ever a body in our taylorised world (356:10)

And *h*oody crow was ere. (360:28)

as *h*e contracted out of the islands empire (362:6)

under *h*eaviest corpusus exemption (362:17)

*h*itch a cock eye (363:2)

I am able to owe it, *h*earth and chemney easy (364:27)

Here endeth chinchinatibus (367:4)

Helping a cubital with a hopes soon to ear (369, *last line*)

And these probenopubbilicoes clamatising for an extinsion on
    his *h*ostillery. With *h*is chargehand bombing their eres.
    (371:24)

*h*ugon come errindwards (371:36)

Horkus chiefest ebblynuncies! (373:12)

Hence counsels Ecclesiast. (374:23)

Hung Chung Egglyfella (374:34)

Hired in cameras, extra! (375:14)

When *h*ives the court to excequer 'tis the child which gives
    the sire away. (375:2)

Head of a *h*elo, chesth of champgnon, eye of a gull! (377:4)

Hang coersion everyhow! (378:27)

poor old *h*aspitable corn and eggfactor (380:11)

in his umbrageous house of a hundred bottles with the radio
    beamer tower and its *h*angars, *c*himbneys and equlines
    (380:15)
got a big buzz for his name in the airweek's honours from
    *h*ome, *c*olonies and empire   (393:13)
O *h*ear, Caller Erin!   (394:33)
*H*ireark Books and *C*hiefoverseer Cooks in their Eusebian
    Concordant *H*omilies   (409:35)
*H*is hungry will be done! On the continent as in Eironesia.
    (411:11)
read the strangewrote anaglyptics of those shemletters patent
    for *H*is *C*hristian's Em?   (419:19)
*H*e*C*it*E*ncy!   (421:23)
House Condamned by Ediles.   (421:2)
under the *h*elpless Corpses Enactment   (423:31)
Femorafamilla feeled it a candleliked but *H*ayes, *C*onyngham
    and Erobinson sware it's an egg.   (434:11)
*h*ome *c*ooking everytime   (455:31)
rural Haun . . . crooner born with sweet wail of evoker
    (471:35)
*h*umeplace of *C*hivitats Ei   (481:20)
  *H*ail him heathen, heal him holystone! Courser, Recourser,
*C*hangechild. . . . Eld as endall, earth . . . (481:1)
*H*ell's *C*onfucium and the Elements!   (485:35)
Heavencry at earthcall, etnat athos?   (494:6)
Holy snakes, chase me charley, Eva's got barley under her
    fluencies!   (494:15)
*h*omosexual *c*atheis of empathy   (522:30)
Hotchkiss Cultur's Everready   (523:14)
Our Human Conger Eel!   (525:26)
Ho, croak, evildoer!   (532:4)
*h*andshakey *c*ongrandyoulikethems, ecclesency   (535:11)
Haveth Childers Everwhere   (535:34)
Hodder's and Cocker's erithmatic   (537:35)
*h*aunted, *c*ondemned and execrated   (544:10)

copious *h*oles emitting mice   (545:8)
Hery Crsss Evohodie   (546:10)
*h*uge Chesterfield *e*lms   (553:19)
*h*er *c*hastener *e*ver   (553:1)
on Holiday, Christmas, Easter mornings when she wore a
   wreath   (556:8)
with a tillycramp for Hemself and Co, Esquara   (557:1)
Do you ever heard the story about Helius Croesus, that white
   and gold *e*lephant in our zoopark?   (564:4)
How *c*himant in effect!   (569:11)
Horsehem coughs enough. Annshee *l*ispes *p*rivily. [HCE and
   ALP]   (571:25)
Honuphrius is a concupiscent exservicemajor who makes dis-
   honest propositions to all.   (572:21) [2]
the *h*eathen church emergency fund   (574:7)
all *h*is *c*ognisances had been *e*streated   (575:30)
Hecklar's champion ethnicist   (578:12)
Hot and cold and electrickery   (579:6)
Herenow chuck english
   *a*nd *l*earn to *p*ray plain [HCE and ALP]   (579:20)
Heinz *c*ans everywhere   (581:15)
*h*uskiest *c*oazing experimenter   (582:3)
*h*igh carnage of semperidentity   (582:14)
And that's how Humpfrey, champion emir, holds his own
   (582:26)
Hokoway, in his hiphigh bearserk! Third position of concord.
 · Excellent view from the front.   (582:29)
*h*ugest commercial emporialist   (589:9)
Humbly to fall and cheaply to rise, exposition of failures
   (589:17)
*h*onoured *c*hristmastyde *e*aseredman   (590:20)
A *h*and from the cloud emerges, *h*olding a *c*hart expanded
   (593:19)
Even unto Heliotropolis, the castellated   (594:8)
the *h*orned cairns erge   (594:24)

Henge Ceolleges, Exmooth   (595:1)

hoseshoes, cheriotiers and etceterogenious bargainboutbar-
    rows   (595:22)

hailed chimers' ersekind   (596:5)

one of the two or three forefivest fellows a bloke could in
    holiday crowd encounter   (596:15)

the hullow chyst excavement   (596:28)

Homos Circas Elochlannensis!   (600:17)

Read Higgins, Cairns and Egen.   (604:5)

Hagiographice canat Ecclesia   (604:19)

Hump cumps Ebblybally!   (612:15)

Health, chalce, endnessnessessity!   (613:27)

Have we cherished expectations?   (614:23)

homely codes, known as eggburst,
    eggblend, eggburial and hatch-as-hatch can   (614:31)

heroticisms, catastrophes and eccentricities transmitted by
    the ancient legacy of the past [HCE and ALP]   (615:33)

as highly charged with electrons as hophazards can effective
    it   (615:7)

the hartiest that Coolock ever!   (616:2)

erect, confident and heroic   (619:14)

And the helpyourselftoastrool cure's easy   (622:13)

hot cockles and everything   (623:8)

Hoteform, chain and epolettes   (623:17)

hardest crux ever   (623:33)

Reverence has so conditioned many of us that some readers
will refuse admittance, on the conscious level, to the over-
whelming Figure that Joyce is drawing. (I, myself, resisted it
for twenty years.) Not until we accept Joyce as a wizard theo-
logian — and the most accomplished blasphemer, too, in all
literature — shall we gain sufficient courage to follow him
wherever he leads. I say this without any disposition to pass
moral judgment on James Joyce, or leap to the defense of
religion. My sole purpose (remember?) is to trace the initials
H.C.E. to their veritable source.

Alive to the depthless metaphor in which we are working, we may legitimately scrutinize any word in the *Wake* that promises to be of assistance. Such a word is "mistletropes" (*p.* 9, l. *19*). "Mistletropes" offers a splendid example of Joyce delving into the "hidmost coignings of the earth" (p. 118, l. 36) to find metals that will prove useful for fresh mintings of sound and meaning.

"This is mistletropes," he says quite simply and opens a door leading to the abyss.

Unafraid, let us take the jump by breaking "mistletropes" into its component parts. "Trope" is the classical term for a figure of speech; hence, figurative language. "Mist" and "Mistle" suggests that Joyce is speaking in mixed and misty metaphors under which he conceals an ever-mistier and more mixed meaning. "Mistle" also suggests "missile" and "Missal." The latter is a book containing all that is said or sung during the Roman Catholic Mass.

But watch out! Joyce will elude us in the fog unless we make the phonetic leap from "mistletropes" to "mistletoe." It was by means of a dart (missile) tipped with mistletoe that Balder, the Norse God of Light, met his death. And now we are grazing the very heart of Joyce's intention, which is to depict both the necessity and futility of the Hero-Victim's death. Protagonist and Scapegoat, he must be slain, murdered, crucified, in order that the race may live by partaking of his body.

Body? Some*body*? (Sum of all body, perhaps?) A certain *stable* some*body*? Where have we heard these words before? And where, if we choose to listen, may we hear them daily?

A thunderhead of dreadful associations is about to break with "majestic instancy" upon our ears. I must confess that I began to shudder with apprehension when I heard Joyce repeating *This is . . . This is . . . This is . . .* fifty-five times in an eighty-seven line passage (pp. 8–10). Two interpretations lay before me and I dared not, for many years, take the profounder one.[3] Scarcely a month ago, I opened the Roman

Catholic Missal that I had read ten thousand times and saw
the fateful line

HOC EST ENIM CORPUS MEUM

Translated into English these words mean "FOR THIS IS MY
BODY." They are uttered when the priest performs the mystery
of Transubstantiation, thereby changing (according to Catholic belief) a wafer of bread into the actual body of Christ.
Scarcely has the priest uttered these words when he elevates
the chalice and says

HIC EST ENIM CALIX SANGUINIS MEI

"THIS IS THE CHALICE OF MY BLOOD."

May I suggest that James Joyce has appropriated to his own
use the innermost mystery of the religion in which he was
bred? It is no part of my program to establish the motive that
drove Joyce to such an action. He needs no apologist. He is *ee*
and no *c*ounter. I feel rather that I owe him an apology for
my failure to recognize, long ago, the source and origin of that
"*stable* [4] some*body*" from whom all H.C.E.'s flow.

I can only strike my breast and say: "Mea culpa Mea culpa,
Mea maxima culpa."

P.S. All crosses are hard to bear, Poorjoist. But yours must
have been the *h*ardest *c*rux *e*ver.

NOTES

1. Because no complete glossary of *Finnegans Wake* exists, it
is impossible to measure the occurrence of H.C.E. against the
probable average occurrence of any other three letters. Should
some control-minded reader care to demonstrate that other
three-letter combinations (excepting A.L.P.) occur with greater
frequency, he is quite at liberty to do so. I except A.L.P. only
because I have already noted some two hundred instances —
apart from her fluvial manifestations — running through the
Wake.

2. The opening sentence of a real shocker; should be approached by initiates only.

3. "*This is* the house that Jack built" and its many ramifications have been admirably treated by Mabel P. Worthington.

4. Read "manger" for "stable" and see what happens: French "*manger*" = "to eat"!

According to a note attached to the frame, this was painted by
Frank Budgen, one of Joyce's closest friends, "in 1918, rather
late in the year." Joyce had met Budgen, British civil servant and
amateur painter, in Zürich in the early summer of 1918.

In 1950 Budgen wrote to H. K. Croessmann in connection
with this painting, "The small picture you possess painted by me
is a study for a portrait I intended painting in the same light key.
That was how I saw him — quiet but alert, birdlike, watchful.
But by the time I was ready to paint the intended bigger portrait,
J. J. was suffering from an eye attack and living in a darkened
room, so I was forced to switch over to the darker key in which
Mrs. Sargent's picture is painted." Mrs. Sargent's painting
appears as the frontispiece of Budgen's *James Joyce and the
Making of "Ulysses,"* London: Grayson and Grayson, 1934. Re-
produced by courtesy of the artist.

Miss Sylvia Beach's book shop, Shakespeare and Company, 12, rue de l'Odéon, Paris, in 1922. The first publishers of *Ulysses*, Mr. John Rodker and Miss Beach, are to the left and right of Joyce.

The first of thirty-three poems of Joyce's *Chamber Music* set to music by Geoffrey Molyneux Palmer (1882–1957), the noted Dublin organist and composer. The manuscripts of all thirty-three are in the Croessmann collection. Reproduced by courtesy of Miss Phyllis A. Palmer and Miss Gladys M. Palmer.

A letter from Joyce to his daughter during her stay in Ireland with Joyce's sister. Italian was customarily used in the Joyce home. Reproduced by courtesy of Miss Harriet Weaver and the Estate of James Joyce.

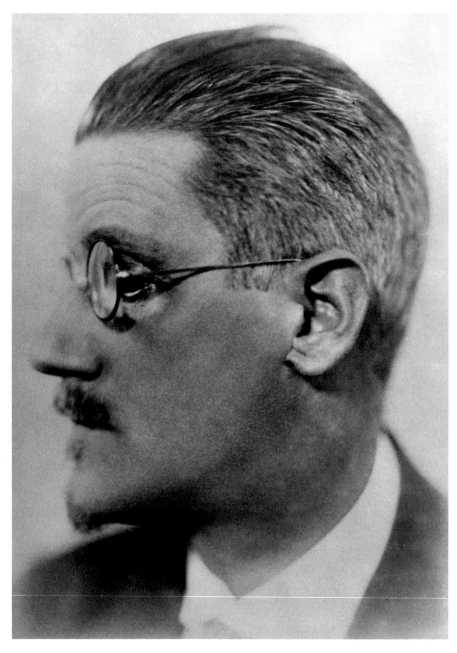

This gift from Joyce to H. K. Croessmann was taken by Paris photographer Henri Martinie. It is signed, "James Joyce/ Paris/ 29 October 1926."

15

The Making of *Finnegans Wake*

WALTON LITZ

W H E N *Finnegans Wake* first appeared in 1939 most readers familiar with *Ulysses* were confounded by what seemed
to be a radical change in Joyce's style and technique. Superficially, the dense language of the *Wake* bore little resemblance to even the most complex sections of *Ulysses*. Only
those who had followed Joyce's *Work in Progress* during the
1920's and 1930's were prepared for the new language, realizing that it had developed gradually and inevitably out of the
style of *Ulysses*. Today we are in a much better position to trace
the evolution of the text of *Finnegans Wake*, since the manuscript drafts and galley proofs presented to the British Museum in 1951 by Miss Harriet Weaver provide complete and
detailed evidence for every stage in the process of composition.[1] It is my purpose in this article "to remount [in Henry
James's phrase] the stream of composition," to describe in
general terms the manner in which Joyce wrote *Finnegans
Wake*, and to discuss briefly a few ways in which his methods
of composition illuminate his stylistic development and aesthetic aims.

Over a year passed after the publication of *Ulysses* before
Joyce could muster the strength and determination to begin
a new work. When *Finnegans Wake* was finally begun, in the
spring of 1923, neither the structure nor the ultimate style of
the book had been determined. Joyce had been preoccupied
for years with many of the *Wake*'s major themes and motifs:

a number of them are foreshadowed in *Ulysses*, most notably
Vico's cyclic view of history and the story of "How Buckley
Shot the Russian General." [2] Nevertheless, the manner in
which these ripening themes would be presented was not
clear.

Joyce's early work on the *Wake* was exploratory, a clarification of basic ideas and stylistic aims. During the spring and
summer of 1923 he composed four short passages which reveal
his concern with Irish history but contain no mention of the
Earwicker family and no hints as to the shape of his new
work.[3] One of these early sketches deals with King Roderick
O'Conor (FW, 380–82), another with St. Kevin (FW, 604–6),
and a third with the story of Tristan and Isolde (FW, II, *iv*).
However, the most interesting of these four sketches is the
one which describes an encounter between St. Patrick and
an Irish arch-druid who turns out to be Bishop Berkeley in
disguise (FW, 611–12). Joyce once told his friend Frank
Budgen that this passage was "the defence and indictment"
of the *Wake* itself.[4] The druid defends in obscure terms the
language and design of *Finnegans Wake*, borrowing his
argument from Berkeley's subjective theory of vision, but
common-sense Patrick dismisses the druid's reasoning and
with it the night-world of the *Wake*. It is significant that
this passage, which ultimately found its place near the end
of *Finnegans Wake*, should have been one of the first written. One might speculate that Joyce in composing it was
debating with himself the advantages and disadvantages of
the task he was about to undertake.

After a brief flurry of revisions in the summer of 1923
these four early sketches were put aside, only to be introduced into the text of the *Wake* fifteen years later during
the last-minute rewriting of 1938. Joyce's work on these
sketches evidently dispelled the depression which had followed the completion of *Ulysses* and confirmed his interest
in the new project, for in the autumn of 1923 he turned
his attention to the Earwicker family and began to draft

episodes with amazing rapidity. During the autumn and winter of 1923–24 six of the eight episodes which now comprise Part I of the *Wake* were begun, in addition to an episode concerning the Four Old Men ("Mamalujo").[5] The various members of the Earwicker family began to assume individuality, and the major themes associated with each were developed. Then in the spring of 1924, with the basic design of Part I already established, Joyce focused his interest on the figure of Shaun and began work on the "four watches" which were later to become Part III of the *Wake*.[6] Although the drafts and revisions for Part I were far from satisfying to Joyce he preferred to start on new material, since it was his method to work on several sections at the same time, allowing the composition of one to illuminate the problems of the others and relying on later revisions to bring the whole work into harmony. Joyce never tried to force his preliminary sketches into a rigid pattern, but patiently waited for relationships to develop. In one of his letters to Miss Harriet Weaver he refers to these early pieces as "not fragments but active elements" which will "fuse of themselves" in time, and in a subsequent letter he speaks of the book as writing itself.[7]

During 1924 and 1925 Joyce worked assiduously on the four chapters or "watches" of Shaun, solving internal problems of structure and gradually developing the character of the blustering twin. Occasionally he would return to Part I in order to prepare one of its episodes for magazine publication, but Shaun remained his chief interest.

However, the further Joyce advanced with his work on Shaun the more puzzled he became by the problem of the *Wake*'s total structure. At first he may have thought of constructing the book in two major parts, but this plan soon had to be modified.[8] The problem was how to effect a transition between the chapters of Part I already drafted and the "four watches" of Shaun. "I am boring through a mountain from two sides," Joyce told a friend. "The ques-

tion is, how to meet in the middle." [9] Finally, however, he
began to see his way clear out of the maze he had created.
In the spring of 1926 he could announce: "I have the book
now fairly well planned out in my head." [10] By this time he
had arrived at a clear conception of the four-part structure
which governs *Finnegans Wake*. He had visualized the four
chapters of Part II, which form a bridge between the *Anna
Livia Plurabelle* episode at the end of Part I and the first
chapter of Part III. He had also foreseen the role of Part IV
as both beginning and end of the book's cyclic structure.
Not only was the *Wake*'s total structure now determined,
but the disposition of material within the major sections
was fairly clear. From 1926 onward the writing of *Finnegans
Wake* entered a second phase, with Joyce laboring like a
mosaic worker on a predetermined pattern, turning first to
one part and then to another of his basic design. During
1927, '28, and '29 he prepared most of the episodes already
written for separate publication. By 1930 Parts I and III of
the *Wake* had been printed in their preliminary forms, and
at this point Joyce felt "a sudden kind of drop" in the
impetus behind his writing.[11] The shaping of Part II proceeded slowly and under great personal difficulties; Joyce
was still laboring on sections of Parts II and IV while Part I
was entering galley proof in 1936 and '37. The entire work
was not completed until 1938, with Joyce making last-
minute revisions on the galley proofs.

Joyce's method of composition, which might best be described as ceaseless elaboration upon a static pattern, was
one he had followed during the last stages of the writing of
Ulysses; as a result of it, his revisions were almost always
expansive rather than selective. The obvious comparison
to mosaic work (like that to the intricate elaborations of
the Book of Kells) was one he encouraged, and one which
emphasizes what I would call the "Imagistic" nature of his
art. Ezra Pound defined the Image as "that which presents
an intellectual and emotional complex in an instant of

time," [12] and it is my belief that Joyce intended the whole of *Finnegans Wake* to be regarded as a single vast Image. The development of the *Wake* is pictorial rather than temporal, and an understanding of any one passage depends as much upon what follows it as upon what precedes it. Ideally the *Wake* should be read many times, since we must hold the entire work in our minds as a single image if any one element is to be fully understood. In effect, Joyce is demanding that the reader visualize the total structure of the book in the same manner as he did while writing it.

But this heavy demand on the reader is not the only result of Joyce's aesthetic aims as revealed by his mode of composition. A process of constant elaboration has no inherent boundaries, and revision tends to degenerate into mere embroidery and lead the reader further and further from central thematic concerns. As Joyce progressed in his revisions his interest in details of texture often overshadowed and even permanently obscured major elements that appear quite clearly in the early versions.

During the first and most important phase of composition, which lasted from 1923 to approximately 1927, Joyce not only discovered the appropriate structure for the *Wake* but developed its "final" style as well. The first sketches begun in 1923 and 1924 differ little from the more complex sections of *Ulysses* in their preliminary versions, but in his revisions of them Joyce was clearly shaping a more intricate style. Their revisions reveal a process which he was later to call "stratification," [13] the expansion and thickening of the text through the addition of related themes and motifs. The ultimate result of this process was the characteristic language of the *Wake,* in which a number of associated ideas are stated *simultaneously* by means of portmanteau words. Joyce's revisions of the period 1923–27 reflect his desire to exploit what might be called the "musical" potentialities of language in two ways: (1) By creating an "orchestrated" prose which sounds a number of themes and motifs "in an instant of time"; and (2) by utilizing the "expressive" powers of language to their fullest extent, so that his prose embodies as many characteristic qualities of its subject-matter as possible. An example of the movement toward an "orchestrated" language may be seen in Joyce's reworking of a passage in the *Haveth Childers Everywhere* section.

That was Communicator a former colonel. A disincarnated spirit called Sebastiam may phone shortly. Let us cheer him up a little and make an appointment for a future date. Hello, Communicate! how's the butts? Everseptic! . . . So enjoying of old thick whilcs, in tall white hat of four reflections he would puffout a smokefull bock.

[1929]

That was Communicator, a former Colonel. A disincarnated spirit, called Sebastion, from the Rivera in Januero, (he is not all hear) may fernspreak shortly with messuages from my deadported. Let us cheer him up a little and make an appunkment for a future date. Hello, Commudicate! How's the buttes? Everscepistic! . . . So enjoying of old thick whiles, in haute white toff's hoyt of our formed reflections, with stock of eisen all his prop, so buckely hosiered from the Royal Leg, and his puertos mugnum. He would puffout a dhymful bock.

[1930] [14]

The revised text has been enriched with several geographical names: the Riviera and Rio de Janeiro ("Rivera in Januero"), Everest ("Everscepistic"), and Eisenstadt ("stock of eisen"). In the latter part of the passage HCE is a white-capped volcano; his snow-white head and smoking cigar are the mountain peak, while ports ("puertos mugnum") lie at his feet. This image has been foreshadowed in the second version by two revisions: the substitution of "buttes" for "butt," and the addition of "deadported" (departed). "Messuages," with its overtones of "messages" and "assuages," as well as its root meaning of "house and lands," is a typical Joycean addition. "Buckely hosiered" combines the image of buckled hose with a reference to Buckley (who shot HCE as the Russian General). The alteration of "Everseptic" to "Everscepistic" is a good example of this compression, for here three attributes of HCE have been merged into the original word. His identification with all mountains is in "Everest"; he is a "sceptic"; he is tainted — "septic" — and at the same time "pistic," pure as the oil with which Mary anointed the feet of Jesus.

There can be no doubt that in revising this passage Joyce multiplied its references and enriched his text, but only at the expense of obscuring some of the original (and important) meanings: "Everseptic" is overshadowed by the more complex "Everscepistic." Too often the process of deformation diffuses the basic effect instead of intensifying it. It is, I think, a valid criticism of Joyce's method that an early version is often the best clue to the meaning of a difficult passage in the final text.

The other major aim revealed by Joyce's revisions, his desire to make language "express" rather than describe its subject, can be illustrated from the evolution of any episode. Thus in revising the *Anna Livia Plurabelle* section he tried to create a prose "expressive" of rivers by working hundreds of river-names into the text. Similarly, when he revised the first (and rather plain) draft of the St. Patrick-archdruid passage during the summer of 1923 he cast it into "pidgin English" in order to "express" the Eastern nature of pre-Christian Irish religion. The first draft opens in this manner:

The archdruid then explained the illusion of the colourful world. . . .[15]

Two stages later in the process of revision this opening statement has been transformed into the following:

Bymby topside joss pidgin fella Berkeley, archdruid of Irish chinchinjoss, in the his heptachromatic sevenhued septicoloured roranyellgreeblindigan mantle finish he show along

the his mister guest Patrick with alb belonga him the whose
throat he fast all time what tune all him monkafellas with
Patrick he drink up words all too much illusiones of hueful
panepiphanal world. . . .[16]

This attempt to exploit the "expressive" potentialities of
language is of course not unique with Joyce, but in the
elaboration of *Finnegans Wake* he carried it to extremes
never before approached in English literature. When the
technique succeeds, as in the wonderful closing passage, the
results are so impressive that they justify its general application. But often Joyce distorted his language only to mirror
some trivial aspect of the subject, as when in the late stages
of revision numerous titles and lyrics from Moore's *Irish
Melodies* were woven into the text.

These trends which emerge quite clearly from a study of
Joyce's revisions were, it must be emphasized, not innova-
tions but rather extensions of stylistic principles which governed much of his work on *Ulysses*. The arrangement of the
time sequence in *Ulysses* aims at simultaneous presentation
of a number of related incidents — Joyce simply carried this
process one step further in the *Wake* by deforming the individual word so that it could present a number of meanings
at the same time. In a like manner, he attempted to intensify the "expressive" qualities of his prose while recasting
Ulysses. When the Aeolus episode (which takes place in a
newspaper office) was revised in 1921, the original version
was augmented with newspaper headlines and numerous
references to wind and rhetoric, all designed to "express" the
setting and subject of the episode.[17]

When one traces Joyce's revisions of a single chapter in
the *Wake*, from early drafts to final version, one is impressed
not only by the risks he was taking but by his own awareness
of these risks. Eugene Jolas tells us that late in the making
of *Finnegans Wake* Joyce "read Coleridge and was interested in the distinction . . . between imagination and
fancy," wondering "if he himself had imagination." [18] It is

not hard to understand Joyce's interest and concern, for
Coleridge's definition of Fancy as a "mode of Memory
emancipated from the order of time and space" [19] could
well apply to the final elaborations of the *Wake*. With the
evolution of a single episode before him, each reader will
choose a different point at which to wish Joyce had halted
his revisions, a point at which allusiveness and evocation
appear to be counterbalanced by an increasing obscurity of
central themes. But Joyce himself would accept no such
compromise, and was not satisfied until he had explored to
the full limits of his genius the "musical" qualities of language.
This point he had reached by 1927, at approximately the
same time that the structural problems of the *Wake* were
solved. When in late 1926 he began work on what is now
the opening passage of *Finnegans Wake*, he rapidly — and
with an obvious sureness of aim — developed the text to a
level of complexity and allusiveness approaching the dense
final version. Here is the familiar opening passage as it appeared at the end of 1926:

brings us to Howth Castle & Environs! Sir Tristram violer
d'amores, had passencore rearrived on a merry isthmus from
North Armorica to wielderfight his peninsular war, nor stream
rocks by the Oconee exaggerated themselse to Laurens
county, Ga, doubling all the time, nor a voice from afire
bellowsed mishe chishe to tufftuff thouartpeatrick. Not yet
though venisoon after had a kidscad buttended a bland old
isaac not yet [though] all's fair in vanessy were sosie sesthers
wroth with twone jonathan. Rot a peck of pa's malt had
Jhem or Sen brewed by arclight & rory end to the regginbrow
was to be seen ringsome [on] the waterface.[20]

When Joyce had reached this stage in the process of composition his exploratory work was over. The next twelve
years were devoted to completing the narrative as already
visualized and recasting the entire work in his achieved final
style.

Chronology of *WORK IN PROGRESS*

1923

March: Joyce wrote his first piece since the conclusion of *Ulysses*, the King Roderick O'Conor fragment (FW, 380–82). See *Letters, p. 202.*

July–August: Joyce drafted the Tristan and Isolde fragment (later included in FW, II. *iv*); the St. Kevin episode (FW, 604–6); and "pidgin fella Berkeley" (FW, 611–612).

September: By the middle of this month Joyce had "finished" a draft of "Mamalujo" (FW, II. *iv*).

The notebook containing rough drafts of all the episodes in Part I except *i* and *vi* (British Museum Add. MS 47471-B) must have been filled before the end of 1923.

1924

January–March: Joyce was working on I. *v*, I. *vii*, and I. *viii*.

"From Work in Progress," *Transatlantic Review*, I, April, pp. 215–23 (FW, II. *iv*).

In March Joyce began the "Shaun the Post" section.

During the remainder of 1924 Joyce continued to revise the episodes in Part I already written, and to compose the "four watches" of Shaun (FW, III. *i–iv*).

1925

The composition of Shaun's "four watches" continued through 1925, interrupted from time to time by the need for revising episodes from Part 1 before their initial publication.

In early April Joyce was correcting copy for the *Criterion*, and late in the month he was faced with the proofs for the *Contact Collection*.

By the end of August Joyce had begun the last watch of Shaun (FW, III. *iv*), and on November 5th he reported that he had "almost made a first draft of Shaun d" (FW, III. *iv*).

"From Work in Progress," *Contact Collection of Contemporary Writers*, Paris, [May], pp. 133–36 (now FW, 30–34).

"Fragment of an Unpublished Work," *Criterion*, III, July, pp. 498–510 (FW, I. *v*).

"From Work in Progress," *Navire d'Argent*, I, October, pp. 59–74 (FW, I. *viii*).

"Extract from Work in Progress," *This Quarter*, I, Autumn–Winter 1925–26, pp. 108–23 (FW, I. *vii*).

1926

In April Shaun abcd (FW, III) was put aside as "finished," after several months of intensive revision.

In the summer Joyce wrote "a piece of the studies" called "The Triangle," later "The Muddest Thick That Was Ever Heard Dump." This eventually became the middle part of II. ii.

In the autumn Joyce drafted the opening episode, FW, I. *i*.

1927

In 1927 Joyce was revising Part 1 for publication in *transition*.

"Opening Pages of a Work in Progress," *transition*, No. 1, April, pp. 9–30 (FW, I. *i*).

In the summer he composed
1. *vi* as a connective episode
between "The Hen" and
"Shem the Penman."

"Continuation of a Work in
Progress," *transition*, No. 2,
May, pp. 94–107 (FW, I. *ii*).

transition, No. 3, June, pp. 32–
50 (FW, I. *iii*).

transition, No. 4, July, pp. 46–
65 (FW, I. *iv*).

transition, No. 5, August, pp.
15–31 (FW, I. *v*).

transition, No. 6, September,
pp. 87–106 f. (FW, I. *vi*).

transition, No. 7, October, pp.
34–56 (FW, I. *vii*).

transition, No. 8, November,
pp. 17–35 (FW, I. *viii*).

1928

In the early months Joyce revised Shaun abc for publication
in *transition*.

In the spring he re-worked
Anna Livia Plurabelle (FW, I.
viii) for publication in book
form.

Trouble with his eyes prevented Joyce from writing during most of the latter half of
1928.

transition, No. 11, February,
pp. 7–18 (FW, 282–304).

transition, No. 12, March, pp.
7–27 (FW, III. *i*).

transition, No. 13, Summer,
pp. 5–32 (FW, III. *ii*).

Anna Livia Plurabelle, New
York, Crosby Gaige, October
(FW, I. *viii*).

1929

Joyce began to revise his "fa-
bles" ("The Mookse and the
Gripes," "The Muddest Thick
That Was Ever Heard Dump,"
"The Ondt and the Grace-
hoper") in late 1928 and continued the process through the
spring of 1929.

transition, No. 15, February,
pp. 195–238 (FW, III. *iii*).

Tales Told of Shem and Shaun,
Paris, The Black Sun Press,
August (FW, 152–59, 282–304,
414–19).

transition, No. 18, November,
pp. 211–36 (FW, III. *iv*).

1930

Joyce began working on II. *i* in September.

Haveth Childers Everywhere, Paris and New York, June (FW, 532–54).

Anna Livia Plurabelle, London, Faber and Faber, June (FW, I. *viii*).

1931

Joyce was virtually idle in 1931, due to personal difficulties.

Haveth Childers Everywhere, London, Faber and Faber, May (FW, 532–54).

1932

Finnegans Wake, II. *i* was completed in 1932, in spite of great difficulties.

Two Tales of Shem and Shaun, London, Faber and Faber, December (FW, 152–59 and 414–19).

1933

During the period 1933–37 most of Joyce's effort was devoted to the composition of FW, II, *ii & iii*.

transition, No. 22, February, pp. 49–76 (FW, 219–59).

1934

The Mime of Mick Nick and the Maggies, The Hague, The Servire Press, June (FW, 219–59).

1935

transition, No. 23, July, pp. 109–29 (FW, 260–75, 304–8).

1936

In July Joyce noted that Part I was "completed." It was submitted to Faber and Faber for printing.

1937

The galley sheets for Part I began to appear in the spring: the sheet for page one bears the printer's date "12 March 1937."

transition, No. 26, February, pp. 35–52 (FW, 309–31).

Storiella As She Is Syung, London, Corvinus Press, October (FW, 260–75, 304–08).

1938

While the galleys for the other sections were being corrected, Joyce was completing parts II and IV. It was not until mid-November that the process of composition came to an end. Corrections and alterations were made up till the last moment, some of them by telegram.

transition, No. 27, April–May, pp. 59–78 (FW, 338–55).

1939

Joyce received the first bound copy of *Finnegans Wake* on his birthday, February 2nd.

Finnegans Wake, London: Faber and Faber, New York: The Viking Press, May 4th.

NOTES

1. I am indebted to Miss Weaver and the administrators of the Joyce estate for permission to use the *Finnegans Wake* MSS.

2. The assassination of the Russian governor-general of Finland, General Bobrikoff, by a Finnish patriot is referred to in the Aeolus episode (*Ulysses,* Modern Library ed., p. 133).

3. For more information concerning the composition of these fragments, see the chronological table at the end of the article. This table is designed to provide a factual outline of Joyce's writing and publication during the years when *Finnegans Wake* was known only as *Work in Progress.*

4. Seon Givens, ed. *James Joyce: Two Decades of Criticism* (New York, 1948), p. 347. From Frank Budgen's "Joyce's

Chapters of Going Forth By Day," *Horizon*, IV (September, 1941).

5. See Chronological Table. The draft of "Mamalujo" (later incorporated in *FW* II. iv) is in British Museum Add. MS 47481.

6. On 15 March 1924 Joyce wrote to Miss Weaver that he hoped to start on "Shaun the Post" in a day or two (from an unpublished letter in Miss Weaver's possession).

7. *Letters of James Joyce*, ed. Stuart Gilbert (New York, 1957), pp. 204 and 213. Letters of 9 October 1923 and 24 March 1924.

8. There are suggestions of a two part plan for the *Wake* in an unpublished letter to Miss Weaver dated 15 March 1924.

9. Givens, p. 24.   10. *Letters*, p. 241.

11. *Letters*, p. 290.

12. *Literary Essays of Ezra Pound*, ed. T. S. Eliot (London, 1954), p. 4. First published in *Poetry*, March, 1913.

13. *Letters*, p. 234. Joyce refers to his first work on III. iv. as "hammer and tongs stratification."

14. The early version comes from *transition*, No. 15 (February, 1929), p. 233; the revised version is found in *Haveth Childers Everywhere* (Paris and New York, 1930), pp. 18–20. This passage is now found on pp. 535–36 of the *Wake*.

15. British Museum Add. MS 47485, p. 99.

16. *Ibid.*, p. 101.

17. The earlier version of Aeolus appeared in *The Little Review*, V (October, 1918), pp. 26–51.

18. Givens, p. 14.

19. *Biographia Literaria*, Chap. XIII.

20. British Museum Add. MS 47482-A, p. 83. For a slightly different version of this passage see *Letters*, p. 247.

16

The Little Known Paul Léon

MARIA JOLAS

W H E N I think of Paul Léon, I recall especially his Buddha-like smile, a smile that rarely broke into real laughter, or so it seemed to me. Nor, and this again is Buddha-like, was it reflected in his eyes, which were usually grave, as though incapable, for all time, of forgetting certain scenes they had witnessed and apprehensive of those they were destined to witness.

For we know now that, after nine months' detention in Drancy, when, as a result of illness, brutal treatment and sheer exhaustion, he collapsed during the long journey eastward to the extermination camp, Paul Léon was shot at arm's length by the Nazi in charge of the convoy. Thus ended the life of the man who, for twelve years, had given unstintingly of his time, his immense erudition, and his friendship to James Joyce.

This gift of time and friendship is known to the majority of Joyce students, and their giver is generally — however erroneously — referred to as "Joyce's secretary." Few, however, outside the circle of Léon's personal friends and collaborators would seem to be aware of the intellectual and temperamental factors that fitted him for this role. How many know, for instance, that at the age of twenty, in St. Petersburg, he devoted his legal thesis to the subject of Irish Rome Rule? Or that, in the course of his career, he wrote learnedly on such widely varied subjects as Mediaeval

225

Jurisprudence and Guild-Socialism; Bakounine, Jean-Jacques
Rousseau, and Benjamin Constant?

These titles alone denote a passionate faith in the individual, in his conscience and in his freedom, and their choice
reflects a temperament that could not but be sympathetic
to Joyce. But if we add to this Léon's extraordinary linguistic gifts, his sceptical, désabusé, yet never bitter, viewpoint, and his capacity for infinite devotion, infinite understanding, I believe that some such expression as *alter ego*
would come nearest to an accurate description of their relationship.

It is good news that the *Centre National de Recherche
Scientifique* are planning to publish his posthumous work
on the *Juridical and Political Thinking of Rousseau*. Meanwhile, it gives me pleasure to present to readers of the *James
Joyce Miscellany* these fragments that constitute, however
briefly, recognizable samples of his own thinking.

*

THE RESTORATION [1] *(Fragment)*

. . . The hatred, leading even to civil war, that followed
the explosion of passions provoked by the episode of the
"Hundred Days," had spread to Parliament, and there
seemed no hope of attaining national unity. Then, dissolu-
tion of the *Chambre Introuvable* [2] unexpectedly revealed
the existence of a power over and above the parties, that
was capable of intervening in favour of this unity. The
rightist parties, having been caught unawares by the inter-
vention of the throne, soon accomplished their regrouping.
Certain of them, the *ultras*, as they were called then, remained firm in their hatred of the new institutions, and
although they accepted Louis XVIII, it was only reluctantly. Others, more clear-sighted and intelligent, made
proposals of their own. They accepted the new institutions:
the Charter, liberty, participation in the government, but

only with the idea of capturing these institutions for their advantage. According to them, only when their final goal had been reached, that is, when the King's very person had been captured in their favour, would national unity be restored. Union of the country reduced to union of the right, such was the dominating idea of the new doctrine that was to be clearly expounded in Chateaubriand's *The Monarchy According To the Charter*. This was not, needless to say, a very firm basis for union of the country, and capture of the King's will (*volonté*) might seem to have been an extremely unreliable course that risked weakening the very doctrine of the new régime. With usage, however, these institutions were to reveal their force, and in the end, become implanted in the country. Constant understood this as soon as he arrived in Paris, and from then on, he devoted himself to politics, which absorbed almost all of the last fifteen years of his life. His activities took place on two different planes: on the one hand, he took practical part in the parliamentary mechanism and, by virtue of his knowledge, intelligence and other excellent qualities, became France's veritable "professor of constitutional law." Indeed, he devoted himself all the more seriously to this task, since he understood clearly that the success of parliamentary government would never serve the aims of the *ultras*. On the other hand, he worked tirelessly in favour of what had always been his most cherished doctrine, and he was, in reality, the actual founder of nineteenth-century liberalism.

Soon after his return, he felt impelled to reply to Chateaubriand, whose real aims he unmasked in terms that were intended as a reply to *The Monarchy According To the Charter*, in a pamphlet entitled *The Monarchy According To the Aristocracy*. This too, however, was done in the hope of creating French unity.

"We have just been through an awful ship-wreck," he wrote, "and the sea is covered with débris. Let us save from this disaster all that is of value: services rendered, valourous actions, shared dangers, aid to the suffering, none of these should be forgotten. Instead of severing the ties that still bind us together, we should create new ties between us, as a result of these honoured traditions."

With this goal in mind, he founded the theory of constitutional monarchy which, according to his idea, would recreate French unity and, at the same time, guarantee liberty for all. He stood apart from the revolutionaries in no uncertain terms:

"I have a horror of revolutions," he wrote. "They sacrifice the individual, destroy character, supplant real responsibilities by factitious ones, substitute blind force for the forces of reason and law. They also pervert justice and do violence to the rights of each citizen."

*

THE EVOLUTION OF THE IDEA OF SOVEREIGNTY BEFORE ROUSSEAU *
(Fragment)

. . . So long as the Christian Church was faced first, with a pagan empire and then, with barbarous tribes in migration, its interior cohesion remained so strong that it could be content with a principle of differentiation ordained from heaven, and a unity whose spiritual leader was the transcendent Christ. But when, not as a Church, but as an institution, as a human group, this unity had no longer to fight for its existence, but rather to accomplish a great civilizing task, then it too became profoundly affected by the process of differentiation, and in the most varied ways. There was, first of all, the differentiation inside the Church itself, between governing and governed, upon which we shall not insist here. But there was also the transformation of the opposition between faithful and infidels into a distinction between spiritual and temporal communities. Historical evolution, however, had already bound these two societies together, and absolute dissociation was therefore impossible.

In order to find a solution it became necessary to let unity descend upon a worldly power, and so the problem arose of the hierarchic relationship between the two powers. Undoubtedly, the vision of unity under a transcendent leader, reflected in worldly matters by collaboration between the two powers, remained very much alive. The Church alone, however, was the "universal city." The Church it was, too, that tried to monopolize universalism, and thus entered necessarily into conflict with the Empire's temporal power. But past interpenetration of both these series of institutions condemned this conflict in advance to become an eternal one. And indeed, absorbed by this struggle for universalism, both the Empire and the Church were suddenly faced with a new social differentiation that broke through the traditional lines of mediaeval society and, at the same time, deprived the contest of its objective. The struggle between the mediaeval Church and the mediaeval Empire had been based on a differentiation founded exclusively on property, that made the rich property owner the defender and consequently the natural representative of the community, as well as the head of its administration. The Church itself had had a direct share in this evolution and its institutions had become so many centers of administration and direction in temporal society. Then, gradually, as concentration evolved towards a more concrete community, tending to dominate functional differentiation and substitute for it the supra-functional idea of the nation, the battle began to be fought around this new unity. Under these conditions the Church could undoubtedly win, but the fruits of victory slipped through her hands when she attempted to establish her spiritual tutelage over the new communities. For the basic elements of the problem proved to be quite different, and it was in fact her own differentiation that was attacked. Since too, she had monopolized spiritual universalism for her own benefit, her decay was soon followed by decay of the very concept of universalism.

*

THE SOCIAL AND POLITICAL IDEAS
OF GUILD SOCIALISM⁴ (*Evolution and Doctrine*)
(*Closing pages*)

The entire evolution of the XIXth Century consisted in conferring upon the human personality traits of concrete individuality that reduced its role of representative of the species, in order to bring out the ties that united it with other groups, ties that at times proved to be stronger, more powerful, deeper, even, than those that bound it to the state society. Political organization no longer sufficed and new, distressing antinomies appeared, that threatened the very foundations of the social structure.

The insufficiency of the old doctrine provoked a reaction in search of a more complete theory of organization that would take all the newly-appeared ties into consideration. In its exaggerated form, collectivism, the theory was unable to go beyond the economic problem; and all it succeeded in doing was to once more sacrifice the individual upon the altars of Leviathan. Even official doctrine was affected by this reaction which took the form of constantly increasing State interference in the life of the citizen. Anarchism alone refused to follow the general movement, but this was much more the result of lack of courage and hopelessness than because of any conviction or new conception of the problem.

Today things are different. When we speak of an institutional conception of legality (Hauriou, Delos), or of legality based on social integration (Gurvitch), it is evident that the problem has been transposed to another plane. In both these conceptions, which I have chosen as being the most characteristic, one member of the juridical equation turns out to be the group itself, conceived either as disposing already of a certain organization (institution) or as possessing only a potential faculty and notion of organization (social legality). In both these examples it is evident that the solution can no longer be political, but that it must de-

velop according to a principle of inner balance that is the
very principle of law. One of the greatest acquisitions of our
time is perhaps the way this idea has penetrated to the very
heart of revolutionary doctrine. (G. H. Cole,[5] as the chief
representative of Guild Socialism, offers a striking example
of this penetration.) The result has been an interest in legal
problems that was unknown to collectivism, but which immediately invites further observation.

There is a page in *Thus Spake Zarathustra* that contains
great poetic eloquence, as well as philosophical insight. Its
essential passage is the following.

Evening is coming on and Zarathustra pauses at the en-
trance to the forest. He is sad. Finally, turning to his dis-
ciples, he says: "The sun is long since down, the field is
damp, from the woods comes a breath that chills.

"An unknown something around me is gazing at me
thoughtfully. What! Are you still living, Zarathustra?

"Why? For what? Through what? Whither? Where?
How? Is it not folly to be still living?

"Ah, my friends, it is evening that questions thus in me!
Forgive me my sadness!

"It is evening now: forgive me that it should now be
evening."

Here we see the master, the super-man, a prey to the
same anguish as the rest of mankind. He excuses himself
that it should now be evening, but we can neither forgive
nor condemn him, for the reason that we neither condemn
nor forgive the fall of night. This is one of the given facts
of human nature, against which we can do nothing. Also,
if evening induces sadness, no organization, no doctrine can
find a remedy for it.

And indeed, if we study the most modern social doctrines, we would appear to be approaching the evening of
our thought. Revolutionary impulse and enthusiasm, faith,
if only in a myth capable of recreating this enthusiasm, seem
to have run dry. A conscious realism has killed the revolu-

tionary impetus, and today a new, more serious atmosphere
reigns in the inner circle of these doctrines, where their
formulators are only too conscious of the limitations that
life itself sets to the realization of ideas. Beside these accepted facts, how hollow and mistaken the proud, ringing
assertions of triumphant collectivism seem today. Also, how
much more sincere, more real and more serious, even though
they be more sad, are the conclusions of the modern sys-
tems, however tainted with relativism. What they seek to
determine is the actual movement, the inevitable evolution,
the necessary development of social organization. It is here,
in fact, that political doctrines go hand in hand with sci-
entific thought. And today, when we proclaim the inade-
quacy of the law, spontaneous regulation of social existence,
independent development of institutions, the primacy of
irrational social legality over that of the organized group,
the same thoughts and the same misgivings always come to
light.

Over and beyond organized and, so to speak, palpable
society, what we seek to discover is the real society, with its
ineluctable features. It is all to the credit of Guild-Socialism
that it should have clearly formulated these thoughts and
these misgivings and thus have placed itself in the forefront
of the social movement. A very general study of this doctrine suffices, however, for us to realize the amount of sadness it contains. Indeed, if Mr. Cole has been led to demand
industrial democracy, it is because he has despaired of political democracy. And he wonders, even, what hope would
remain to him if he were to come to despair, as well, of the
new forms of democracy (*Self-Government,* p. 199).

*

A musician once said to me that he could think of no
more beautiful *Requiem* for a civilization than *Finnegans
Wake*. For Joyce, too, it was evening. But just as in every
Requiem there is a note of hope of a life to come, so in the

very title of Joyce's great work we find assurance of a re-awakening, only this time, to take place in this world, not in the next.

During the last twelve years of *Work in Progress*, Paul Léon was Joyce's close companion. And I can't but think that, despite his scepticism, despite his refusal of every sort of mystification, he too believed that a to-morrow would follow the evening he had so clearly recognized.

(*These fragments from writings by Paul Léon were chosen and translated by Maria Jolas.*)

NOTES

1. From *Benjamin Constant*, Paris: Editions Rieder, 1930. Later re-issued by the Presses Universitaires de France.

2. Ironic epithet for the ultraroyalist Chamber of 1815–1816.

3. "L'Evolution de l'Idée de la Souveraineté avant Rousseau," published in *Archives de philosophie du droit et de sociologie juridique*, Cahier Double nos. 3–4, 1937. Recueil Sirey, 22 Rue Soufflot, Paris.

4. "Les Idées sociales et politiques du Guild Socialisme," *Archives de philosophie du droit et de sociologie juridique*, Cahier Double nos. 3–4, 1931. Recueil Sirey, 22 Rue Soufflot, Paris.

5. Author of *The World of Labor* (1913), *Self Government in Industry* (1917), *Social Theory* (1920), etc.